Study Guide

T0355101

Religious Education
for CSEC®

Pippa Durn
Sister Marlyn James
Pandita Indrani Rampersad
Pauline Raymond
Shaikh Shazad Sookram
Reverend Paul Douglas Walfall

OXFORD
UNIVERSITY PRESS

Great Clarendon Street, Oxford, OX2 6DP, United Kingdom

Oxford University Press is a department of the University of Oxford.
It furthers the University's objective of excellence in research, scholarship,
and education by publishing worldwide. Oxford is a registered trade mark of
Oxford University Press in the UK and in certain other countries

First published by Nelson Thornes Ltd in 2012
This edition published by Oxford University Press in 2015

British Library Cataloguing in Publication Data
Data available

978-1-4085-1634-8

23

Printed and bound by CPI Group (UK) Ltd, Croydon, CR0 4YY

Acknowledgements

Cover photograph: Mark Lyndersay Digital, Trinidad
www.lyndersaydigital.com
Illustrations: Paul McCaffrey and Andrew Elkerton (both Sylvie Poggio
Agency); Simon Rumble and Richard Jones (both Beehive Illustration);
David Russell Illustration.
Page make-up: Integra

Throughout the book the terms BCE (before Common Era) and CE (Common
Era) are used instead of BC (before Christ) and AD (Anno Domini).

In Islam the words 'peace be upon him' are used whenever the Prophet
Muhammad is mentioned. For ease of reading we have omitted this, but no
disrespect is intended.

Contents

Introduction   1

Part A

Section 1 Essentials of religion

1.1 Definitions and features of religion   2

Section 2 God in religion

2.1 A Christian understanding of God   8
2.2 Major manifestations of God in Hinduism   10
2.3 Relationship with Allah in Islam   12
2.4 The nature of God in Judaism   14
2.5 The concept of God in Caribbean indigenous religions   16

Section 3 Places of worship

3.1 Christian places of worship   18
3.2 Sacred places in Hinduism   20
3.3 Places of worship in Islam   22
3.4 Places of worship in Judaism   24
3.5 Places of worship in Caribbean indigenous religions   26

Section 4 Major religions: locations and origins

4.1 Locations of major religions   28
4.2 How major world religions came to the Caribbean   30
4.3 How the Caribbean indigenous religions developed   34

Section 5 Sources of authority

5.1 Sources of authority in Christianity   36
5.2 Hindu holy scriptures   38
5.3 Sources of authority in Islam   40
5.4 Jewish holy scriptures   42
5.5 Sources of authority in Caribbean indigenous religions   44

Section 6 Major teachings and beliefs

6.1 Major teachings of Christianity   46
6.2 Major teachings of Hinduism   48
6.3 Major teachings of Islam   50
6.4 Major teachings of Judaism   52
6.5 Major teachings of Caribbean indigenous religions   56

Section 7 Festivals

7.1 Festivals in Christianity   58
7.2 Festivals in Hinduism   62
7.3 Festivals in Islam   64
7.4 Festivals in Judaism   68
7.5 Festivals in Caribbean indigenous religions   72

Contents

Section 8 Religious practices and rites of passage

8.1 Practices and rites in Christianity 74
8.2 Practices and rites in Hinduism 78
8.3 Practices and rites in Islam 80
8.4 Practices and rites in Judaism 82
8.5 Practices of Caribbean indigenous religions 86

Section 9 Similarities and differences

9.1 Comparing religions 88

Part B

Option A: Christianity

A.1 Human life issues 92
A.2 The Bible 98
A.3 God 102
A.4 Concept of sin and salvation 104

Option B: Hinduism

B.1 Human life issues 106
B.2 The *Ramayana* and Bhagavad Gita 112
B.3 The Absolute and avatars 114
B.4 Concept of sin and liberation 116

Option C: Islam

C.1 Human life issues 120
C.2 The Holy Qur'an 128
C.3 The concept of Allah (God) 134
C.4 Concept of sin, punishment and reward 140

Option D: Judaism

D.1 Human life issues 144
D.2 The Tenakh 150
D.3 God 156
D.4 Festivals and observances 160

Exam tips 166
Part A Practice exam questions 169
Part B Practice exam questions 178
Glossary 180
Index 184
Acknowledgements 188

This CSEC® Religious Education Study Guide has been developed exclusively with the Caribbean Examinations Council (CXC®) to be used as a resource by candidates and teachers following the Caribbean Secondary Education Certificate (CSEC®) programme.

This Study Guide has been written to meet the requirements of the CSEC® in Religious Education. The contents provide comprehensive coverage of the CXC® Religious Education syllabus.

Designed to help you achieve your best in the examination, this guide has been written by experienced teachers and examiners who have included features to make it easier to master the key concepts.

At the end of the book you will find a comprehensive glossary of all the key terms and their definitions, as well as practice exam questions for each section to test your knowledge.

Included with this Study Guide is an accompanying CD, which includes electronic activities that are designed to help you with your exam technique:

- **On your marks** activities are designed to provide experience of exam questions and offer guidance on improving grades. Each **On your marks** will provide you with an examination-style question, an example candidate answer and feedback from an examiner to show where the example candidate did well and how their answer could be improved.

- **Test yourself** activities are specifically designed to provide you with experience of multiple-choice exam questions. In addition to this, helpful feedback refers you back to the guide so that you can revise problem areas.

1 Essentials of religion

1.1   Definitions and features of religion

Definitions

Religion

Religion is a system of beliefs and practices that people follow in order to make sense of life, to bring meaning to their existence and to bring them comfort and guidance. Religions help to explain the creation of the world and recognise and meet the needs of the human spirit. Religions teach that a supreme or higher power is at work in the world – whether this is God, gods or spirits. Religions also provide a moral code to live by. There are many different religions in the world, but four of the world's major religions found in the Caribbean are Christianity, Hinduism, Islam and Judaism. This guide looks at each of these religions, as well as Caribbean indigenous religions.

Denomination

Denomination describes the various beliefs and practices between different branches of the same religion. Denominations tend to emerge gradually over time and are officially recognised in society. All of the Christian denominations have the same core beliefs, but they may interpret some teachings differently or emphasise a particular belief or practice above others. Examples of this include the teaching of the Methodist Church to abstain from alcohol, and the practice in the Roman Catholic Church of praying to the saints.

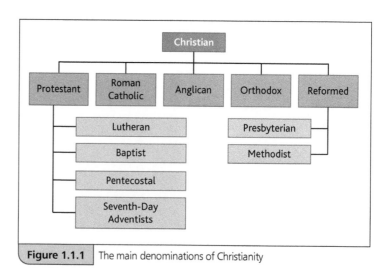

Figure 1.1.1 | The main denominations of Christianity

Sect

Sects are different groups within established religions that follow a system of belief (or doctrine) that differs from others within their religion. Sect and denomination are often used to mean the same thing.

For example, Hindus may worship God without form (nirguna) or with form (saguna). Within this categorisation, there are many different groups including Shaiva, Vaishnava, Shakteya and Kali Mai. During rituals, followers of the different groups wear particular markings to show which group they belong to.

ACTIVITY

Give definitions of 'denomination' and 'sect' in your own words, and cite examples of each within one of the major religions.

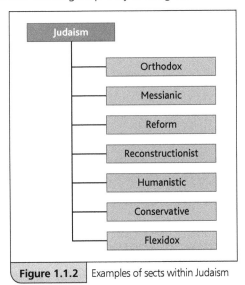

| **Figure 1.1.2** | Examples of sects within Judaism |

Cult

A cult is a small, recently created religious group. It is not a variation of an established religion, it is a new religion, and it is often founded by a charismatic leader. Cult leaders often have a high level of control over their members. Many people think that cults are dangerous and that they brainwash their followers. However, many cults are harmless and are made up of people who may be disillusioned with established religion. Often cults are radical in the way they live out their beliefs – for example, followers may live together in communes, dress in a particular way and choose to separate themselves from society.

Features of religion

Prayer

Prayer features in all religions. It is the means by which humans communicate with God, gods or spirits. Prayer may be in the form of liturgy (written words and movements) or people may use their own words to pray. Particular prayers are often read at significant times. For example, Christians say a prayer for forgiveness before they receive Holy Communion. Many people pray before eating to remind themselves to thank God for His provision of food. People pray in many different ways:

- Together in groups
- Individually
- Prayers spoken out loud
- Silently inside their own minds
- By way of meditation
- By serving people
- Ritual movements

People can pray on their own or in a group

Some religions have specific rules regarding prayer. For example, Muslims must pray five times a day as they face Makkah (Mecca). Jews pray three times a day – in the morning, the afternoon and the evening. Jesus taught Christians to pray using the Lord's Prayer. Hindus pray twice a day, at dawn and dusk. The one common factor that unites prayer in every religion is that it enables humans and God to communicate with each other and have a relationship.

Places of worship

LINK

There is more about places of worship in Section 3, Places of worship, beginning on page 18.

Many religions have a particular place of worship where followers can meet to pray and worship together. For Christians this place is called a church, for Hindus it is a mandir (temple) or a shrine at home, for Muslims it is the masjid (mosque) and musallah, for Jews it is the synagogue. Many Caribbean indigenous religions also have a meeting place, church, chapel or hall. Religions use different sacred objects and features within their buildings to aid worship.

Belief systems

Religious belief systems have been developed through holy scriptures and through a long history of teachings. A belief system is a set of core beliefs and practices that a person has that influences how they live, what they believe and what they value. Often these beliefs are linked to a particular religion. What a person believes about God, others and themselves will influence the decisions that person makes, how they relate to others, what they value and how they spend their time.

Rituals

Rituals prescribe particular ways of carrying out worship within different religions. For example:

- Muslims, some Hindus and Caribbean indigenous groups may offer meat from an animal as a sacrifice during some special ceremonies.
- Some Hindus also give offerings of flowers and fruit to their gods.
- In Islam, Muslims wash before prayers (called wudu in Arabic).

Different religions originated in different geographical areas. For this reason, particular languages remain important to religions.

Worship

Worship is a way of showing love, obedience and devotion. In religion, this love and devotion is shown to God. People worship in various ways. In Christianity, people often worship using songs and through written and spoken prayers. In Orisha, chants are often used in worship. Dance is an important element of worship in Revivalism.

Symbols

Symbols are objects or signs that carry a meaning. Religions often use symbols to help them worship. Symbols can also represent a religion or a particular aspect of a religion. The Star of David is the symbol of Judaism, and the cross in Christianity reminds Christians of how and why Jesus died. In Hinduism, the symbol for the sacred sound Aum signifies different states within Hinduism.

However, there are no symbols in Islam. Islam teaches its followers not to use symbols or pictures.

Figure 1.1.3 Can you state which religion these symbols are connected with?

Sacred writings

Sacred writings are books or pieces of writing that people believe are inspired by God. These writings help people to understand God and His purposes for humankind as well as giving guidance on how we should live. Sacred writings may also help to explain the origins of particular religions. Examples of sacred writings are the Bible for Christians, the Tenakh for Jews, the Qur'an for Muslims and the Holy Piby for Rastafari. Hindus have many sacred writings. The Ramayan of Tulsides is the best known in the Caribbean.

ACTIVITY

Match the language to the religion that it is connected with:

Arabic, Hebrew, Greek, Sanskrit, African/Creole

Christianity, Hinduism, Islam, Judaism, Caribbean indigenous religions

DID YOU KNOW?

- All Muslims are required to learn their holy language, and the language of the Jews is still used today.
- Hinduism uses its holy language in rituals and worship. Hindus also often use Hindi-related languages in their devotions, particularly in the Caribbean.
- Caribbean indigenous religions use mainly English, but this is sometimes mixed with words from African and Caribbean language forms.

Deities

Deity is another term for God. It is also the term used for multiple manifestations of God shown in Hindu gods and goddesses such as Brahma, Lakshmi and Durga. However, Islam does not use the term 'deity'.

Festivals

Within religions, festivals take place to mark a particular event within a religion's history or to celebrate a particular time of year. Festivals are usually celebrated with a special period of worship followed by people coming together and often giving gifts. Festivals are normally a time for celebration, but they also can be a time to think seriously about your religion and beliefs.

Rites of passage

Rites of passage are religious customs that mark a particularly significant time in a person's spiritual or physical life. Examples are:

- a Hindu child receiving their sacred thread. This can happen at any time from the age of eight and it marks the beginning of the Hindu child's spiritual education
- bar mitzvah (for boys) and bat mitzvah (for girls) in Judaism to mark their entry into adulthood
- Christian babies being christened when they are born to welcome them into God's family
- the Aqeeqah in Islam, where a baby is named, has their head shaved and (for boys) is circumcised seven days after birth
- the mourning ceremony for Spiritual Baptists where they focus on their spiritual rather than physical needs.

LINKS

There is more about sacred writings in Section 6, Major teachings and beliefs, starting on page 46, as well as within Option B, Hinduism.

There is more about religious festivals in Section 7, Festivals, starting on page 58.

There is more about rites of passage in Section 8, Religious practices and rites of passage, starting on page 74.

Human needs

You can learn about the principles and practices that make up a religion, but what makes someone choose to follow a religion? What is it that makes people need to believe in some power higher than them? And how do people choose which religion to believe in? There are many reasons why people follow a religion. Some of them are covered on the following pages.

Quest for personal identity

Religion gives an explanation for the existence of human beings – it explains where we have come from and why we are on the earth. Whichever religion you belong to, your purpose is to worship, to obey and to have a relationship with God. Religion teaches that we are God's creation – that is our identity. Belonging to a particular religion also provides you with a set of views and beliefs. It can ground you and help to make sense of life's issues and challenges.

To belong to a particular religion is to have a clear identity – to know what you believe in and how you should live. For most religions, being part of a worldwide group, with other believers, also helps the followers to have an identity and a sense of belonging.

Quest for personal fulfilment in life

Followers of religion argue that human beings are created to worship God, and that if we do not do this we will always have a sense of being incomplete. Knowing that you are following God's purposes for your life and living in a close relationship with Him can bring great personal fulfilment. Millions of people who follow religions have found that ultimate and lasting fulfilment and peace can only be found through God.

Search for harmony with nature and in human relationships

Religions teach us to be in harmony with, and to respect, nature as God's creation. This means protecting the world and not purposely harming or spoiling our environment. Religious people feel that this is because God created the world for us to enjoy. Judaism, Christianity and Islam believe God originally created a paradise called Eden for humans to enjoy. It could be that our souls are still trying to connect with that Eden today. Hindus see the earth as a manifestation of God's creative energy. Many Hindus worship Mother Earth and perform rituals to purify the atmosphere.

The onset of climate change has generated greater awareness of and responsibility towards nature and humanity together, as many people are suffering due to more extreme weather. Many religious people feel that they have to take action on climate change because it has been caused largely by humans and because it is damaging both the environment and human lives.

Religion is about building happy human relationships. Many religions provide teaching and advice on marriage, family relationships, how to deal with conflict and what our attitude should be to others. Following these teachings can bring inner peace and harmony.

Personal fulfilment

If I discover within myself a desire which no experience in this world can satisfy, the most probable explanation is that I was made for another world.

C.S. Lewis, 1898–1963, Christian writer and theologian

Many people who follow a religion feel that they have an obligation to care for the world

ACTIVITY

What other benefits can you think of that belief or faith brings to an individual? Make a list.

Seeking spiritual meaning

One of the biggest reasons people follow religion is to find spiritual meaning. It may be hard to try to follow the ideals and values of a particular religion, or to believe in something that you cannot see. However, many people feel that it would be harder still to believe that there is no meaning to life and that our experiences are insignificant. Not believing in any god is called **atheism**. Religion gives purpose to life, with all of its challenges, pain, sorrows and joys. Believing that whatever happens to us can be used for good – either to strengthen us or to help someone else or to bring us closer to God – brings comfort and strength. Knowing that there is life after we die, and that how we respond to events on earth can impact our eternal life, affects how we live and the decisions we make.

Providing moral codes as a guide for life

As touched on already, religion provides guidelines for life. The Tenakh contains the Ten Commandments, the Bible contains the Sermon on the Mount, the Qur'an contains teachings on good conduct and how to treat others. Caribbean Hindus rely on the Vedas, the Ramcharitmanas and Bhagavad Gita, among others, as their main guides for living a moral life. All of the world's religions regard human life as precious and as coming from God. Therefore, all people should be respected, cared for and treated with dignity. In this sense, religion is a positive contributor to society.

ACTIVITY

Write a short summary of your personal beliefs. What do you see as your religion?

KEY POINTS

1 All religions include key concepts such as worship, prayer, belief systems and rituals.

2 Religion can provide identity through explaining the origins and purpose of humankind. Belonging to a group of people also helps to bring identity.

3 Many followers of religion have found that ultimate personal fulfilment can only come from a relationship with God.

4 Religion teaches that we should respect our environment and fellow human beings.

5 Religion can bring meaning to life. Religion teaches that God can use our situations for good purposes – even if it is only to strengthen our faith. Many people who follow a religion believe that God ultimately shapes and directs our life if we allow Him to.

6 Religion can provide moral codes to live by.

2 God in religion

2.1 A Christian understanding of God

DID YOU KNOW?

'With the Lord a day is like a thousand years, and a thousand years are like a day.'
2 Peter 3:8

Some people believe that verses such as this one show how the biblical creation account and the science of evolution (animals and humans developing and changing over millions of years) can work together.

Creator

Christianity derives much of its understanding about God from Jewish beliefs, since Christianity grew out of Judaism. Christians believe in a single creator, God, who made the world and all living things in it. Belief in a single God is called **monotheism**.

The Bible describes how God created order from chaos just by speaking His instructions:

• On the first day, God created periods of light and darkness, which became day and night.

• On the second day, He created the sky.

• On the third day, He gathered the water into oceans and created areas of dry land. On this dry land He commanded plants and trees to grow.

• On the fourth day, He created the sun, moon and stars to give light to the earth and create the seasons.

• On the fifth day, He created fish and birds and told them to multiply and fill the skies and the oceans.

• On the sixth day, God created animals and people. God was very pleased with all that He had made.

• On the seventh day, He rested.

Christians believe that God created a perfect world where God and human beings were in harmony. Sin entered the world as a result of Adam and Eve (the first humans) disobeying God. With the arrival of sin came sickness, disaster and evil. The Old Testament section of the Bible is full of accounts of how God's people suffered in a broken world, and of the troubled relationship between God and man.

Despite all of their sin, God loved His people (the Israelites). He delivered them from slavery in Egypt and led them to freedom in a land He had promised them (Exodus 3:7–8). Even after God's people reached this new land though, it did not take long for sin, disobedience and separation from God to build again. To break this cycle, the Old Testament promises a future deliverer or liberator who will bring freedom from sin for ever.

The Bible says that God created the world and everything in it in six days

Jesus Christ – Deliverer and Liberator

Christians believe that Jesus Christ is the Deliverer and Liberator that the Old Testament speaks about. Christians believe that God came to earth in the human form of Jesus. Christians call this 'incarnation'. God came to earth in human form to restore the relationship between God and people and to bring freedom from sin, sickness and death. While he was on earth, Jesus healed people, forgave their sins and even brought people back to life after they had died. (You can read about these things in the biblical gospels Matthew, Mark, Luke and John.) But Jesus' ultimate act was his death and resurrection. Christians believe that the consequence of sin is death – physically and spiritually. Through his sacrificial death, Jesus, who was perfect and had never sinned, defeated sin and therefore death. Jesus' sacrifice shows that God could forgive people's sin and He goes on forgiving today.

Holy Spirit

After Jesus' death, the Bible teaches that he came back to life and returned to heaven. Christians believe that God then sent His spirit, the Holy Spirit, to be His presence in the world. The Holy Spirit is one of the three persons of the **Trinity**. The Holy Spirit came to the first Christians at Pentecost. The Holy Spirit lives in the believer and brings comfort, guidance, peace and strength.

God as father and mother

The Bible says that human beings were made in God's image. This means that the human qualities we have – such as a conscience, morality, spirituality, love, personality, dominion and creativity – are reflections of God. Since God made both man and woman in His image, many Christians believe that He must have both male and female characteristics.

Christians believe that God loves them as a loving parent loves their child and that, like a parent, He also has to discipline them, teach them and help them to grow. In Matthew 23:37 the Bible describes God as wanting to gather His people under His wings as a mother hen gathers her chicks. And Matthew 7:11 compares God to a loving father who wants to give good gifts to His children.

Major manifestations of God in Hinduism

The majority of Hindus believe in many different deities (male and female divinities) who have appeared in different forms or incarnations. Each of these gods and goddesses derive from **Brahman**, who is the Ultimate Reality or God. Some people see Hinduism as a polytheistic or pantheistic religion (believing in more than one god). Others see Hinduism as a monotheistic religion, since all Hindu gods descend from Brahman.

The central Hindu gods, as descended from Brahman, are Brahma, Vishnu and Shiva (called the Brahman Trinity or Trimurti). The central goddess is Shakti. All other gods and goddesses are incarnations, spouses or offspring of these major gods and goddess. There are many different traditions or branches of Hinduism and different traditions may believe slightly different things about the gods. Also, not all Hindus worship all of the gods. Generally, Hindus choose one or two of the Hindu gods to focus on and worship, and will probably build a shrine to these deities in their home, as per family tradition or personal choice.

The Trimutri: Brahma (left), Vishnu (middle) and Shiva (right)

Brahma

Brahma is the Creator. Hindus believe Brahma created the world but, once creation was complete, Brahma's work was finished. Brahma is not worshipped as it is thought that he is responsible for distracting people from nourishing their soul and thinking instead about their physical desires.

Vishnu

Vishnu is the preserver and protector of creation. He is full of mercy and goodness. Vishnu maintains life and the cosmic order of creation. Vishnu has many incarnations to redress the balance of **dharma** and **adharma**.

Shiva

Hindus believe Shiva (or Mahesh) is the destroyer god. Along with Brahma and Vishnu, he is responsible for the ongoing cycle of creation, preservation and destruction of the world. Shiva is considered the god of change. His destruction is not always bad – it may bring death but it can also bring freedom from our ego (self) and from bad habits.

Lakshmi

Lakshmi is the goddess of health, beauty, wealth and good fortune. She is Vishnu's wife and is very beautiful. Each time Vishnu incarnates, Lakshmi incarnates with him as his companion (or consort).

Saraswati

Saraswati is the goddess of knowledge, music and the creative arts. During their examinations, students worship this goddess in the hope she will help them do well!

Ganesh

Ganesh is an elephant-headed god who represents wisdom and intellect. Many Hindus worship him when they want to remove obstacles in their life – perhaps obstacles to belief or to their happiness or success. The fact that Ganesh has an elephant head encourages Hindus to look beyond outer appearances and to the spiritual side of life. Ganesh is the god who is called on at the start of every Hindu ritual.

Saraswati (left), Lakshmi (middle) and Ganesh (right)

Hanuman

Hanuman is the monkey god, an incarnation of Shiva. He is known for his courage, strength and devotion. Hanuman teaches Hindus of the power that lies in every person. In times of trouble, many Hindus will chant the name Hanuman or sing his chalisa (hymn) to gain strength and perseverance.

Surya

Surya is the Hindu sun god. Since Surya controls light and warmth, he is an important god in terms of influencing the seasons and therefore is worshipped in relation to blessing crops.

Durga

The goddess Durga was created by Hindu gods who each formed a different part of her body. Durga is the warrior aspect of Shakti and was created to fight evil forces who were overpowering the gods. Durga signifies the unity of all the gods. In some Hindu traditions, Durga is the wife of Shiva.

Hanuman

Surya

Durga

KEY POINTS

1 Brahman is the Ultimate Reality or God in Hinduism. All other gods are manifestations of Brahman. Each of these gods, in turn, has multiple avatars or incarnations. Although Hinduism is often described as polytheistic because of its many gods, this labelling is not strictly true since all gods derive from a single God.

2 The central Hindu gods are Brahma, Vishnu and Shiva (the Brahman Trinity) and the central goddess is Shakti. All other gods and goddesses are manifestations, spouses or offspring of these main gods and goddess.

3 Different traditions of Hinduism prioritise different gods. Hindus worship different gods at different times in their lives, although many Hindus also have a favourite god.

Relationship with Allah in Islam

Muslims, like Christians and Jews, believe in only one God. Their belief in the Oneness of God is called **Tawhid**. They call God Allah, the Arabic word for God. The Qur'an and **Hadith** refer to Allah in 99 different ways, each revealing something about His attributes.

Creator and created

Al-Khaaliq means Allah the Creator. Muslims believe that Allah created the universe and everything in it. Humans are the most important part of Allah's creation. The Qur'an states that the first human was made out of clay. Today Allah continues to create human beings through the human reproduction process, which He oversees (see Surah 23:12–14).

All living things depend upon Allah for their existence, therefore humans should submit to Allah as a servant submits to his master. This is such a central belief to Muslims that the word 'Islam' literally means submission to Allah. Submission is not meant to be difficult or painful. The relationship between Allah and His servants is one of obedience and love. Submitting to Allah is to put your life into the hands of an all-powerful God who loves and cares deeply for you. Hadith number 19 of An-Nawawi's 40 Hadith speaks of how everything that happens is under Allah's control.

Allah's love and mercy for man

Surah 2:21–22 gives examples of how Allah shows love for His people through providing for them. These verses also tell readers that they should love Allah. Although Allah is all-powerful and holy, He does not judge people harshly when they do wrong. Surah 3:31 tells how Allah is ready to forgive and show mercy. In response, Muslims should show their love for Allah by living lives dedicated to Him. Surah 9:24 talks about how Allah should be more important to Muslims than any worldly wealth, possession or pleasure. Man should value his relationship with Allah above all else. This means loving Allah, living a life that pleases Him and following the Five Pillars of Islam (Shahadah – the Muslim declaration of faith; salah – prayer; zakah – giving to the poor; sawm – fasting; and hajj – pilgrimage to Makkah).

| The Shahadah | Salah | Zakah | Sawm | Hajj |

Figure 2.3.1 The five pillars support the 'House of Islam'. Through putting the five pillars into practice, Muslims uphold their religion.

Worshipped and worshipper

The relationship between Allah and Muslims is one of worshipped and worshipper. To worship means to show obedience, adoration and devotion to God. Muslims believe that Allah should be worshipped as the one true God who is above all things. He is holy, almighty, compassionate and all-knowing. He is far beyond our understanding or our power. He is infinitely bigger than us and therefore our only response should be to worship him. Worship can come in many forms – it is shown through the rites and ceremonies that Muslims perform such as salah (prayer) and wudu (ritual washing). But worship is also shown through the way Muslims live their lives – through zakah, through kind acts and through living honourably and peacefully. In these ways, Muslims worship Allah.

Hadith

The Hadith are the sayings, actions and silent approvals of Muhammad, which do not appear in the Qur'an but which were written down by his followers. An-Nawawi was an Islamic scholar who lived in Damascus. He was born in AH 631 (1234 CE) and died in AH 676 (1278 CE). During his 44 years of life he wrote many Islamic texts. The best known is the An-Nawawi 40 Hadith. This is a collection of 42 Hadith that An-Nawawi collected and sourced. These 42 Hadith are considered the core Hadith for Muslims.

Human and race relations

As well as loving and worshipping Allah, Muslims show their faith by the way they treat other human beings, regardless of their race or religion. Islam teaches that Muslims should not intentionally cause harm to anyone. A well-known Hadith is: 'Fear Allah wherever you are, and follow up a bad deed with a good one and it will wipe it out, and behave well towards people' (An-Nawawi 40 Hadith number 18).

DID YOU KNOW?

Muslims follow a lunar calendar (controlled by cycles of the moon). Each year in the Islamic calendar is designated AH (which stands for the Latin term Anno Hegirae (in the year of the Hijra)) or BH (before Hijra). AH time began the year Muhammad migrated from Makkah to Medina (this migration, or journey, is called the Hijra).

KEY POINTS

Muslims believe that:

- there is one God, Allah, who created the world and humanity
- we should worship Allah and submit to His will. All of life is controlled by Him
- Allah is full of love and mercy towards mankind and He expects His followers to show love towards each other.

The nature of God in Judaism

The one and only God

Like Christians and Muslims, Jews believe in a single God. A very important verse of the Tenakh to Jews is Deuteronomy 6:4. Jews call this verse **Shema**. It declares that the Jewish God, Yahweh, is the one God. The verse also reminds Jews that they are God's chosen people (**elected**). Jews say this verse twice a day (morning and evening).

One in His works

Jews believe that Yahweh is the single creator of the world. Genesis 1:1 states that 'In the beginning God created the heavens and the earth'. As well as scriptural evidence, Jews believe that the beauty and complexity of nature prove that God must have designed it. As well as creating the world, Jews believe that God controls and sustains it.

One in His attributes

Jews believe that God is incorporeal – that is, He is spirit rather than a physical being. The fact that He is spirit means that He is not bound by time and space – He can be everywhere at the same time.

Jews also believe that God is eternal. God has existed since before time began and will go on existing forever. God's nature is also eternal in the sense that He never changes.

Omni is the Latin word for 'all'. Jews believe that God is omnipotent (all-powerful), omniscient (all-knowing) and omnipresent (all-present/everywhere) by His spirit. The Tenakh tells of powerful acts of God, such as when He divided the Red Sea (Exodus 14) and created the world.

> Hear O Israel, the Lord is our God, the Lord is One.
>
> Deuteronomy 6:4

God also knows His creation intricately. He knows the movements of planets and when volcanoes will erupt, as well as the thoughts and desires of every human heart. Psalm 139 is a very well-known passage that talks about God knowing everything about us.

Finally, since God is omnipresent, Jews believe He can be everywhere, with everyone, at the same time. Jews also believe that, since all of nature was created by God, all of nature must reflect His handiwork.

Compassionate and merciful judge

The Tenakh states that God is compassionate and merciful. However, God is also holy and all-powerful. Two of the Hebrew names for God, 'Elohim' and 'Adonai', describe God's authority and role as Master. He demands obedience and devotion and judges all actions.

Sacredness of God

The sacredness of God's name is very important in Judaism. The Hebrew name for God is Yahweh. Jews believe that God's name is so holy that it cannot be spoken or written down. Therefore, when writing God's name, Jews write YHWH or G-d. Another example of

God's judgement

The righteousness of the righteous will be credited to them, and the wickedness of the wicked will be charged against them. But if a wicked person turns away from all the sins they have committed and keeps all my decrees and does what is just and right, that person will surely live; they will not die.

Ezekiel 18:20b–21

Jews respecting God's sacredness is that, when they read the Torah, they use a silver pointer (a yad) to follow the words so that their fingers do not touch the sacred pages.

God's covenants with Abram, Moses and David

Throughout history, God made covenants with His people. A covenant describes an exchange of promises. God promised Abram (Abraham), that he would be the patriarch (father) of a great nation and that the Jews would bring blessing to the earth. The covenant was renewed with Abram's son Isaac and Isaac's son Jacob. God also promised that He would be with Abram and his descendants. In return, Abram and his descendants must always remember God and keep His laws, including being circumcised. Abram also had to go to a land that God directed him to. In Abram's old age, his wife Sarah gave birth to a son, Isaac – this was the start of the Jewish nation. When Abram died, God's blessings were passed on to Isaac and then to Isaac's son, Jacob. God told Jacob:

> you will have descendants as many as dust! … and all the nations of the earth will be blessed through you and your descendants.

Genesis 28:13–14

Although God promised to bless Abram, Isaac, Jacob and their descendants, this did not mean that life would always be easy. One period when it may have seemed to the Jews that God had forgotten His promise was when the Jews were slaves in Egypt.

After helping the Israelites to escape from Egypt, God gave Moses instructions for how the Jewish people should live. These form the Torah that Jews follow today. The best known of these laws are the Ten Sayings (Christians call these the Ten Commandments) recorded in Exodus 20:1–17.

David was a Jewish king who ruled Israel for 40 years. He made mistakes, but God was with him, and blessed him and the Jewish people through him. God promised that David's son would make the Jewish kingdom strong. He again renewed His promise to be with the Jewish people and to love them, and He promised that the Jewish people would have an Everlasting Kingdom. It was through David's lineage that the Messiah would come. David's son, Solomon, built a Jewish Temple in Jerusalem. Today, only one wall of the Temple remains after it was destroyed by the Romans in 70 CE. This wall is known as the Western or Wailing Wall.

Jews use a yad (a silver pointer) when they read from the Torah. This is so that their flesh does not touch the Jewish scriptures, which are considered sacred.

God kept His covenant with Moses and led the Jews out of Egypt to a land He had promised them

KEY POINTS

Jews believe that:

- there is one God, Yahweh, who created the world
- God is incorporeal (spirit), eternal, all-knowing, all-powerful and present everywhere
- God is a compassionate judge
- God is holy and should be worshipped but He also wants a relationship with His people. He has made covenants through the ages that outline His promise to bless Israel and be with the Jewish people, in exchange for obedience and love from them.

ACTIVITY

Read in Exodus about how God kept His covenant with the Jews during their time of slavery and led them out of Egypt. What were the 10 plagues that God sent on Egypt?

The concept of God in Caribbean indigenous religions

Bible verse that Rastafari believe refers to Haile Selassie

I, Jesus, have sent my angel to you to tell the churches all these things. I am both David's root and his descendant. I am the bright morning star.

Revelation 22:16

Haile Selassie was the final Emperor of Ethiopia. Rastafari believe he was the final incarnation of God on earth.

Rastafari

Rastafari believe that Ras Tafari is the living God, **Jah.** This is the same God that Christians and Jews believe in. Some Rastafari believe that Jesus Christ was God on earth. However, unlike Christians, orthodox and theocratic Rastafari believe that Haile Selassie, the final Emperor of Ethiopia, was the reincarnated Christ.

The belief in God coming to earth in various forms is one that the Rastafari religion shares with Hinduism. Rastafari believe in the Trinity of God as the Father, Son and Holy Spirit (the name Haile Selassie means 'the power of the Trinity'). They believe that God lives in the human heart and soul in the form of the Holy Spirit. This presence of the Holy Spirit creates oneness with God and oneness (equality) with other people. This concept is expressed in the term 'I and I' that Rastafari use instead of 'we'.

Rastafari believe Emperor Haile Selassie to be the Supreme Being. Rastafari believe that the titles 'King of Kings', 'Lord of Lords' and 'Conquering Lion of the Tribe of Judah', given to him at his coronation, link Selassie to the biblical use of the titles, and therefore confirm him as a deity. Other titles for him are His Imperial Majesty or HIM. Rastafari believe that Haile Selassie was divine. They cite verses such as Revelation 22:16 and Psalm 87:4 as evidence of Haile Selassie's divinity.

Rastafari, like Christians and Jews, believe that God (Jah) created the world and everything in it. However, unlike Christianity and Judaism, Rastafari believe that Jah created the plant marijuana, which is used as a sacrament in some of their services, to be used to help gain spiritual enlightenment.

Revivalism

Revivalism has many ties to Christianity. It believes in the Bible and, in this sense, believes some of the same things about God as Christianity does. There are two forms of Revivalism – Zion and Pukumina. Zion has closer links to Christianity and Pukumina has closer links to African religion. Unlike Christianity though, Revivalism focuses on three levels of spirits: heavenly, ground and earthbound spirits.

Heavenly spirits in Revivalism are the Christian deities such as God, archangels, saints and angels. Earthbound spirits are fallen angels who have been expelled from heaven. These include Satan and evil spirits. Finally, ground spirits are spirits of people's ancestors. Revivalists believe that if ground spirits are honoured they will take care of you in this life. However, of the three types of spirit, Zion Revivalism mainly focuses on the heavenly spirits, while Pukumina focuses on ground and earthbound spirits.

Vodun

Vodun has much of its roots in ethnic African practices and Roman Catholic Christianity. However, it veers away from Christianity in some of its practices – particularly animal sacrifice and possession by many spirits.

Vodun believes in one God who is known as **Grand Maitre** (the Great Master/Creator) or Bon Dieu (Good God). Grand Maitre has many helpers (or **orishas**). Vodun believes that the chief God, Olorun, authorised a less-powerful God, Obatala, to create the earth.

Vodun believes in hundreds of minor spirits that are present in nature and can possess human beings. These spirits are known as loas or lwas. Some of these loas came with Vodun from Dahomey (what is now the West African country Benin). Dahomey spirits are called Rada loas. Other loas were added to Vodun at a later date. Many of these are thought to be the spirits of deceased leaders. These are called Petro loas.

Orisha

Like many of the Caribbean indigenous religions, Orisha originated from Africa. However, when it arrived in the Caribbean, it mixed with the beliefs and practices of Roman Catholicism to form its own distinct religion.

Orisha believes in one Supreme Being – Olodumare. Followers of Orisha believe that Olodumare has many smaller gods (or orishas) who carry out his work. The god Obatala created the world and humanity. Shango is the warrior god of thunder, lightning, fire, drums and dance. The god Oshun rules over the waters of the world and embodies love and fertility.

Spiritual Baptist

Spiritual Baptists have the same view of God as Christians. They believe in the Trinity of God with an emphasis on the Holy Spirit. They believe that there are other spirits, such as the Orisha spirits, but they do not believe that any god should be worshipped other than the God of Christianity.

Santeria

Santeria, like Orisha, also believes in Olodumare as the one Supreme God. Followers of Santeria believe that Olodumare is the source of Ashe – the life force that runs through all things and controls what happens in life. Followers of Santeria obtain Ashe through their conduct and good character, which also gives them inner peace.

Santeria also believes in orishas (lesser gods). Male and female priests in the religion are thought to have been possessed by a particular orisha. This gives them spiritual powers, such as being able to see into the future and bring healing to people.

Spiritual Baptists dance, drum, ring bells, sing and shout in their worship. Their churches can be very loud and lively places!

3 Places of worship

3.1

Christian places of worship

Christians believe that God is everywhere and lives within a person through the Holy Spirit. A person does not have to be in a church, chapel or cathedral to be close to God. In fact, many people feel closest to God when they are enjoying the nature that He created, or through seeing God within other people. However, places of worship within Christianity give a focal place for people to come to worship God. Buildings also enable group worship to take place. Many people find great comfort and encouragement through worshipping together.

A church building

This is the most common place for Christians to worship. It is used on Saturdays and Sundays for Christians to gather for services, which include prayer, singing and teaching. Churches are also often used during the week for meetings, Bible study and community activities. Some churches, particularly Roman Catholic and Anglican ones, are highly decorative and are designed with features such as a font (for baptising babies), a pulpit (a raised area to preach from), a nave (the central area where people sit) and an altar (an area to kneel and receive **Holy Communion** or prayer). Other churches may be small, simple halls. Some church groups do not meet in a specially designed building but rent out a building, such as a school, to meet in.

Worshippers at a church service

Temples

In Jesus' time, the Temple was a common place of worship for Jews in Jerusalem. The Temple was also the place where Jews would meet to study. There is a famous account in the Bible of Jesus turning over tables in the Temple in Jerusalem (Matthew 21:12). Traders were using the temple to deceive and make money from people. For Christians today, a temple is another name given to a church, although there are not many Christian temples in existence.

Tabernacles

During the Israelites' escape from Egypt, it was necessary for them to transport the Ark of the Covenant (a sacred chest that contained the Ten Commandments, written on tablets of stone). This was too holy for men to touch, so a tabernacle (a tent-like structure that could be carried) was created to contain the Ark. Today, many Christian churches are given the title of tabernacle. Christians believe that God is always with them, but naming a church a tabernacle reminds worshippers that the church is a holy place where God should be the focus of their thoughts. The chest or box on a church altar that contains the sacraments for Holy Communion is also referred to as a tabernacle.

Cathedrals

In the Anglican denomination, churches in a geographical area are grouped together into diocese. A cathedral is the head church in a diocese (group) of churches. It is the place where the bishop of a city or area is based. Roman Catholic and Orthodox traditions also have cathedrals. Many cathedrals are very old and often contain beautiful architecture. St Michael's Cathedral in Bridgetown, Barbados is a very old cathedral. St George's Cathedral in Georgetown, Guyana is the tallest wooden building in South America.

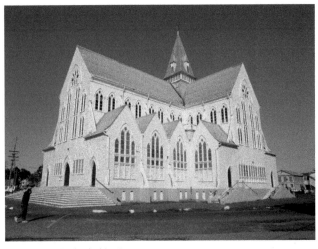

St George's Cathedral in Guyana

Basilica

A basilica is a church with architecture similar to the basilicas of ancient Rome. It has aisles on each side of a central area (the nave), a colonnade and an apse at one end (a large open area with a domed or arched roof). A church can also be named a basilica by the Pope – usually this is because the building is a **pilgrimage** site or contains relics of a saint or significant religious object. Services in basilicas are generally very formal and traditional. The Minor Basilica of the Immaculate Conception is found in Castries, St Lucia.

Assembly halls or tents

An assembly hall or tent is a less formal place of worship than a church. Assembly halls are normally simple halls that have chairs and usually a piano, drums or guitar. Often these halls are also used during the week by the congregation and community. Assembly halls are most often found in villages or small towns. Tents are used for Christian worship when no building is available (sometimes temporarily), or when an event is taking place that the public are invited to. A tent can give more space than a hall and has the advantage that it can be set up anywhere. Many church groups run community events or services in tents in public places.

'Assembly' is the term used to describe a gathering of worshippers. An assembly may meet in a building, in a tent or in the open air. Churches often run services in the open air in order to **evangelise**.

Chapels

A chapel is a small and usually very simple church building. Chapels are often found in villages. A chapel can also be a room in a public place that is allocated for worship and prayer. Hospitals, airports and funeral homes contain chapels where people can be quiet to reflect and pray. Many cemeteries, universities and large places of work also contain chapels. Methodist churches are also often called chapels.

Sacred places in Hinduism

LEARNING OUTCOMES

In this topic you will learn to:

- identify the sacred places of worship and teerthas in Hinduism.

Hindus believe that Brahman, the Ultimate Reality, is in all things and is present in all of creation. This is one reason why there are so many sacred objects in Hinduism, including trees, rivers, mountains, animals and plants. It is important to Hindus that they have a focal point to worship their chosen god and to offer gifts to him or her. A collective place of worship is not as important to Hindus as it is to followers of other religions.

Home altar

Hindu worship (puja) mainly takes place at a **home altar** or **shrine**. Hindus will designate a part of their home (or somewhere close to it) for worship of their god and will set up a shrine containing a statue or image of the god that they worship. Each morning, an elder of the family will present fresh flowers and other gifts on the shrine (such as incense and fruit). Each person in the family will then carry out their own worship in front of the shrine before their day begins.

Mandirs

Many Hindus travel to a temple (known as a mandir) to worship too. Mandirs contain a shrine that may have one or more deities. Inside the mandir, Hindus sit on the floor and face the shrine to worship. During worship, music is played, bhajans sung and sacred scriptures are recited. As well as being centres for collective worship, some mandirs are centres for religious teaching and schools as well as being social centres for the Hindu community to gather.

The temple in the sea in Trinidad

Teerthas

As well as places that people have created (buildings and shrines), nature is very important in Hinduism and many aspects of nature are considered sacred. Many natural places become places of pilgrimage (**teerthas**) that Hindus travel to in order to gain spiritual enlightenment and good karma.

Holy rivers

Rivers are particularly significant in Hinduism. Hinduism has seven holy rivers. Hindus believe that if you bathe in any of these rivers, bad karma (bad deeds from your past) will be washed away. Hindus also believe that if their ashes are scattered on a holy river when they die, their soul will be able to move quickly on to the next life and perhaps escape the cycle of birth, death and rebirth that all people are caught up in. Hinduism's most holy river is the Ganges in India. Every 12 years a bathing fair called a Kumbh Mela is held at the River Ganges where it meets the Yamuna and Saraswatti rivers. People bathe in the river to have their past sins washed away, and people who are ill believe that bathing in the river may make them well. Situated on the banks of the Ganges, Varanasi is one of the oldest cities in the world. It is the most sacred city for Hindus. It is also considered to be the dwelling place of Lord Shiva.

Spiritual Hindu bathers at the River Ganges

Sacred plants and trees

Certain plants or trees have special significance in Hinduism and are considered sacred. There are many sacred trees and plants in Hinduism. Three of the most sacred are as follows:

- The tolsi tree is found at many Hindu temples, especially those dedicated to Vishnu and Krishna. It is also in every Hindu home.
- The neem tree has many curative properties. Ancient Hindus attributed this to the fact that a drop of heavenly nectar fell on it. The flower of the neem tree is offered to God and its bitter leaves are chewed on New Year's Day to symbolise accepting the good with the bad.
- The lotus flower symbolises beauty, purity and divinity. Many Hindu gods are shown with a lotus flower. The lotus flower symbolises the goddess Lakshmi and is one of the incarnations of the goddess Devi. The lotus flower also symbolises spiritual enlightenment. Most Hindu homes will have one in the home.

Sacred animals

All animals are respected in Hinduism since Brahman, the Ultimate Reality, is thought to reside in every living thing. However, certain animals are considered more important than others. The cow is the most sacred animal to a Hindu and Hindus are forbidden to eat beef (many Hindus do not eat any meat at all). Cows are considered sacred as they are very gentle creatures and because they represent sacrifice through providing milk to humankind. Milk is essential for our health and well-being. Also, milk is needed for ghee (clarified butter), which is a very important offering made to the gods in worship.

The cobra is another sacred animal in Hinduism. It is thought to symbolise power and represents the cosmic energy coiled and sleeping in every person.

ACTIVITY

What are the names of Hinduism's seven holy rivers? Can you find out any interesting facts about them?

Many of Hinduism's holy plants also have strong medicinal qualities. Tulsi is said to be a powerful stress reliever and antiviral remedy.

DID YOU KNOW?

Everything the cow produces – milk, curds, ghee butter, urine and dung – can be used in Hindu worship. For example, cow dung can be used as disinfectant, as a building material and in place of firewood.

KEY POINTS

1 Hindus believe Brahman (the Ultimate Reality) is present everywhere.

2 Hindus worship at home shrines and Hindu temples (mandirs).

3 Nature is very important in Hinduism. Many natural objects are considered sacred.

Places of worship in Islam

The Kaaba in Makkah, Saudi Arabia

LINK

There is more about the hajj in Section 6.3, Major teachings of Islam, starting on page 50.

Masjidul Aqsa, Jerusalem

Masjidun Nabi, Saudi Arabia

Worship in Islam is not confined to any particular place. The Prophet Muhammad stated that the entire earth is a masjid (mosque). Therefore, Muslims can pray anywhere, except for toilets and dirty places. Muslims should always be conscious of Allah and be in submission to Him. At the call to prayer, Muslims are required to stop what they are doing and, wherever they are, put down a prayer mat, face the direction of Makkah and pray. That said, masjids are important places for Muslims. They allow for congregational worship and teaching, as well as providing a place for the Muslim community to meet and support one another. Three of the most important masjids are Masjid al-Haram, which houses the Kaaba, Masjidul Aqsa and Masjidun Nabi.

Masjids

Masjid al-Haram

The Kaaba is a cube-shaped building situated in the masjid in Makkah in Saudi Arabia. Muslims believe that Abraham built the Kaaba with his son Ishmael after Ishmael had settled in Arabia. Very few people are allowed in the Kaaba itself, but people are allowed in the masjid built around the Kaaba, called the Masjid al-Haram. The Masjid al- Haram is the largest masjid in the world. One of the Five Pillars (the central beliefs) of Islam is that all Muslims should go on a pilgrimage to the Kaaba at Makkah at least once in their lifetime. This pilgrimage is called the hajj.

Masjidul Aqsa

Masjidul Aqsa is the masjid situated on Temple Mount (known to Muslims today as Haram al-Sharif) in the old city of Jerusalem. The Dome of the Rock is also located here. Muslims believe that the dome of the masjid covers the place (the rock) from which Muhammad ascended to heaven. It is believed that Muhammad was transported from Masjid al-Haram to the site of Masjidul Aqsa during his **Night Journey.** The Masjidul Aqsa was the second place of worship built to Allah, according to Muslim belief. The Kaaba, built by Abraham and Ishmael, was the first.

Masjidun Nabi

Masjidun Nabi is the masjid that the Prophet Muhammad helped to build and worshipped in. It is located in Medina, Saudi Arabia (after the Prophet moved to this city its name was changed from Yathrib). Masjidun Nabi is the second most holy site in Islam (after Masjid al-Haram). It is here that Muhammad is buried. A green dome has been erected in the centre of the mosque over his tomb.

Features of a masjid

Outside the masjid

- Minaret: The minaret is the tower from which the mu'adhdhin gives the call to prayer (called the Adhan) five times a day. The tower is tall so that the mu'adhdhin's voice can carry and be heard across the community, as well as to show the importance of the Adhan. Today, the Adhan is called by a person over a loudspeaker from the minaret.
- Dome: Domes are built over the prayer hall. This helps the acoustics (quality of sound) in the masjid.

Inside the masjid

- Prayer area: Masjids contain one large open space where Muslims pray. This area is carpeted and often contains decorated rugs but no cushions or seating. The prayer itself makes all Muslims to be equal in prayer before God. People from all walks of life stand shoulder to shoulder as equals before God.
- Qibla wall: The qibla wall shows the direction of the Kaaba in Makkah. This is important because Muslims must always face Makkah when they pray.
- Mihrab arch: Within the qibla wall is the mihrab arch – the imam faces into this arch (towards the direction of Makkah) to lead prayers. The sound echoes back from the arch and enables worshippers to hear the imam's words. The mihrab arch is decorated with patterns and Islamic calligraphy (writing).
- Minbar: The minbar is a raised platform from which the imam speaks to the congregation during Friday prayers. The minbar allows everyone in the mosque to see and hear the imam.
- Washing area: Most masjids have a washing area for worshippers to perform wudu (ritual washing) before praying.
- Clocks: Most masjids display a row of clocks showing the times that prayers will be held each day (this varies depending on where in the world the masjid is and what time the sun rises and sets).

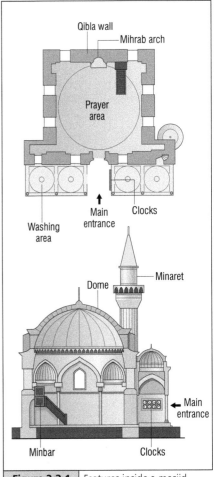

Figure 3.3.1 | Features inside a masjid

DID YOU KNOW?

Caribbean masjids are built with the front of the masjid facing Makkah. This means that Muslims face the front of the masjid to pray and do not need a qibla wall.

Islamic centres

As well as masjids, Muslims often meet in Islamic centres (sometimes mosques double up as Islamic centres too). These centres provide community and religious services, such as Islamic schools and libraries, and often act as a kind of community and advice centre for Muslims. Worship can take place in Islamic centres too.

KEY POINTS

1. Muslims pray five times each day.

2. Masjids (mosques) are important centres for worship and community support.

3. The three most important and sacred masjids are Masjidul Aqsa, Masjidun Nabi and Masjid al-Haram.

4. All masjids have common features, such as a minaret and a minbar.

Places of worship in Judaism

Temples and synagogues

The Jewish Temple in Jerusalem was destroyed by the Romans in 70 CE. The Temple was the central and most important place for Jews to worship God. This is where Jews would gather on important religious occasions. However, with the destruction of the Temple, synagogues that had been used for Jews to worship in locally in their towns and villages became more important. Today, Jews worship in synagogues.

Like Christian churches, synagogues are normally used for far more than worship. They are also used as community centres – for example for senior citizens clubs and youth clubs, and for the study of Jewish traditions, beliefs and customs.

Synagogues can vary greatly in their outward appearance. The most important feature is that they are built facing the direction of Jerusalem.

The Sha'are Shalom synagogue in Kingston has sand on the floor to remind the Jews of their flight from Egypt

Features of a synagogue

• Prayer hall: Inside a synagogue is a central prayer hall. In some Orthodox synagogues men and older boys sit on the ground floor while women and children sit on the balcony. However, these days in the reform tradition many families all sit together on the ground floor. Synagogues contain four main features for worship:

  – Aron Hakodesh/the Ark: The Ark is a large cupboard or alcove in the wall that faces Jerusalem. The Ark contains the scroll on which the Torah is written.

  – Ner Tamid/the perpetual light: Above the Ark is a light that never goes out. It signifies the light in the original Jewish Temple in Jerusalem that always burned. It also gives reassurance to worshippers that God is always with them.

- Sefer Torah/scrolls of the Torah: This is the scroll that is taken out of the Ark to be read to the congregation during a service in the synagogue. A particular passage on the scroll will be selected for that day's reading.
- Binah/platform: This is a raised area in the front or centre of the synagogue from which the Sefer Torah is read out to the congregation.

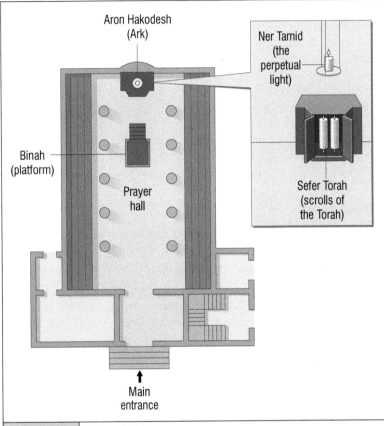

The Congregation Mikvé Israel-Emmanuel synagogue in Willemstad, Curaçao. Built in 1692, it is the oldest synagogue in use in the Western Hemisphere and contains several copies of the Torah that are more than 300 years old.

Figure 3.4.1 | Features inside a synagogue

ACTIVITY

Why do many people refer to the Western Wall of the Jewish Temple in Jerusalem as the Wailing Wall? Many Jews and Christians believe that the Temple in Jerusalem will be rebuilt before the Last Days. Find out more about these beliefs.

KEY POINTS

1 Synagogues are used by Jews for worship and as community centres.

2 Although synagogues may look very different from the outside, they have certain common features. These include a prayer hall and a Binah.

Places of worship in Caribbean indigenous religions

Rastafari

Rastafari believe that their body is the Temple of Jah so they do not need special buildings in which to worship. However, Rastafari do use some buildings – called temples or tabernacles – for worship. Often these buildings are situated in camps where Rastafari live communally. The Bobo Shanti Community in Bull Bay, Jamaica is an example of a Rastafari camp, with their worship taking place in August Town square. Rastafari respect nature and so will often sit outside to worship and learn more about their faith. Rastafari worship through meditation, prayer, drumming, chanting and **reasoning.** The Nyabhingi group of Rastafaris in particular use chants, rhythm and drums in their worship. These chants have had a big influence on ska, reggae and rocksteady music.

Revivalism

Revivalists gather together to worship on a Saturday or Sunday and throughout the week in either churches or mission houses. Revivalist worship includes singing, Bible reading and sometimes spirit possession.

Special Revivalist services include the Table where a table is spread with food and lit with candles. Worshippers dance anticlockwise around this table to encourage spirit possession. Revivalists also meet during the week for healing services (at a place called the balm-yard), and prayer meetings.

Vodun

Vodun ceremonies are usually held in the homes of followers. However, worship also takes place in Vodun temples. Vodun temples are called hounfour. Hounfours are usually quite simple buildings with a mud floor. At the centre of a hounfour is a poteau-mitan. This is a pole where spirits communicate with worshippers. Vodun temples usually contain an altar or table decorated with candles, pictures and symbolic items. Drums are very important in Vodun worship as the drumming is used to take worshippers into a trance. This then enables them to be possessed by a loa (spirit).

The hounfour is the geographical district that the Vodun priest (houngan) or priestess (mambo) is responsible for.

Vodun temples (or hounfours) are usually simple buildings. Their main feature is a central pole where spirits communicate with Vodun followers.

Orisha

Orisha worship takes place in an Orisha leader's yard. In this yard is a palais (palais is the French word for palace but, in reality, a palais for Orisha worship is a simple hall/building). Orisha worship takes place in the palais and is lively with singing, drumming, chanting and dancing. Ceremonies, particularly spirit possessions, also take place outside in the yard where there is plenty of room for dancing.

The leader's yard also has a chapelle. This is a special shrine room containing an altar and pictures of saints, as well as objects of the Powers (symbolic implements of the saints and gods such as candles, beads, cups of water and flowers).

Spiritual Baptist

Spiritual Baptists worship in specially designed church buildings. Many features of these churches are the same as Christian churches. There are pews for people to sit on and a pulpit for the minister to preach from. The symbol of the cross also features in churches of Spiritual Baptists. However, Spiritual Baptist churches differ from Christian churches in that they include a centre pole that is decorated with flowers, candles and containers of water to attract the spirits.

Santeria

There are not many buildings designed specifically for Santeria worship. Many forms of Santeria worship take place in hired halls or in the homes of senior priests (santeros). These homes are called Casa de Santos. Santeria devotees belong to a particular Casa de Santo, with the chief male or female priest acting as their leader and spiritual guide. Casa de Santos often contain altars where rituals take place to attract or please the orishas (spirits).

Followers of Santeria can also go to the Casa de Santo for consultations with a santero (priest) when they need advice and guidance.

Spiritual Baptist church service

ACTIVITY

Many places of worship in Caribbean indigenous religions contain a pole to attract or communicate with the spirits. Why do you think a pole is used for this purpose? (Clue – where is the pole reaching from and to?)

KEY POINTS

1 Followers of some Caribbean indigenous religions often gather in outside spaces or in people's homes to worship.

2 Some Rastafari live together in communal camps. These camps often have a specific space set aside for worship.

3 Tables (altars) and poles are used in some Caribbean indigenous religions to attract spirits.

4 Major religions: locations and origins

4.1

Locations of major religions

In this topic you will learn to:

- identify the major locations where Christianity is practised
- identify the major locations where Hinduism is practised
- identify the major locations where Islam is practised
- identify the major locations where Judaism is practised
- identify the major locations where each Caribbean indigenous religion is practised.

Map of the world showing where major religions are concentrated

This map shows the countries where Christianity, Hinduism, Islam and Judaism are practised. It is likely that every country of the world contains some followers of the major religions, even if only in very limited numbers. However, this map focuses on where each major religion is concentrated (present in large numbers). The key also tells you how many followers of each of these religions there are in the world.

ACTIVITY

1 Look at the map of the world in Figure 4.1.1. Can you identify regions of the world where each of the major religions are concentrated? Can you find any regions where a major religion isn't present?

2 List the major religions in order of their largest geographical presence across the world.

3 Conduct some research to discover where, around the world, the different major religions are on the increase/decrease.

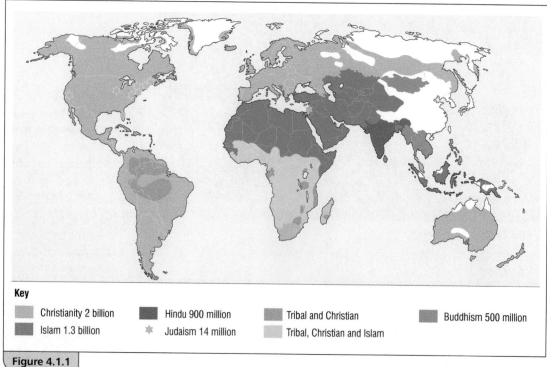

Key

Christianity 2 billion	Hindu 900 million	Tribal and Christian		Buddhism 500 million
Islam 1.3 billion	Judaism 14 million	Tribal, Christian and Islam		

Figure 4.1.1

Map of the Caribbean showing where different indigenous religions are concentrated

This map shows the countries where different indigenous religions are practised in the Caribbean.

Although religions such as Rastafari and, some believe, Spiritual Baptist, originated in the Caribbean, these indigenous religions are now also found widely across the United States and Europe.

Since many Caribbean indigenous religions originated from Christianity, and then fused with African tribal religions, the concentrations of Caribbean indigenous religions shown on this map also indicate how widespread the influence of Christianity was across the region.

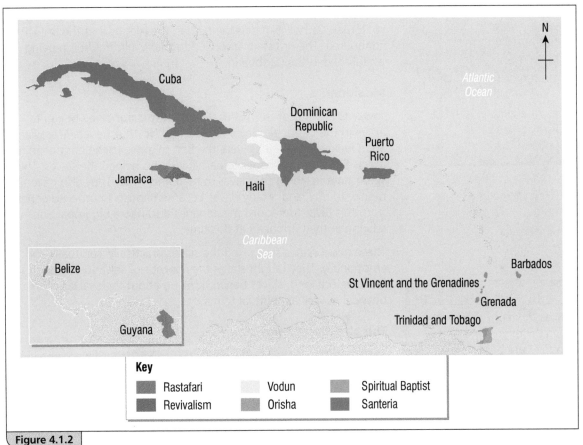

Figure 4.1.2

How major world religions came to the Caribbean

In this topic you will learn to:

- explain how Christianity came to the Caribbean through Christian mission and its establishment in the region
- explain the ways in which Hinduism came to the Caribbean
- explain the ways in which Islam came to the Caribbean
- explain the ways in which Judaism came to the Caribbean.

DID YOU KNOW?

As well as the many different Christian denominations that exist in the Caribbean, many Caribbean indigenous religions are based on Christian beliefs.

KEY POINTS

1 Roman Catholicism was the first denomination to exist in the Caribbean.

2 Later, the British invasion meant that Protestant Christianity was the dominant religion.

3 Missionaries in the Caribbean converted African and Indian (Hindu) slaves to Christianity.

How Christianity came to the Caribbean

The first denomination of Christianity to arrive in the Caribbean was Roman Catholicism (Catholics) in the late 15th century (around 1493). The European explorer Christopher Columbus, along with Spanish invaders, were responsible for establishing Roman Catholic churches across the region.

In 1655 the British invaded the Caribbean. Britain was Protestant and so Roman Catholicism was banned on the islands that the British conquered. The British invasion led to the Anglican Church being established in the Caribbean.

Missionaries

Towards the end of the 1600s, Christian **missionaries** began to arrive in the Caribbean from Europe and North America. Moravian and Quaker missionaries were the first to arrive in the Caribbean. But it was Baptist missionaries in particular who helped the slaves. They spent time teaching the slaves to read and write. They also gave them money to buy land. Many slaves became Baptists in order to benefit from this help. Methodist missionaries also had a big impact on religion in the Caribbean at this time.

These missionaries supported the slaves practically, spiritually and emotionally. They taught slaves the concept of salvation through faith. Before long, slaves began thinking about their salvation in physical as well as spiritual terms.

The abolition of slavery

Slavery was abolished (emancipation) in 1834 (the Slavery Abolition Act was signed in 1833). After that time, **indentured** labour was brought in from India and West Africa to replace the freed slaves. The many Indians that were brought to the Caribbean in the 1800s were mainly Hindu, and there were some Muslims. They lived in very poor conditions in the Caribbean and were often abused by their employers. During this time, two Canadian missionaries, John Morton and Kenneth Grant, built schools for the Hindu and Muslim indentured workers. They also built churches. However, many indentured workers were forced to convert to Christianity as a result of social pressure, for example, in order to get jobs or housing.

Christianity in the Caribbean today

Today, Christianity has by far the largest number of followers in the Caribbean – across the Caribbean islands, 87 per cent of the population are Christian.

More recently, newer denominations of Christianity have arrived in the Caribbean. These include Pentecostalism, Seventh-Day Adventists and Jehovah's Witnesses.

How Hinduism came to the Caribbean

Hinduism arrived in the Caribbean in the early 1800s. Indian Hindus travelled to the Caribbean to replace slaves as indentured workers. Often these indentured workers were not paid a wage but were given meagre food, clothing and shelter, as well as passage to the Caribbean, in exchange for their work. They lived in very squalid conditions and were often badly mistreated by their employers.

Life in the Caribbean was very hard for Indian immigrants. They lived and worked in difficult conditions. The landlords who employed them discouraged the Indian workers and their families from meeting together and there were no mandirs. During this time, Indian Hindus, particularly the women, ensured that the Hindu faith continued through the oral tradition. They told their children stories about the Hindu gods and built shrines in their homes where family members could worship and make offerings to their gods.

Indentureship

Once Hindu workers had completed their contracts and were free, they began to build mandirs in which to worship, pray and support one another. The building of mandirs developed significantly when the first period of indentureship ended in the mid-1800s. As life improved for Hindus, families grew, increasing the number of Hindus on the islands.

Indentured Hindus arrived mainly in Trinidad and Guyana, as these were the last islands to become colonies and so contained fewer slaves but more indentured workers.

Hinduism in the Caribbean today

Today Hindus in the Caribbean are mainly concentrated in:

- Trinidad and Tobago (around 23 per cent of the population)
- Suriname (around 27 per cent of the population)
- Guyana (around 30 per cent of the population).

There are also significant Hindu populations in Jamaica, Barbados, Grenada, St Lucia and Martinique.

Just over 1 per cent of the population across the Caribbean are Hindu.

LINK

There is more about Divali and Holi in Section 7, Festivals, starting on page 58.

The Caribbean benefits from a mix of different religions and cultures. The annual Hindu festival of Phagwa (Holi) brings colour, music, fun and dancing to the streets of Trinidad.

DID YOU KNOW?

Outside their homes, most Hindus in the Caribbean have a sacred space where they plant their jhandis after a puja. Jhandis are sacred bamboo poles that fly flags symbolic of the deity worshipped in the puja. These are considered very important in the Caribbean Hindu world.

ACTIVITY

The joyous festival of Phagwa (Holi) is one benefit that Hinduism brings to the Caribbean. What others can you think of?

KEY POINTS

1 Hindus came to the Caribbean as indentured workers.

2 Hinduism in the Caribbean grew following the end of indentureship.

3 Hindus in the Caribbean are mainly concentrated in Trinidad and Guyana.

Many Muslims arrived in the Caribbean on slave ships from Africa

How Islam came to the Caribbean

There is some evidence to suggest that when Columbus 'discovered' the Caribbean towards the end of the 15th century (around 1493), many Caribbean people already followed Islam. Some people think that Islam had probably been brought to the Caribbean by Spanish explorers and West African travellers and traders hundreds of years earlier.

Slavery

When Columbus arrived in the Caribbean, he brought the influence of Christianity with him. The British invasion in 1655 also contributed to the dominance of Christianity. By the time slaves began arriving in the Caribbean in large numbers, during the 1600s, there were few Muslims left in the Caribbean.

When the slave ships from Africa arrived in the Caribbean, they brought a new generation of Muslims with them. These Muslim slaves were dispersed throughout the islands (although concentrated in Trinidad). Since these slaves were the only Muslims in the Caribbean, surrounded by Christians and followers of local religions, many of them pretended to follow other religions in order to avoid persecution. As Muslims integrated with these other religions, many of them did actually convert. By the time slavery was abolished in 1833 there were very few Muslims left in the Caribbean.

Indentureship

As in the case with Hinduism, indentureship brought many Muslims to the Caribbean from India. Muslims arriving in the Caribbean during indentureship came from many different parts of India. Although their cultures and traditions were different, these people shared common goals. This produced strong ties between the different Muslim groups.

Following indentureship, many workers settled in the Caribbean and had large families. This caused Islam to grow. Arab traders and Muslim merchants also began to travel to the Caribbean to trade and sell. Many of them stayed and influenced others to convert to Islam.

Once they were free, Muslims built masjids across the Caribbean. Masjids were used as places to socialise, support one another and learn, as well as being places for prayer and worship.

Islam in the Caribbean today

Today Muslims are found across the Caribbean but particularly in Trinidad and Tobago (6 per cent of the population) and Guyana (10–12 per cent). There are Muslim schools in the Caribbean, as well as shops selling halal meat and Muslim clothes.

How Judaism came to the Caribbean

Judaism arrived in the Caribbean around the same time as Christopher Columbus (1493). At this time, Jews were being persecuted and killed in Spain, and later in Portugal, as part of the **Inquisition**. Many of them fled to the Caribbean. It is thought that some Jews formed part of the crew of Christopher Columbus' ships. Jewish people found peace and freedom to practise their religion on the Caribbean islands.

Emigration from Brazil

Most of the Jews who came to the Caribbean were Sephardic Jews. These are Jews who originate from the Iberian Peninsula (modern-day Spain, Portugal, Andorra, Gibraltar and France). Other European Jews came to the Caribbean during the Second World War.

Around 1664, large numbers of Jews began arriving in the Caribbean from Brazil. These Jews had fled to Brazil to avoid persecution in Portugal during the Inquisition that began there in 1532 (half a century after the Spanish Inquisition). They had settled in Brazil as this was a territory of Portugal, so they could speak their own language and integrate easily. Jewish people were successful in Brazil, establishing trade routes between Portugal and Brazil and farming the land.

A Jewish family in the Caribbean

However, Judaism was still forbidden in Brazil and so Jews set up secret societies in which to practise their religion. During the 1630s Holland successfully invaded part of Brazil. During Dutch rule, Jews were allowed to worship freely.

Following the recapture of Brazil by Portugal in 1664, many Jews did not want to return to the days of hiding their religion. Instead they chose to flee – and since they were geographically close, many of them travelled to British territories in the Caribbean.

In particular, Jewish people moved to Suriname. At this time, Suriname was a British colony. The British wanted to attract Jews to the colony to develop its economy. Jews were offered British citizenship, recognition of their Sabbath and 10 acres of land on which to build a synagogue. This attracted many Jews to Suriname. When it became a Dutch colony in 1667, most Jews moved to other British colonies, such as Jamaica and Barbados, in order to retain their British citizenship.

Judaism in the Caribbean today

Jews have brought wealth and development to the Caribbean islands and in exchange they have found freedom to thrive and practise their religion. In particular, the Caribbean islands of Jamaica, Barbados and Puerto Rico have significant Jewish populations.

ACTIVITY

Are there any distinguished Jewish people in your community? Do some research to find out.

KEY POINTS

1 Judaism arrived in the Caribbean around 1493. Jews were escaping persecution in Europe.

2 A large number of Jews arrived in the Caribbean in 1664, again to escape persecution.

3 The former British colonies of Jamaica, Puerto Rico and Barbados have large numbers of Jews.

How the Caribbean indigenous religions developed

Marcus Garvey was an early influence on Rastafari

Caribbean indigenous religions formed from a combination of Christian and African religious beliefs. These religions were formed though the influence of Christianity on the islands as well as African traditions and beliefs that were brought over with African slaves. When slaves arrived in the Caribbean they were forbidden to practise their African religions and forced to convert to Christianity. However, many continued with their traditional practices in secret.

Rastafari

Rastafari began in Jamaica in the 1930s in the slum areas of Kingston, Jamaica. It was a people movement against the harsh conditions that blacks lived in (no housing, no jobs and no political representation). The black rights' promoter and cultural leader, Marcus Garvey, told people to 'look to Africa when a black king shall be crowned, for the day of deliverance is at hand'.

Shortly after this prophecy, Haile Selassie was crowned Emperor of Ethiopia in 1930. Rastafari believed that this was the fulfilment of Marcus Garvey's prophecy. L.P. Howell then founded the first branch of Rastafari in Jamaica and preached about the divinity of Haile Selassie.

Rastafari theology developed from Protestant Christianity mixed with African religious practices. Rastafari emerged as a reaction against the harsh realities of life for poor blacks. Rastafari believe in the Christian Bible but apply a different translation to some parts of it. They also believe in the supremacy of the black people.

Revivalism

Revivalism also began in Jamaica, in Watt Town, St Ann. It was adapted from a religion called Myalism, brought to the Caribbean by African slaves. In 1760 a slave leader called Taki led a rebellion among Myalists against their slave owners. During this time Myalists formed into groups for worship and healing services, which helped to further strengthen the religion. Following the Great Revival of 1860–61, which started in Christian churches, Myalists joined with the Christian Native Baptist Movement and the American Baptist Movement to form Revivalism. The **fusion** of Myalism and Christianity led to the formation of the new religion Revivalism. Revivalism is split into two groups: Zion, aligned more with Christian practice, and Pukumina, representing more African elements.

Vodun

Vodun originated in the West African country of Benin (formerly Dahomy). It was brought to Haiti by slaves. Vodun is a mix of Roman Catholicism and Dahomean (African) religious practices. Early Vodun followers in Haiti practised their religion at night since slaves were not allowed to meet together in groups and African religions were banned by the Roman Catholic Church. Slaves forced to convert to Roman Catholicism brought many elements of Roman Catholicism into Vodun. Some slaves escaped from their owners and lived together in rural communes. Over time, as Africans of different religions mixed, Vodun adapted again. Today, the vast majority of Vodouisants in Haiti are also Roman Catholics.

Orisha

Orisha originated in Trinidad, where it was known as Shango. It was brought to the island by African slaves who combined their traditional African Yoruba beliefs with Roman Catholicism and Baptist Protestantism. Dancing, drumming and spirit worship are aspects of Orisha that came from Africa. Respect for the saints is an influence of Roman Catholicism. Orisha grew significantly during the indentureship when a new influx of Africans arrived in Trinidad.

Dancing, drumming and spirit worship are aspects of Orisha that originated in Africa

Spiritual Baptist

It is thought that the Spiritual Baptist movement began in St Vincent in the early 1800s. African slaves originally brought the religion to the Caribbean from the Yoruba area of Africa. Like many of the other African religions, once in the Caribbean it combined with Christian beliefs (both Protestant and Roman Catholic) to form a new religion. Today there are Spiritual Baptist congregations around the world.

Santeria

Santeria is a fusion of the Yoruba religion (brought to the Caribbean by African slaves), Roman Catholicism (from the Iberian Peninsula) and Native Indian traditions (brought to the Caribbean by indentured workers). Santeria developed mainly in Cuba, from where its influence reached other Caribbean followers.

5.1 Sources of authority in Christianity

In this topic you will learn to:

- identify the written source of authority for Christianity.

1 Corinthians 14:35–36 has been the cause of much controversy and discussion in the worldwide Christian church. The verses state that women should not speak in church. Some people take this teaching literally as meaning that women should not fill any public role in church, while others believe that this was just a teaching specific to the time and context that Paul was speaking to in Corinth at the time.

The Bible

The Bible is the written source of authority for Christians. Along with the guidance of the Holy Spirit, Christians believe that the Bible is the main way in which God communicates with people. The Bible also tells the story of God's relationship with humankind throughout history and records Jesus' teaching and actions while he was on the earth. The **Old Testament** part of the Bible gives people an explanation of how the earth came into being and the purpose of human life. It also gives instructions for how to live a godly life, provides comfort and encouragement, and tells of events still to come (prophecy).

Christians believe that the Bible was inspired by God and written by people. God told people what He wanted them to write. In this way, the Bible transmits the Word of God to earth. The Bible also gives an account of Jesus' life and teaching while he was on the earth. As well as recording the miracles that Jesus performed, the Bible also tells the stories (called parables) that Jesus used to communicate his messages. Jesus often used stories to explain a point. Using stories of everyday situations and happenings helped people to understand Jesus' teaching and remember his message.

In the parable of the Good Samaritan, Jesus teaches that we should love everyone and show this in practical ways. In Matthew 5:43–45 he takes this idea further, stating that people should love their enemies and pray for those who persecute them. The account of Jesus' life, recorded in the Bible, shows this type of love in action. Christians try to follow the example of loving others that Jesus gave.

Throughout the Bible, God repeatedly tells His people not to worship other gods or idols (statues); they should only worship Him. The Bible gives specific instructions for worship. For example, in the book of 1 Corinthians, the Apostle Paul explains how the different gifts of the Holy Spirit should be used in worship (1 Corinthians 14).

However, the Bible teaches that loving God and other people is more important than how people worship or the rules they follow (Micah 6:6–8). Jesus reminds people of the importance of love in the **New Testament** (Matthew 22:37–40).

> Love the Lord your God with all your heart and with all your soul and with all your mind. This is the first and greatest commandment. And the second is like it: Love your neighbour as yourself.
>
> Matthew 22:37–39

Instructions for living

The Bible also gives some specific instructions about how people should live:

- It states that people should forgive (Matthew 18:21–22). This passage in Matthew goes on to record Jesus' parable of the unforgiving servant. He was forgiven his huge debt but would not forgive his debtor a small debt. As a result, the servant is thrown into jail by his master. This story illustrates the huge debt (of sin) that God has forgiven in each of us. If we don't forgive others the relatively small sins they have committed against us, God cannot forgive us our sin.

- It states that Christians should show their faith through love and compassion in their actions (James 2:14–17).

- It gives advice on how men and women should support each other in marriage (Ephesians 5).

- It teaches that Christians should look to God to supply their needs and not worry about material provision. Above all else, the Bible teaches, Christians should focus on the Kingdom of God. If they do this, the things they need each day will be provided. This coming to God to meet daily needs is reflected in the Lord's Prayer which states: 'Give us this day our daily bread.' (Matthew 6:11).

Christian congregations also place great importance on the teachings of their pastor or vicar to interpret and apply what the Bible says.

LINKS

There is more about prophecy and the other types of writing in the Bible in Option A, Christianity, starting on page 98.

There is more about biblical teaching on daily life in Option A, Christianity, starting on page 92.

ACTIVITY

Paul's letters to the early churches give lots of advice about how Christians should conduct themselves in life and in worship. Read Ephesians Chapters 5 and 6 and 1 Corinthians 14 for examples of this. Choose one of these chapters and select three or four instructions. Rewrite these instructions for modern-day life.

KEY POINTS

1. The Bible is the main source of authority for Christians. Christians believe that it contains the inspired words of God.

2. The Bible explains the origins of the earth and the purpose of human life, as well as giving guidelines for life, instructions for worship, work, comfort and encouragement.

3. Christians also rely on the insight of pastors and Christian teachers to help them understand the Bible and the Christian faith.

Christians study the Bible to discover more about their faith, God's nature and the teachings of Jesus

Hindu holy scriptures

In this topic you will learn to:

• identify Hindu scriptures.

A person can achieve everything by being simple and humble.

Rig Veda

DID YOU KNOW?

One school of thought in Hinduism believes that only the Samhitas contain the revealed knowledge from Brahman and can be classed as Shruti. This school believes that the Brahmanas, the Aranyakas and the Upanishads are philosophical writings of rishis and are therefore Smriti.

Several holy scriptures are used in Hinduism. These give insight, knowledge and understanding to Hindus about the spiritual universe and how to conduct themselves. Hindu texts are also used in worship and for reflection. Much of the Hindu scriptures contain beautiful language and imagery. The Hindu scriptures are divided into **Shruti** and **Smriti**. Hindu scriptures are the oldest in the world – the first written records are believed to date from between 1500 BCE and 1200 BCE, although the scriptures were in existence orally thousands of years before this. Hindus describe their scriptures as existing from 'the dawn of creation'.

Shruti

The Hindu term 'Shruti' means 'what is heard or revealed'. It is used to describe the ancient Hindu scriptures that contain the four Vedas and the Upanishads. The four Vedas are the Rig Veda, the Yajur Veda, the Sama Veda and the Atharva Veda. Hindus believe that the Vedic texts were revealed directly from Brahman to holy men (called rishis) in India. The rishis handed down what they had received from Brahman orally for hundreds of years before their words were written down in **Sanskrit**. Each Veda is divided into four sections that contain different types of writing:

• **Samhitas:** mantras used for chanting

• **Brahmanas:** explaining the Hindu hymns and rituals

• **Aranyakas:** containing writings that focus on a category of rituals relevant to one who has renounced the world

• **Upanishads:** revealing knowledge about the Vedic texts, the human spirit and the universe.

The Rig Veda is the best-known and most important Veda. The Yajur Veda is mainly used in ceremonies involving sacrifice. The Sama Veda is often used for chanting, and the mantras of the Atharva Veda are used to bring good luck during difficult times.

Smriti

Smriti are writings that have been composed by enlightened Hindus (rather than coming from Brahman directly). These Hindus are believed to have reached the ultimate level of spirituality. The Smriti writings are a collection of Hindu laws, beliefs, thoughts and practices – often communicated through stories. Unlike Shruti scriptures, Smriti writings are constantly changed and adapted to relate to modern life.

Dharma Shastras

The Dharma Shastras are the writings in the Smriti that record laws and rules. These laws outline how a Hindu should behave in relation to the community, their family and the nation. The laws in the Dharma Shastras can be adapted to reflect the requirements of the time. For example, certain laws may become outdated and, as science and culture progress, other laws may need to be added. The law-giving Smriti are named after the people who collected those laws together. The most famous lawgiver was Manu – his writings are called the *Manusmriti*.

> Where women are honoured, there the devatas (gods) are pleased; but where they are not honoured, no sacred rite yields rewards.
>
> *Manusmriti, 3:56*

LINK

There is more about Hindu scriptures and how they apply to daily life in Option B, Hinduism, starting on page 106.

The *Ramayana*

The *Ramayana* is a sacred poem set in the Second Age when the forces of adharma were attacking the world but dharma was prevailing. The story is of the Lord Rama coming to earth and marrying Princess Sita. The princess is abducted by Ravana, who takes her to Sri Lanka. With the help of the monkey god, Hanuman, Lord Rama builds a bridge from India to Sri Lanka and rescues Princess Sita. This story shows how, although adharma threatens order and happiness, dharma or righteousness overcomes.

ACTIVITY

The *Ramayana* has been retold in many languages and forms, including films and plays. The *Ramcharitmanas* written by Tulsidas is the most popular version in the Caribbean. What other versions of the story can you discover?

The *Mahabharata*

This is the longest and oldest poem in history. It is set in the Third Age when adharma was engulfing the world. In essence, the story tells of two cousins who go to war to decide who should be king. One of the cousins, Arjuna, decides to turn back during the final battle as he does not want to kill people whom he loves. However, Arjuna's chariot driver is Krishna. He tells Arjuna that sacrifice must be made in order to achieve victory and righteousness, and that the souls of those who die will live again in another life. Arjuna's resolve is strengthened by Krishna's words and he goes on to fight and win the war. The recorded words that Krishna speaks to Arjuna are called the Bhagavad Gita (meaning the Song of the Lord). This is a very famous piece of sacred literature.

Puranas

These are a series of Hindu stories and poems that celebrate the life and work of the gods. There are 18 poems – six for each god of the Trimurtri: Vishnu, Shiva and Brahma.

This illustration from the *Mahabharata* shows Arjuna being comforted and strengthened by Krishna's words

KEY POINTS

1 The Shruti are the Hindu scriptures that contain the four Vedas and the Upanishads. They are believed to come directly from Brahman.

2 The Smriti are the secondary sacred texts. They are the writings of rishis and philosophers and are there to guide and inspire humans in accordance with the teachings of the Vedas.

Sources of authority in Islam

In this topic you will learn to:

- identify the written source of authority for Islam.

DID YOU KNOW?

There are two main sources of guidance in Islam:

- the Qur'an – the revealed Word of God to the Prophet Muhammad
- the Hadith/Sunnah – the recorded life of the Prophet.

There are four main sources of Islamic jurisprudence (sources of law):

- the Qur'an
- the Hadith/Sunnah – the sayings, actions and approvals of the Prophet
- the Ijma – consensus of the scholars
- the Qiyas – analogical reasoning.

Praise be to Allah. Lord of the Universe.

The Compassionate, the Merciful.

Sovereign of the Day of Judgement!

You alone we worship, and to You alone we turn for help.

Guide us to the straight path,

The path of those whom You have favoured.

Not of those who have incurred your wrath,

Nor of those who have gone astray.

Surah 1:1–7

Shariah

Shariah means 'straight path' in Arabic. It is the term used to describe the laws of Islam. These laws are based on the **Qur'an** and the **Sunnah**. Islamic schools of law also influence Shariah. Shariah is used by Muslims alongside the laws of the country in which they live. However, in some Muslim countries, such as Saudi Arabia and Iran, most of their laws are governed by Shariah law.

The Qur'an

The Arabic word 'Qur'an' means 'that which is read or recited'. Muslims believe that the Qur'an contains the direct words of Allah, as communicated to Muhammad. Muhammad received revelations from Allah from 610 CE until his death in 632 CE. The Qur'an was compiled orally in Muhammad's lifetime and, before his death, Muhammad instructed his followers on its order and arrangement and parts of it were written down. After the Prophet's death, his Khalifah (successor) Abu Bakr, commissioned a written compilation of the Qur'an, using the oral and written compilations that already existed. The Qur'an contains:

- explanations for the purpose of the world and of humankind
- instructions for living in a way that pleases Allah and brings blessing to yourself and others
- historical references and stories of past nations
- encouragement and comfort at difficult times.

The Qur'an is divided into surahs (chapters) each with a different theme. The best-known surah in the Qur'an is the first surah. Muslims recite this surah at least 17 times each day during the five prayers. Muslims believe that, because the Qur'an contains the direct words of Allah, it can never be added to or have anything taken away from it.

The Sunnah

The Sunnah is made up of Hadith and Muhammad's biography. The Qur'an outlines how a Muslim should live, but it can be difficult to know how to apply these rules to daily life. The Sunnah (in Arabic 'the practical example' or 'the way') records the actions and sayings of Muhammad during his life. The Qur'an *tells* Muslims how to live and the Sunnah *shows* them how to live. The Sunnah is recorded as Hadith, the short passages that record Muhammad's sayings, actions or silent approvals. The approvals are the actions or attitudes that Muhammad approved of in others. The Sunnah complements the Qur'an by showing how its teachings can be put into practice in daily life. The Qur'an tells Muslims to follow the example of Muhammad's life (the Sunnah).

ACTIVITY

In your own words, explain why it is important that Muslims have the Sunnah as well as the Qur'an to guide them.

LINK

There is more about the Qur'an and the Hadith in Option C, Islam, starting on page 131.

Fiqh

Fiqh describes Islamic **jurisprudence** – the methods of interpreting and applying Islamic law. There are four main schools of thought (Madhhabs) as to how Islamic law should be interpreted. These are considered below.

Hanafi

This interpretation is based on the legal views of the Iraqi scholar Abu Hanifa an-Nu'man who lived between AH 699 and AH 767 (1299–1365 CE). This is the oldest school of thought regarding Islamic law and it is the most popular. It is the most liberal (relaxed) of the four Madhhabs and has the largest number of followers. It is the main school of thought followed in the Caribbean, Iraq, Afghanistan, Pakistan, Bangladesh, India, China, Turkey and the Balkans.

Maliki

The Maliki is the second-largest of the four schools of thought regarding the interpretation of Islamic law. It is followed by around 25 per cent of Muslims, mostly in North Africa, West Africa, the United Arab Emirates, Kuwait and in some parts of Saudi Arabia. This school of thought was founded by Malik ibn Anas in Medina. All Islamic schools use the Qur'an and the Sunnah as their first reference point regarding Islamic law. However, the Maliki school differs from the others in that it also uses the recorded teachings and practices of the Muslims of Medina, including the Muslims that lived there immediately following Muhammad's death.

Shafei

The Shafei school of thought is named after the Islamic scholar Imam ash-Shafei. Imam Shafei was born in Gaza in AH 760 (1358 CE). At that time, there were two different interpretations of Islamic law: one was independent reasoning based on the teachings of the Qur'an and Sunnah, and the other was literal interpretation of these teachings. Imam Shafei also taught that if a practice was widely accepted and followed by the Muslim community then it became acceptable in the eyes of Islamic law.

Hanbali

The Hanbali school of jurisprudence was established by the students of Imam Ahmad ibn Hanbal. Hanbali jurisprudence (law interpretation) is the strictest and most conservative of the four schools. This is the Islamic law interpretation that is followed in Saudi Arabia, Yemen and the Palestinian territories. It also forms the main laws to be followed in the holy sites of Makkah and Medina.

Islamic law gives guidance about how women should dress – although Muslims interpret this in different ways. Some Muslim women cover themselves completely, including their faces, while others leave their faces and the palms of their hands uncovered.

KEY POINTS

1 The Qur'an and the Sunnah are the main sources of authority for Muslims.

2 The Hadith are the sayings, actions and silent approvals of Muhammad.

3 Fiqh is the term used to describe Islamic jurisprudence (law interpretation).

4 There are four main schools of Islamic jurisprudence.

Jewish holy scriptures

In this topic you will learn to:

• identify the written sources of authority for Judaism.

LINK

There is more about the Tenakh in Option D, Judaism, starting on page 150.

The scroll on which the Torah is written is treated with great respect by Jews. This scroll, which belongs to a synagogue in Kingston, is protected and decorated by an ornate cover and silver crowns.

The Lord said, 'It is because they have forsaken my law, which I set before them; they have not obeyed me or followed my law. Instead, they have followed the stubbornness of their hearts; they have followed the Baals, as their ancestors taught them.' Therefore this is what the Lord Almighty, the God of Israel, says: 'See, I will make this people eat bitter food and drink poisoned water.'

Jeremiah 9:13–15

The Tenakh

The **Tenakh** is the name for the Jewish Holy Scriptures. It is the same as the Old Testament part of the Bible, although the books are arranged in a different order. The books within the Tenakh are grouped into three sections, the Torah, the Nev'im and the Ketuvim, according to their content.

The Torah

The **Torah** contains the law books. It is made up of the first five books of the Old Testament (Genesis, Exodus, Leviticus, Numbers and Deuteronomy). These first five books give an account of how the world was created and how the Jewish people were chosen by God. The Torah also contains all of the laws that Jews should live by. Jews believe that these laws were spoken directly from God to Moses. The Torah is considered the most important Jewish scripture and is treated with great respect. The Ten Commandments contained in the Torah are considered the most important laws for Jews to follow.

As well as the Torah referring to the first five books of the Bible, the term is also used by some Jews to mean the whole collection of Jewish scriptures and the commentaries that interpret and apply these teachings to daily life. Writings by rabbis and scholars that attempt to interpret and explain Jewish scriptures and teachings are called Midrash.

The Nev'im

The Nev'im records the lives and teachings of the prophets. The Nev'im is divided into two parts: the Former Prophets and the Latter Prophets. The Former Prophets records the lives and spiritual journey of the Israelites after Moses' death. The Latter Prophets contains prophecies and teachings from important figures such as Isaiah and Jeremiah, as well as from 12 minor prophets including Micah and Habakkuk. These prophets brought messages from God to the Israelites. The messages were often reprimands – reminding the Jewish people to only worship God and to live a moral life (see the example from Jeremiah opposite). The messages often contained warnings of what would happen if the Israelites did not change their ways. However, the prophetic writings also contain passages that tell of God's love and care for His people and His longing for them to turn back to Him.

The Ketuvim

The Ketuvim contains all of the other writings contained in the Old Testament – this includes the Psalms, Proverbs, philosophical writings (such as Job and Ecclesiastes) and poetic writing such as the Song of Solomon.

Other sources of authority in Judaism

Mishnah

The Mishnah contains Jewish laws that were not included in the Torah. These were originally passed on orally but, in around 200 CE, Rabbi Judah the Prince wrote these laws down.

Gemara

The Gemara is a **commentary** on the Mishnah. It explains laws and teachings recorded in the Mishnah and helps people to apply these to their everyday lives. It also contains writings on subjects not covered in the Mishnah.

Talmud

The Talmud brings the writings contained in the Mishnah and the Gemara together into one book. Some Jews believe that the contents of the Talmud (the Mishnah and the Gemara) were spoken directly from God to Moses.

Mishneh Torah

The Mishneh Torah summarises and provides a commentary on the teachings contained in the Torah and Talmud (an example of Midrash). It was written by the Jewish rabbi and philosopher Moses ben Maimon in 1167 CE and helps Jews to decipher the laws and teachings contained in the Talmud. There are other commentaries on the Talmud, but the Mishneh Torah is one of the most widely respected and authoritative.

Apocrypha

The Apocrypha (from the Greek word meaning 'hidden') are Old Testament writings that were not officially selected to be included in the Tenakh. Nevertheless, some Jews consult these books for information and teaching.

DID YOU KNOW?

The 613 commands recorded in the Torah are called mitzvot.

Moses ben Maimon lived in the 2nd century and wrote the respected commentary on the Talmud, called the Mishneh Torah

ACTIVITY

Find out which 15 books make up the Apocrypha. How many of these books were written by women? Choose two or three of the Apocryphal books and find out more about them. What type of writing is contained in them? And why are they not accepted as God-inspired scripture by Jews and Christians?

KEY POINTS

1 The Tenakh is the main collection of Jewish Holy Scriptures. It contains the Torah, the Nev'im and the Ketuvim.

2 The Torah (containing the Jewish laws) is the most important source of authority for Jews.

3 The Talmud contains extra Jewish laws not contained in the Torah. Opinion differs as to how important these laws are.

Sources of authority in Caribbean indigenous religions

Rastafari

The Holy Piby is the main source of authority for Rastafari. This is also often known as the Blackman's Bible. It puts an emphasis on black supremacy, Africa as Zion (the promised land) and the destruction of Babylon (white rule). The Holy Piby was compiled by Robert Athlyi Rogers and published in 1924.

After the Holy Piby, the Bible is the next source of authority for Rastafari. Rastafari use the King James translation of the Bible as they believe other translations are corrupt and that the King James is closest to the original manuscript. However, although Rastafari refer to the Bible as their authority, they interpret some passages differently to Christians.

Rastafari also take authority from their own self (**I and the plural I-N-I**). Through meditation, reasoning together and studying scripture, they can come to know the truth through revelation from Jah.

Revivalism

Since Zion Revivalism is close in its origins, beliefs and practices to Christianity, its main source of authority is the Bible. The Pukumina branch of Revivalism also uses books of magic, dreams and possession by spirits as its source of authority. Zion Revivalists also believe that God can speak to them through dreams and visions but believe that only the Holy Spirit should possess them.

Vodun

Vodun uses the Bible as its main source of authority for worship and guidance on day-to-day living. However, Vodun also places a strong emphasis on spirit possession. Followers of Vodun believe that spirits that possess them can bring messages and guidance to them and to others through them. Sometimes Vodun followers seek spirit possession in order to find an answer to a specific question, to seek guidance on a particular matter or to discover the future (prophecy).

Orisha

Due to its connections with Roman Catholic Christianity, Orisha uses the Bible as a source of authority. The Bible provides followers of Orisha with direction, strength and answers to life's questions. However, for specific questions and difficulties, Orisha followers take direction and guidance from divination and from the Odu Ifa. This is a collection of writings making up 16 books that are believed to give advice on all situations, circumstances, actions and consequences. Orisha priests use **divination** to select passages from the Odu Ifa that they believe will provide insight and guidance to individuals in particular circumstances. In addition, like followers of other Caribbean indigenous religions, followers of Orisha use spirit possession to gain spiritual enlightenment and guidance.

When eyes are two, they watch events unfold

When legs are two, they walk with heavy treading

The rumps are two, they sit on a mat

One hand does not jingle

Also, one leg will not walk with fast treading

Odu Ifa

Spiritual Baptist

The links that Spiritual Baptists have with Christianity mean that the Bible is their main source of authority on issues of worship and day-to-day life. In particular, Spiritual Baptists take from the Bible their practice of baptising their members. Baptism is the practice of immersing believers in water. Spiritual Baptists also take authority from communication with God and the Holy Spirit – this may be through dreams, possession or a sense of God speaking to them.

Santeria

Santeria beliefs have been passed on orally through the generations. These oral traditions use stories to convey the beliefs and practices of the religion. Santeria also emphasises communication with spirits of ancestors and deities as a means to gain knowledge, insight and direction.

Many Caribbean indigenous religions teach that God and spirits can speak to people through dreams and visions. Often dreams can show people what to do in a particular situation.

KEY POINTS

1 The Holy Piby is the main source of authority for Rastafari. They also take guidance from the King James Version of the Bible.

2 Followers of Revivalism, Vodun, Orisha and the Spiritual Baptists refer to the Bible as their source of authority.

3 Santeria relies on oral tradition for its authority.

4 Many of the Caribbean indigenous religions see dreams, visions and spirit possession as sources of authority. However, Zion Revivalists and Spiritual Baptists only believe in possession by the Holy Spirit.

6.1 Major teachings of Christianity

Jesus' crucifixion redeemed mankind's relationship with God

Almighty creator God

The Bible teaches that there is only one God (monotheism). This God is Yahweh – the God of the Old and New Testament.

The Bible instructs Christians to worship only God and not bow down to any other god, statue, idol or earthly possession. This theme carries over into the New Testament where Jesus warns that a person cannot love both God and money (Matthew 6:24).

Christians believe that God created the world and everything in it. They believe that God is almighty – He controls the universe and sustains life. But God is also gentle, kind and righteous. Christians trust Him to protect, love and provide for them.

The Trinity

The Trinity is the three persons contained within one God. It is a holy mystery. The Trinity is made up of God the Father, God the Son, and God the Holy Spirit.

The Father

God the Father created the universe and is the ultimate authority. Jesus and the Holy Spirit submit themselves to Him. Jesus himself says:

> Very truly I tell you, the Son can do nothing by himself; he can do only what he sees his Father doing, because whatever the Father does the Son also does.
>
> John 5:19

The Son

God the Son came to earth as Jesus to redeem mankind and restore God's relationship with man. Since Jesus lived on earth and was fully human, he understands our joys and temptations, our pains and our sorrows. At the same time, Jesus was God. He lived a perfect life and never sinned. Christians often pray to Jesus, rather than God the Father as they can connect with Jesus' humanity.

The Holy Spirit

Before he died, Jesus told his followers that God the Father would send them a helper. This helper, the Holy Spirit, would guide and comfort people when Jesus had left the earth. God sent the Holy Spirit at Pentecost. The Holy Spirit entered into the spirits of the first Christians and gave them boldness. Today, Christians testify that the Holy Spirit gives them boldness, wisdom, understanding and comfort.

He is the presence of God inside every Christian and many Christians claim to sense the Holy Spirit speaking to them. The Holy Spirit is also responsible for the spiritual **gifts**, which include speaking in tongues, prophecy and words of knowledge.

Man, sin and salvation

Sin has plagued the relationship between God and man since it entered the world through Adam and Eve. The Old Testament contains many accounts of God punishing people for their sin. But with Jesus came salvation – the means for man's sin to be forgiven and the relationship between God and man to be restored.

Jesus Christ is redemption

During Jesus Christ's time on earth, he healed the sick, performed miracles, forgave sins and taught about God. But Jesus' ultimate purpose was **redemption**. Sin had damaged the relationship between God and man. The Old Testament contains accounts of animals being sacrificed to pay for people's sin and bring forgiveness. But no sooner had a sacrifice been made than people would sin again. God's holiness meant He could not get close to sin so the only solution was for a perfect and final sacrifice to be made to pay for humanity's sin. This sacrifice was Jesus. Only he had lived a perfect life on earth. The Bible teaches that Jesus' death paid for sin forever. With sin dealt with, the relationship between humans and God was restored. Christians still sin but, because of Jesus' sacrifice, God can forgive.

Judgement, punishment, forgiveness and reward

The Old Testament contains many accounts of God punishing people for their sin. Christians believe that this cycle of laws and punishment was broken by Jesus' sacrifice. However, the Bible teaches that there will be a final judgement for everyone after death:

- Those people who have accepted Jesus and had their relationship with God restored will go to heaven. Their rewards in heaven will depend on the life they have lived on earth.
- Those people who have not believed in Jesus' sacrifice and do not have a restored relationship with God will not enter heaven. They will face eternity separated from God.

Concept of the Second Coming and last days

The Bible teaches that Jesus Christ will come to earth a second time. Christians call this the **Second Coming**. During this time, Jesus will take up to heaven all Christians left on the earth. This is called the Rapture. Before this time comes, the New Testament Book of Revelation warns of difficult times of famine, wars and natural disasters. The Bible also warns of an Antichrist who will rule the world and try to turn people against God. But the Bible encourages Christians to hold fast to their faith because, when these troubles come, it means Jesus' return is near.

ACTIVITY

What are some of the signs of the last days, as recorded in the Book of Revelation?

For it is my Father's will that everyone who sees His Son and believes in him should have eternal life – that I should raise him at the Last Day.

John 6:40

LINK

Christian beliefs and practices, and the impact of these on daily life, are covered in more depth in Option A, Christianity, starting on page 92.

KEY POINTS

1 The one God created the earth.

2 The Trinity contains God the Father, God the Son, and God the Holy Spirit.

3 Jesus Christ brought redemption from sin and restored God and man's relationship.

4 God will judge everyone, based on their acceptance of Jesus. People's actions on earth determine their heavenly rewards.

5 Jesus will return to earth and take Christians to heaven. As this day draws near, life on earth will become more troubled.

Major teachings of Hinduism

Hindus use yoga and meditation to try to connect with their atman (their spiritual soul or self)

The original name of Hinduism was Sanatana Dharma, meaning 'Eternal Truth that sustains and upholds'. Hinduism is the oldest major religion and has many laws that Hindus believe uphold and sustain life.

Nature of atman

Atman (sometimes called atma) is the Hindu term for the soul or spiritual self. Hindus believe that atman is the eternal part of every living thing. Atman can easily be forgotten in the day-to-day activity of life. Hindus perform meditation to connect with atman.

Forms of life

Hindus believe that Brahman is present in all of creation. They also believe that all forms of life have a soul (including humans, animals and plants). Hindus believe that every soul experiences life in different forms through reincarnation.

Dharma

Dharma is a Sanskrit word meaning 'that which supports'. It refers to the duties, responsibilities, values and guiding principles that help Hindus achieve moksha while also maintaining order, peace and harmony on the earth and in society.

Sanatana dharma – the laws of the universe and duties of people. Individuals have personal dharma according to their stage in life.

Karma

Karma is the Sanskrit word for 'deeds' and it is the collective actions of a person throughout their different lives on earth. If a person lives well and follows dharma, they will earn good karma. The amount of good or bad karma that a person has determines what form their life takes through reincarnation.

Incarnation

Incarnation in Hinduism describes the different forms that Hindu deities have taken on the earth. For example, the god Vishnu has been incarnated as a fish (matsyavatara), a dwarf (vamanavatara) and many other forms, such as Ram and Krishna.

Reincarnation

Hindus believe that, following death, they return to earth in another bodily form. This is called reincarnation. If a Hindu has earned good karma in their life, they will be reincarnated into a higher **caste** or even as a guru. It is the ultimate aim of Hindus to escape the cycle of life and rebirth (called **samsara**) and to achieve moksha.

The four yugas

The four yugas are the four different ages (or eras) within a cycle of time in Hinduism. During each era, dharma (righteousness) decreases and adharma and disease increases. As humanity becomes increasingly unrighteous, the length of human life decreases. The four yugas are: Satya Yuga, Treta Yuga, Dapara Yuga and Kali Yuga.

The four stages of life

Hinduism teaches that there are four different stages to a person's life. A Hindu may not necessarily enter each stage (these days it is not expected). However, progression through the four stages is the ideal. The stages are:

- Brahmacharya: the period of education, including spiritual education. Their life is simplistic and emphasis is on spiritual attainment. This stage normally lasts up to age 25.
- Grihastha: home and family life. Individuals pursue religious merit, wealth and pleasure.
- Vanaprastha: a person's hair turns grey and his grandchildren are born. During this stage, a person should move into a simple dwelling in a forest. Life should be devoted to spiritual growth, retirement from the world and devotion to spiritual matters.
- Sannyasin: a person breaks all worldly ties and wanders alone, without possessions. He/she relies on charitable giving for survival. His/her soul prepares to leave the earth.

The four goals of life

The four life goals for Hindus are:

- Dharma: as a Hindu matures, the pleasures of sexual relations, power and wealth fade. Spiritual connection and peace of the soul, through following dharma, become more important.
- Artha: the pursuit of power, fame and wealth.
- Kama: seeking worldly pleasures (including sexual satisfaction) and recreation. This must comply with morals governed by dharma.
- Moksha: to escape from samsara (the continual cycle of death and rebirth) into spiritual enlightenment and union with God.

Maayaa

Maayaa (or Maya) is a power that causes us to focus on our physical and mental state, rather than our spiritual existence. Hindus believe it blinds us to the real nature of the self, creation and Brahman, and the relationship between each of these. Maayaa causes people to look inwards into themselves and prevents them seeing beyond their desires and feelings. Hindus believe humans are one tiny part of a bigger picture – like a tiny drop of water in an ocean. Hindus try to rise above Maayaa and achieve spiritual enlightenment through connecting with the universe of which they are a part.

DID YOU KNOW?

The Hindi word 'paap' means to move away from dharma (the guiding principle of Hinduism). Adharma is the closest equivalent to sin.

LINK

Hindu beliefs and practices, and the impact of these on daily life, are covered in more depth in Option B, Hinduism, starting on page 106.

KEY POINTS

1. Every living being has a soul (atman) – the atman is eternal and is like Brahman in its nature.
2. All Hindus should follow the moral and ritual duties of dharma.
3. Karma determines a person's rebirth.
4. Hindu gods can be incarnated into earthly forms. The god Vishnu has been incarnated on the earth many times.
5. All human souls are reincarnated after death, unless they have achieved moksha (a Hindu's ultimate goal).
6. There are four yugas (cycles) of time, four stages of life and four goals in life.
7. Hindus believe that Maayaa blinds us to the real nature of the self, creation and Brahman, and the relationship between these three realities.

Major teachings of Islam

The Shahadah
There is no god but Allah, and Muhammad is His messenger.

Muslims performing salah

The five pillars of Islam

Muslims believe that there are five crucial actions (pillars) that a person must live out. The entire Muslim faith rests on these pillars.

The Shahadah

Muslims make this declaration of faith several times a day. It should be the first thing a Muslim hears after birth and the last thing they hear before they die. To become a Muslim, a person says the **Shahadah** three times in front of witnesses.

Salah

Salah (prayer) is crucial. The Qur'an teaches that Muslims should pray five times a day facing Makkah. Muslims perform wudu (ceremonial washing) before they pray. The mu'adhdhin calls Muslims to prayer and the prayers are led by an imam. Muslims pray at home individually or wherever they are if they cannot reach the masjid.

Zakah

Zakah is charitable giving. Muslims are commanded to give donations of money to other Muslims who are suffering. The minimum amount a Muslim family should give is 2.5 per cent of money left over once all basic requirements have been met. However, money left over must exceed a minimum requirement, called the **nisab,** to have zakah paid on it.

Sawm

Sawm (or saum) is the fast during Ramadan. This takes place during the ninth month of the Muslim year and remembers Muhammad's revelation of the Qur'an. During sawm, a Muslim abstains from food, drink and sexual relations during daylight hours.

Hajj

Hajj is the pilgrimage to Makkah that each Muslim should try to make in their lifetime. This pilgrimage involves a number of symbolic acts recalling the life of Ibrahim. In particular, it remembers Ibrahim's willingness to sacrifice his own son to Allah.

The six articles of faith

Tawhid

Muslims believe that Allah is the one and only God. Allah has no partner, equal or rival. He alone created and controls the world and demands to be worshipped. This belief in the Oneness of Allah is called Tawhid. Muslims believe that Allah's attributes are perfect and greater than any worldly attributes.

Belief in angels

Muslims believe that angels are spiritual, heavenly beings created from light by Allah, with specific jobs to do. The angel Jibril spoke the Qur'an to Muhammad. The angel Mikhail gives daily sustenance. There is an angel that brings death, and an angel to blow the trumpet on Judgement Day. Angels in Islam provide protection and blessing for Muslims. Even the angel of death brings blessing by taking Muslims into a place of peace to await Judgement Day.

Belief in prophets

The Qur'an lists 25 prophets that Muslims believe in. Prophets are also called messengers. Not all prophets are messengers, but all messengers are prophets. Many prophets in Islam are the same prophets that Christians believe in, including:

- the first prophet – Adam
- the first messenger and prophet – Nuh (Noah)
- Ibrahim (Abraham)
- Musa (Moses).

However, Christian and Islam belief differs with regard to Isa (Jesus) and Muhammad. Muslims believe that Isa was a prophet and not God. Muslims also believe that Muhammad was the most important and final prophet. Prophets receive messages from Allah – usually through angels – then reveals these messages to the world.

Belief in the Revealed Books

Muslims believe that there are four known Revealed Books that have been revealed directly by Allah to different prophets. These are:

- the Torah – revealed to Musa (Moses)
- the Psalms (in Arabic Zabur) – revealed to Dawud (David)
- the Gospels (in Arabic Injeel) – revealed to Isa (Jesus)
- most importantly the Qur'an – revealed to Muhammad.

Muslims believe that only the Qur'an is the absolute, unspoilt Word of God. Muslims believe that the other Revealed Books were altered by humans. Muslims also believe that there are ancient scrolls that contain direct revelation from Allah.

Belief in Al Qadr

Belief in **Al Qadr** is the belief in predestination or fate. Muslims believe that everything that happens is the will of Allah and that Allah knows every human heart. He knows what people will do before they do it and He sees every person's life before they live it.

Belief in Al Akhirah

Belief in life after death is called Al Akhirah. Muslims believe that after they die they stay in their graves until the Day of Judgement. This period of time is called barzakh. On Judgement Day, earthly life ends, the dead are resurrected and both the living and the dead are judged. Those whose good deeds outweigh their bad enter paradise. Those whose bad deeds outweigh their good go to hell. Ultimately, it is the mercy of Allah that will allow a person to enter paradise.

LINK

Islamic beliefs and practices, and the impact of these on daily life, are covered in more depth in Option C, Islam, starting on page 120.

And to every soul will be paid in full (the fruit) of its deeds; and (God) knows best all that they do.

Surah 39:70

KEY POINTS

1 Islam contains six major articles of faith: belief in the unity of Allah, belief in angels, belief in prophets, belief in the Revealed Books, belief in life after death and belief in predestination.

2 Islam is built on Five Pillars, or practices, which every Muslim should try to carry out. These Five Pillars are: the declaration of faith, prayer, giving to charity, fasting and pilgrimage to Makkah.

Major teachings of Judaism

God is one, Almighty creator

Like Christians and Muslims, Jews believe in one single creator God (monotheism). Unlike Christians, Jews do not believe in the Trinity. They believe that God is a single being whose spirit is present in the world. They do not believe that Jesus Christ was God. Judaism teaches that God:

• is almighty
• is present in all of creation
• has no rivals
• controls human activity
• is present with us
• is omnipresent (everywhere).

Jews and Christians have the same beliefs about how God created the world. Both religions follow the same creation story, recorded in Genesis of the Bible and the Tenakh.

There is judgement, punishment, forgiveness, reward

Judaism teaches that everyone will be judged. God will reveal to every person what their life could have been like if they had sinned less and loved God and people more. Jews believe that a person's punishment is the shame and sadness they feel at opportunities they have missed on earth. Jews believe that this shame of life not being lived well is the burning punishment that the Tenakh speaks of. However, Judaism also teaches that God is forgiving and will show mercy. After the 'punishment' of shame, human souls enter God's presence (heaven). Judaism teaches that there are different levels in heaven. Souls will be rewarded and sent to different levels, depending on their holiness. Each level brings a soul closer to the presence of God.

Converse to the reward of living for eternity in the presence of God is the punishment of being cut off from God forever. This fate is reserved for souls who have shown themselves to be evil on earth.

Concept of humanity, sin and salvation

Jews believe that the human soul has three parts:

• The animating spirit – this is connected to the physical body
• The 'you' – a person's intellect, personality, desires, etc.
• The Holy – the presence of God within us all

Judaism teaches that all humanity is created by God and should be submitted to Him. Our job on earth is to grow closer to God through our actions, thoughts and worship. However, Judaism teaches that we all sin (disobey God's commands) and need God's mercy and forgiveness. Jews believe that it is this mercy and God's love for humanity that brings their salvation.

ACTIVITY

According to Jewish belief, the human soul has three parts. For each part of the human soul, think of a situation where that part might be particularly active. In what ways might the animating spirit and the 'you' sin?

Concept of second coming and last days

Jews do not believe in a 'second coming' because they do not believe that the Messiah has visited the earth a first time yet. Orthodox Jews are still waiting for the promised Messiah, who they believe will establish God's kingdom on earth and rule humanity in the Last Days. Reform Jews view the Messiah, spoken about in the Tenakh, as being a time (the Messianic era) rather than a person. During the Messianic era, all humanity will live in peace and follow the one true God.

According to what is written in the Tenakh (particularly in the Book of Isaiah), Jews believe that there are a number of prophecies to be fulfilled during the Messianic age. These include the following:

- The Messiah will be descended from King David (Isaiah 11:1).
- Knowledge of God will fill the world (Isaiah 11:9).
- All Israelites will be returned to their homeland (Isaiah 11:12).
- All of the dead will rise again (Isaiah 26:19).

Opinion differs within Judaism regarding what happens to the earth after the Messianic era, or the reign of the Messiah. Some believe that human souls exist in another spiritual place. Others believe that the earth continues, but that it becomes an intensely spiritual place. Belief in life after death though is a widely held Jewish belief.

A bazaar in the West Bank, Palestine. Many Jews believe that one of the signs of the Messianic age is that all Israelites will return to Israel. This is a sensitive issue as Palestinians have lived in the land for centuries. Currently, around 3 million Palestinians live in Israel and view the country as their homeland.

Varying beliefs of the major Jewish sects

Orthodox Jews

- Orthodox Jews believe that the Torah came directly from God via Moses.
- They believe that the 613 mitzvot (commandments) in the Torah should be followed exactly.
- Modern Orthodox Jews observe halakhah (Jewish law), while integrating into modern society. Ultra-Orthodox Jews live outside of modern society.

Messianic Jews

- Messianic Jews believe that Yeshua (Jesus' original name in Hebrew) is the Messiah.
- They believe that Yeshua completes their Jewish faith and is the new covenant spoken of in the Tenakh.
- While having the same core beliefs as Christianity, Messianic Jews retain and practise their Jewish identity.
- Messianic Jews follow the whole Bible, including the Torah, the Prophets, the Writings and, unlike other Jews, the New Testament.
- Messianic Jews do not believe they have to follow halakhah (Jewish law) since Yeshua introduced a new covenant between God and people.

Reform Jews

- Reform Jews believe that the Torah was written by different human sources.
- Reform Judaism began in Germany in the early 1800s. Some Jews felt that the rigid nature of Orthodox Judaism was unhelpful. At the same time, Germany society was becoming more liberal, which was influencing many Jewish people.
- They are not controlled by halakhah, although they do follow some Jewish practices and maintain Jewish values.
- Reform Judaism is the most liberal expression of modern Judaism.

Reconstructionist Jews

- Reconstructionist Jews believe that Judaism must evolve.
- They do not accept the traditional Jewish beliefs of God.
- They follow halakhah to retain their Jewish identity.

Humanistic Jews

- Rabbi Sherwin Wine established the first Humanistic Jewish congregation in 1963. He also helped set up the Society for Humanistic Judaism in 1969.
- Humanistic Jews either do not believe in the concept of God or consider His existence irrelevant. Humanistic Jews believe that humans, not God, have the power to bring change and solve the world's problems.

Conservative Jews

- Conservative Jews believe that God gave people original thoughts and ideas that were developed in the Torah.
- They follow halakhah but believe that the law should adapt, within reason, to modern times.

Flexidox Jews

- Flexidox Jews follow a very new form of Judaism (established in 2003).
- They embrace the spirit of Orthodox Judaism but give themselves flexibility to move beyond specific and outdated constraints of Jewish law.

LINK

Jewish beliefs and practices, and the impact of these on daily life, are covered in more depth in Option D, Judaism, starting on page 144.

Teachings concerning the Sabbath

The fourth of the Ten Commandments is:

> Remember the Sabbath day by keeping it holy.
> Six days you shall labour and do all your work,
> but the seventh day is a Sabbath to the Lord
> your God. On it you shall not do any work,
> neither you, nor your son or daughter, nor
> your male or female servant, nor your animals,
> nor any foreigner residing in your towns.

Exodus 20:8–10

Sabbath (in Hebrew Shabbat) begins at sunset on Friday and finishes at sunset on Saturday. The Sabbath is a day to rest and focus on God. Orthodox Jews mark the start of the Sabbath by lighting candles, blessing bread and wine, reciting prayers and reading scripture. Many Jewish families celebrate the Sabbath with a meal on Friday evening. On the Sabbath, families attend a service together at the synagogue. It is generally forbidden for Jews to carry out any kind of work on the Sabbath. There are 39 types of forbidden 'work' including travelling in a vehicle, cooking and writing. However, Reformed and Liberal Jews do not follow all of these laws.

In some parts of the Caribbean, such as Jamaica, there is flexibility around observing the Sabbath due to work demands.

Orthodox Jews believe that even travelling in a vehicle or cooking are forms of work and should not be performed on the Sabbath

KEY POINTS

1 God is one – the Almighty creator.

2 Everyone will be judged and rewarded or punished according to how they have lived. Only evil people will be expelled from God's presence.

3 All humanity sins, but there is salvation through God's mercy and forgiveness.

4 In the Messianic age there will be peace on earth and all people will know God. Judaism teaches life after death. Some believe life will continue on earth, others believe souls enter a spiritual realm.

5 The Jewish sects differ in their beliefs on the sacredness of the Torah, the literal following of halakhah (Jewish law) and the need for Judaism to adapt to the modern world.

6 The Sabbath should be kept holy. Jews rest and nurture their spirit.

ACTIVITY

Do you think there should be work or employment that a Jew should be free to perform on the Sabbath? If yes, what work or employment would you argue should be allowed? Do you think Jews in professions such as medicine or policing who don't want to work on the Sabbath should be required to? Give reasons for your answers.

Major teachings of Caribbean indigenous religions

Rastafari

Rastafarians believe that:

- Haile Selassie was God incarnated in a human body. They believe that he was the Messiah, whose coming was predicted in the Bible. Some Rastafarians also believe that Jesus Christ was God on earth in human form, but that Haile Selassie was God come to earth a second time

- all Rastafarians should live in Africa since this is the nation that the descendants of most Rastafarians came from

- there should be reparation (compensation) for the wrongs committed during the slave trade. This compensation could come in the form of money, investment in countries where the slave trade took place, repatriation of slave descendants, etc.

- black people are the true Israelites, whose history is recorded in the Bible

- Ethiopia is a sacred land – the 'black man's heaven', since this is where Haile Selassie ruled

- the King James Bible is the correct version of the Bible to refer to

- Babylon is a term to describe any government, regime or rule that goes against Rastafarian teaching and beliefs, and the will of Jah

- ganja was given by Jah as medicine and to prompt wisdom

- the body is a temple for God and should be kept healthy. Diet should be natural, unprocessed and vegetarian

- reflection and meditation are needed to feed the spirit and gain insight

- they should respect the environment

- **Pan-Africanism** is something that can and should be achieved.

Revivalism

Revivalists believe:

- in the existence of two words: the temporal (what is physically here on earth now) and the spiritual

- that the universe is occupied by three groups of spirits: the heavenly, the earth-bound and the ground spirits

- that the human body can be possessed by spirits

- that Revivalists can travel to the spirit world, receive spiritual gifts and communicate with the spirits

- that ancestors can communicate with Revivalists through dreams and visions

- that sometimes spirits communicate with them using colours. Devotees will also wear a particular colour based on their rank within the religion

- in **baptism by water** (or baptism by immersion).

Revivalists and Spiritual Baptists believe in the Christian practice of baptising believers by submerging them in water

Vodun

Followers of Vodun believe:

- in loas (spirits of ancestors) and saints. Some believe that these are the same thing and others believe that they are two distinct groups of spirits
- that loas communicate with followers of Vodun through dreams and visions
- that the dead can reward or punish you on earth so must be honoured
- that people with special talents or gifts must be **degraded** when they die so that they do not torment their living relatives
- that spirits can possess the bodies of Vodun followers.

Orisha

Followers of Orisha believe:

- that gods possess the bodies of Orisha followers and can be identified through the physical effect they have on the body
- that ancestors play an important role in life – they can bring good or harm to people
- that the dead have a soul, as well as a shadow or spirit
- that the gods speak to Orisha followers through dreams, visions and **divination**
- in the giving of offerings or sacrifices, such as animals and herbs.

Spiritual Baptist

Spiritual Baptists believe:

- that the Holy Spirit lives within them to guide, empower and comfort them
- that the Bible and prayer are powerful and can change situations
- in **baptism by the Holy Spirit** as well as baptism in water
- that when a person sins, they can be cleansed through repenting, fasting and mourning
- that ancestors communicate with the living through dreams.

Santeria

Followers of Santeria believe:

- in five different levels of power. These are Olodumare (the high god), the orisha (lesser gods), human beings, human ancestors and plants, animals and natural and man-made items
- that Olodumare is the one Supreme God
- that they communicate with the orisha through prayer, divination and offerings (including fruit, flowers, sweet foods and ebo-sacrifice such as an animal or animals' blood)
- that 11 commandments were given to Obatala (the eldest orisha, who created the world) to keep people from evil and help them to live prosperous lives.

7 Festivals

7.1 Festivals in Christianity

Christmas

Advent

Advent is the period that starts on the fourth Sunday before Christmas Day and ends on Christmas Day. In many churches around the world, a candle is lit each week of Advent. In the Caribbean this is only recognised in some traditions, such as Roman Catholic and Anglican. This symbolises lighting the way for Jesus' birth. During Advent, Christians remember Christ's promise that he will come to earth again to judge humanity. Many Christians use Advent as a time to focus on their relationship with God.

CASE STUDY | The day arrives!

At Christmas it is traditional to give out presents to each other to remember how Jesus was God's gift to the world

It's 6am on 25 December and the Williams family in St Vincent are already up and very excited! Mum is busy cooking ham, baked chicken and rice and preparing salads and black cake (fruitcake in Jamaica) for Christmas dinner. Dad is making final alterations to the decorations. The Williams family are Christians and, for them, today is Christmas Day – the day when Christians celebrate Christ being born on earth to save humankind from their sin and restore the relationship between God and people.

Ten-year-old Patricia and her 14-year-old brother Winston have been opening the doors on an Advent calendar each day during December, excitedly counting down the days to Christmas. Yesterday, on Christmas Eve, the family attended a service at their Anglican church. Soon, everyone will dress in their best clothes for the Christmas Day service at church. They will sing carols – with a distinctive reggae beat – and hear readings from the Bible about Jesus' birth. It will be a very joyful service, thanking God for Jesus' arrival on the earth.

Patricia and Winston are looking forward to seeing their cousins later, when the whole family will have a special meal together. After everyone has eaten, it will be time to give out presents. Presents symbolise the gift of Jesus that God sent to the world. This is the part of the day that Patricia and Winston are looking forward to most of all!

Epiphany

The account of Jesus' birth tells of wise men (or magi) who travelled many miles to worship Jesus (scholars think they travelled from Iraq, Iran or India). The Greek word **epiphany** means manifestation, and Christians consider Epiphany to be the manifestation of Christ to the **Gentiles**. The visit of the magi shows that, from his birth, Jesus came to save all people, not just the Jews. Epiphany also marks the end of the 12 days of Christmas and, for some Christians across the Caribbean, it is the time to take down decorations and officially end the celebrations.

CASE STUDY | Going without

Lent lasts for 40 days in the run-up to Easter and is a time when traditionally Christians show penitence and self-restraint to commemorate Christ's fasting in the wilderness. During the 40 days of Lent, Patricia and Winston's mother, Merlene, has decided to give up meat. She hopes that this will help her to understand more about how it felt for Christ to go without food and drink when he was in the wilderness. Merlene also hopes that, by denying her body some of the luxuries of daily life, she can focus more on her spiritual life.

Ash Wednesday

Ash Wednesday marks the first day of the abstinence of Lent. It is a time for repentance and cleansing of the soul. Roman Catholic and Anglican churches hold sombre services in which people's foreheads are marked with ash. This ash symbolises sorrow for sin and the death that sin has brought into the world.

Holy Week

This is the most sombre week of the Christian Calendar. It is the week in which Christians remember Jesus' death and the events leading up to it. The week incorporates Palm Sunday, Maundy (or Holy) Thursday and Good Friday. Some of these days are public holidays in many Caribbean countries.

Palm Sunday

On Palm Sunday people remember Jesus' triumphant arrival in Jerusalem. People cheered and waved palms to welcome him. Yet, only five days later, the public called for him to be killed. Palm Sunday marks the start of Holy Week.

Maundy or Holy Thursday

On this day, people remember Jesus' Last Supper with his disciples. During this meal, Jesus washed his disciples' feet – showing the importance of humility, love and service. Maundy Thursday also marks the origins of Holy Communion, when Jesus told his disciples to remember the sacrifice of his death and celebrate the new covenant with God through eating bread and drinking wine.

Good Friday

This is the day when Christians remember Jesus' crucifixion. Churches hold three-hour services for people to reflect on Jesus' suffering and on their own sin, which contributed to his death. Although it seems a strange name, the day is good because Christians believe that Jesus' death paid for their sin and restored the relationship between God and man.

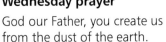

Traditional Ash Wednesday prayer

God our Father, you create us from the dust of the earth.

Grant that these ashes may be for us a sign of our penitence, and a symbol of our mortality.

And he took bread, gave thanks and broke it, and gave it to them, saying, 'This is my body given for you; do this in remembrance of me.'

In the same way, after the supper he took the cup, saying, 'This cup is the new covenant in my blood, which is poured out for you.'

Luke 22:19–20

Kite flying is popular on many Caribbean islands all year round. On Good Friday though, the activity takes on special meaning. Kite flying represents Jesus' ascension into heaven that occurred a few weeks after his death. In Bermuda, Barbados, Trinidad and the Grenadines, kite flying over the Easter weekend remains a strong tradition – although, for many, its links to Christianity have been lost.

Paschaltide

Paschaltide (sometimes written Paschal Time) covers the time from Easter Sunday to Pentecost (seven weeks later) and includes the following events.

Easter Saturday

This is the day after Good Friday. It is a sombre time for Christians as, following his crucifixion on Good Friday, Christ's followers were filled with sorrow over his death.

Easter Vigil

In the early hours of Easter Sunday, the day that Christ rose from the dead, many Christians hold a vigil. They meet together to pray, worship and read the Bible as they wait for the sun to rise. The sun rising marks the start of Easter Sunday, when those attending the vigil will celebrate Christ's resurrection together. The vigil may end with a shared breakfast.

Easter Sunday

On Easter Sunday, Christians celebrate Jesus rising from the dead and leaving an empty tomb

When he had led [the disciples] out to the vicinity of Bethany, he lifted up his hands and blessed them. While he was blessing them, he left them and was taken up into heaven.

Luke 24:50

CASE STUDY	Easter Sunday and the resurrection of Jesus

It is Easter Sunday and Patricia and Winston are enjoying church. The church is decorated with flowers and there is an atmosphere of celebration. There have been Bible readings telling of the empty tomb and Mary Magdalene's encounter with the risen Jesus on Easter morning. Lots of joyful hymns have been sung about Jesus defeating death. Christians believe that Jesus' resurrection (him coming back to life after he died) is further proof that Jesus was God. Jesus' resurrection also symbolises the new spiritual resurrection between God and humanity.

Easter is also a time to celebrate life and new birth. Patricia and Winston have already eaten many Easter buns over the weekend. Today they have been given chocolate eggs. These eggs symbolise new life and Jesus' empty tomb.

After church, Patricia and Winston's neighbours are coming round for lunch. Then they are all going to fly kites on the beach.

Ascension Day

Jesus spent 40 days on earth with his disciples after rising from the dead. After this time, Jesus returned to heaven. The Bible tells that Jesus will return to earth one final time in the last days to take his people (Christians) up to heaven. This only applies to some denominations.

Pentecost and Whitsuntide

Jesus' return to heaven did not mark the end of his influence on the earth. Before Jesus was taken back to heaven, he promised to send the Holy Spirit to the disciples.

The role of the Holy Spirit was to comfort, guide and strengthen the disciples when Jesus was no longer with them. The Holy Spirit still comforts, guides and strengthens Christians today. The Bible teaches that gifts of the Holy Spirit, such as speaking in tongues and prophesying, are for all Christians at all times. Many of these gifts of the Holy Spirit are seen in churches today – particularly **non-denominational churches** and Pentecostal churches. Another word for Pentecost is Whitsuntide.

> When the day of Pentecost came, [the disciples] were all together in one place. Suddenly a sound like the blowing of a violent wind came from heaven and filled the whole house where they were sitting. They saw what seemed to be tongues of fire that separated and came to rest on each of them. All of them were filled with the Holy Spirit and began to speak in other tongues as the Spirit enabled them.
>
> Acts 2:1–4

ACTIVITY

What other gifts of the Holy Spirit are there? What are the benefits of these? If you are able, try to visit a Pentecostal church – you may see some of the gifts of the Spirit actually occurring.

Trinity Sunday

Trinity Sunday occurs on the first Sunday after Pentecost. It provides a chance for Christians to focus on the concept of the Trinity (God the Father, God the Son and God the Holy Spirit). Sermons in church often focus on the Trinity on this day and children will learn about the Trinity in Sunday school. Congregations in Anglican churches often say the Nicene Creed together, which is a statement of belief including what Christians believe about the Trinity.

Corpus Christi

This day occurs on the first Thursday after Trinity Sunday (although some church traditions have moved the day to the first Sunday after Trinity Sunday). The day celebrates the Eucharist (the service of Holy Communion). It is a mainly Roman Catholic tradition, although some Anglican and Lutheran churches mark the day too.

KEY POINTS

1. During Advent Christians prepare, spiritually and practically, for Christmas.

2. Christmas celebrates Christ's birth.

3. Epiphany marks the visit of the magi to Jesus. It celebrates Jesus coming to redeem all people, not just the Jews.

4. Lent marks the 40 days Jesus spent without food or water in the wilderness. It is a time of penitence and self-restraint. Lent begins on Ash Wednesday.

5. During Holy Week, Christians remember Christ's death. This week includes Palm Sunday, Maundy Thursday and Good Friday.

6. Paschaltide marks the Easter season, which runs from Easter Sunday to Pentecost (seven weeks later).

Festivals in Hinduism

In this topic you will learn to:

- describe some of the important Hindu festivals and reasons for their observance.

Ramesh and Kamala light the deeyas that represent the lights that guided Rama home

CASE STUDY	Divali/Deepavali

It is late October in Guyana and, for 12-year-old Ramesh and 14-year-old Kamala, the five-day festival of Divali is coming to an end. A week ago, they helped to clean the house to welcome the goddess Lakshmi into their home. Hindu custom teaches that Lakshmi will bring prosperity and good fortune to the family. Most Hindus perform pujas to the goddess Lakshmi.

Divali is the festival of lights, so Ramesh and Kamala decorated their home with tiny deeyas (lights in small clay pots). They also have spectacular lights in the window every evening. These lights represent the lights that guided Rama home after he had rescued his wife Sita from the demon king Ravana.

Kamala's favourite part of the five-day festival has been the new clothes and beautiful necklace that she has been bought to wear for the celebrations. Ramesh has enjoyed listening to traditional stories about Hindu gods, particularly the *Ramayana*, and watching the motorcades drive through town the day before Divali. The whole family has enjoyed pujas (sacred rituals), sharing of meals and sweets with neighbours, singing praises to the deities in their mandirs and homes', and, of course, Ramesh and Kamala have enjoyed receiving presents. But now they are ready for life to calm down again – they need some sleep! The lights that form the centrepiece of Divali celebrations are a reminder that darkness can be driven away by light and that, in the same way, adharma can be driven away by dharma.

Phagwa/Holi

Phagwa/Holi, after the spring month Phalguna, in which the festival falls, is when Hindus remember the story of Holika and her nephew Prahlada. Holika tried to kill Prahlada because she did not like the devotion he showed to the god Vishnu. By repeatedly speaking the name Vishnu, Prahlada was saved from death – instead it was Holika who died in a bonfire.

Find out more about the festival of Krishna Janam Ashtmi. What is the significance of midnight?

This story teaches Hindus the importance of having faith in the god Vishnu, as well as confirming the Hindu belief that good will triumph over evil. It also provides a great reason for Hindus to celebrate the festival with bonfires! Fertility, connected to spring and new life, is also an important aspect of Holi celebrations. Holi also celebrates the god Krishna who was an avatar of Vishnu. Krishna has a playful side and Hindus remind each other of this during Holi by throwing coloured dye and powder at one another. They enjoy singing songs, praising the deities (especially Krishna), and making the streets very colourful during Holi.

Rama Naumi (or Rama Navami) takes place in March or April (Vaishakha in the Indian calendar) and celebrates the birth of Lord Rama, an avatar of Vishnu on earth. Lord Rama was the hero of the *Ramayana*. For around a week leading up to Rama Naumi, the book is recited continually. On the day of the festival, highlights of the story are read in the temple. Pujas and devotional songs are also performed.

Kamala is helping to clean and decorate the house for the festival. Yesterday, Ramesh bought fruit and Kamala collected flowers for the family shrine to Lord Rama. Today the children will perform pujas, recite devotional songs and visit the mandir. They will also rock a cradle containing an image of the infant Rama and lay flowers in the cradle around the figure.

Afterwards, Ramesh and Kamala are looking forward to a feast using the sacred food offered to Rama.

Ramesh and Kamala lay flowers around the figure of the infant Rama

Maha Sivaraatri

Maha Sivaraatri is celebrated every year on the 13th night/14th day of the Hindu month of Phalguna (March), which is a moonless night. Hindus believe that there is a high level of divine energy present on the night of Maha Sivaraatri. During the night they keep vigil, fast, offer prayers and sing devotional songs called bhajans to Shiva. During the day, Hindus offer bael leaves to Lord Shiva, fast, and practice yoga and meditation in order to achieve greater spirituality.

Krishna Janam Ashtmi

This festival falls in the Hindu month of Bhadra (August/September) and celebrates the birth of the god Krishna. Re-enactments are performed of rocking the infant Krishna's cradle and of Krishna being born. Traditional songs are sung and special pujas (rituals) are performed in the minutes leading up to midnight. At midnight, there is singing and dancing, and sweets are shared out.

Find out more about the festival of Krishna Janam Ashtmi. What is the significance of midnight?

Nava Raatri

This festival celebrates God in the feminine form as Shakti. The festival remembers Shakti's **incarnations** as nine different Hindu goddesses. The festival takes place for 10 days between September and October. During the festival, different stories of Shakti in her various forms are retold, in particular the story of the goddess Durga defeating Mahishasura the Buffalo Demon. Ram Lila is a very popular performance in communities at this time as a re-enactment of the life of Ram.

Nava Raatri means nine nights in Sanskrit. This is because the festival takes place for 10 days and nine nights.

1   Divali means 'festival of lights'. This festival celebrates the goddess Lakshmi and it is a time for new beginnings.

2   Phagwa/Holi celebrates the triumph of good over evil and the importance of faith. It is also a time for fun.

3   During Maha Sivaraatri, Hindus fast, perform yoga and meditate to achieve higher spiritual revelation.

4   Krishna Janam Ashtmi celebrates Krishna's birth.

5   Rama Naumi celebrates the birth of Lord Rama.

6   Nava Raatri celebrates the mother goddess or energy Shakti in her nine different forms as Hindu goddesses.

Festivals in Islam

In this topic you will learn to:

- recall the purpose of selected festivals and observances in Islam.

During Eid ul Fitr, Muslims celebrate with a feast after the long weeks of fasting during Ramadan

CASE STUDY | Eid ul Fitr

Today is Eid ul Fitr and a national holiday in Trinidad. Muslims have been **fasting** for the last 30 days during Ramadan. Going without food and drink all day in the heat has been a big challenge. People who are young, old, frail or pregnant have not followed the fast. Today, everyone is happy and celebrating because Eid ul Fitr marks the end of the fast. Maryam has fasted, but her brothers Muhammad and Aadam are still to young to fast all day. Instead, they have missed one meal each day to prepare them for when they too will go without any food or drink during daylight hours in Ramadan.

Yesterday, the children's father went to the masjid to pay zakah. This is a donation of around 3.8 kg of rice for each member of the household. The children's father donated 23 kg (since the children's aunt lives with them too). During Ramadan, Muslims, however rich or poor, become equal. Everyone experiences how it feels to go without food. This morning, Maryam, Muhammad and Aadam recited the Salatul Eid ul Fitr, a special prayer to mark the start of Eid ul Fitr, at the masjid. Maryam, Muhammad and Aadam followed the procession of people travelling to the masjid one way and travelled back home by a different route, as the Prophet Muhammad taught.

Now it is time for the feasting and celebrations to begin! Maryam, Muhammad and Aadam are wearing their best clothes. Their house is filled with **Eid Mubarak** cards and brightly coloured decorations. Maryam, Muhammad and Aadam have been given presents and sweets from family, neighbours and friends and later they will share in the Eid ul Fitr feast with their family.

ACTIVITY

As well as to benefit others, there is another reason behind families donating food at the end of Ramadan. Find out what this reason is.

1 Why is this benefit particularly significant during Ramadan?

2 Why do Muslims believe it is easier to perform good deeds during Ramadan?

DID YOU KNOW?

Not only does Eid ul Fitr mark the end of the fast of Ramadan, it is forbidden for Muslims to fast on this day.

Eid ul Adha

Eid ul Adha is known as the festival of sacrifice. It commemorates Ibrahim's willingness to sacrifice his son Ismail to Allah. This showed that Ibrahim was willing to obey Allah completely, even when it was hard. Once Ibrahim had shown his obedience, Allah provided a ram for Ibrahim to sacrifice instead of Ismail. It is unlikely that Allah would ever ask anyone today to sacrifice their son, but it is this same obedience and sacrifice that all Muslims should show towards Allah.

Eid ul Adha starts on the tenth of Dhulhajj (the last Islamic month), and animal sacrifices are made. The festival occurs at the same time as the hajj pilgrimage.

Eid ul Adha begins with a special prayer that is recited in the morning. Later, an animal is sacrificed. This must be a healthy animal and it is usually a sheep, goat, bull or, in Arab countries, a camel. In Muslim countries it is often the father of a family who slaughters the animal but, in the Caribbean and other non-Muslim countries, the animal is slaughtered professionally in the courtyard of the masjid. There are strict rules for how the animal should be slaughtered in order for it to be **halal**:

- It must not be frightened.
- It must be turned to face the direction of Makkah while the slaughterer declares the name of Allah.
- The animal is killed with a very sharp knife that is drawn across its jugular (main) vein in its neck. All of the blood is drained from the body.

Once the sacrifice has been made, the family keep one-third of the meat for a feast for themselves and share the rest among relatives and the poor.

During Eid ul Adha, sacrificed meat is shared among relatives and the poor in order that everyone can join in the celebrations

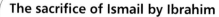

> **The sacrifice of Ismail by Ibrahim**
>
> when the son reached the age of serious work with him, he said, 'Oh my son! I see in vision that I offer you in sacrifice; now see what is your view!' (The son) said: 'Oh my father! Do as you are commanded: you will find me, if God so wills, one practising patience and constancy!'
>
> So when they had both submitted their wills (to God), and [Ibrahim] had laid him prostrate on his forehead (for sacrifice), We called out to him, 'O Ibrahim! You have already fulfilled the vision! – thus indeed do we reward those who do right. For this was obviously a trial.'
>
> Surah 37:102–106

Ashura

The Ashura festival occurs on the tenth day of the Islamic month of Muharram. Sunni Muslims fast on either the 9–10 or 10–11 Muharram to remember both Nuh leaving the ark and Musa and the Israelites being saved from the Egyptians.

Imam Hussein

For Shia Muslims, Ashura is also the day they mourn the martyrdom of Imam Hussein.

- Hussein was a grandson of Muhammad who fought against the ruler of the Islamic community in the 7th century CE.
- Hussein was killed in battle, together with many of his followers, in 680 CE at Karbala in modern-day Iraq.
- Hussein's death led to the two distinct sects of Islam – Shia and Sunni.
- During Ashura, Shia men and women dress in black and march in the streets slapping their chests and chanting. Many of the men share in the suffering of Imam Hussein by hitting themselves with chains (self-flagellation).

Miladunnabi

The twelfth day of Rabiul Awal celebrates the birthday of the Prophet Muhammad in 570 CE. On this day, many Muslims remember the life of the Prophet Muhammad and his wisdom, bravery, leadership and teaching. Parents tell their children stories from the Hadith and religious leaders make speeches about Muhammad's life. Some Muslims do not celebrate Miladunnabi as there is no evidence that Muhammad celebrated his birthday and they believe that only practices instructed in the Qur'an and Sunnah should be followed.

Lailatul Miraj

This festival, celebrated by some but not all Muslims, marks Muhammad's Night Journey when the Prophet travelled from

Makkah to Jerusalem in a single night. From Jerusalem, Muhammad was taken up to heaven by Allah. In heaven he met the prophets who had gone before him and he also met with Allah. This is when Allah told Muhammad that Muslims should pray five times a day. This festival is also known as Lailatul Isra.

Lailatul Qadr

This festival is a single night in Ramadan that is a solemn, reflective night of prayer (also called the Night of Power), which marks the night when the angel Jibril (Gabriel) revealed the first verses of the Qur'an to the Prophet Muhammad. The festival, which falls during Ramadan, is a time for prayer and study of the Qur'an. Some Muslims spend all night praying and reciting from the Qur'an. It is also a time to seek forgiveness from Allah for your sins.

Almost one million pilgrims visit Makkah to pray on Lailatul Qadr, one of the holiest nights of the Islamic calendar

Lailatul Bara'at

This festival, known as the Night of Forgiveness, falls on 15 Sha'ban, the eighth month in the Muslim calendar. Not all Muslims observe this festival, but those who do believe that their life for the coming year is determined on this night. Therefore, many Muslims stay up all night praying for guidance and for God's mercy and grace. Some Muslims also fast during the day to prepare for their night of prayer. Muslims often give charitable donations on this day and visit the graves of dead relatives to pay their respects.

The Night of Power

We have indeed revealed this (Message) in the Night of Power:

And what will explain to thee what the Night of Power is?

The Night of Power is better than a thousand months.

Therein come down the angels and the Spirit by Allah's permission, on every errand:

Peace! … This until the rise of morn!

Surah 97:1–5

KEY POINTS

1 Eid ul Fitr marks the end of the 30-day fast during Ramadan.

2 Eid ul Adha, the festival of sacrifice, remembers Ibrahim's willingness to sacrifice his son Ismail.

3 Ashura commemorates Musa being saved from the Egyptians. For Shia Muslims it is also a day to sanctify the death of Imam Hussein.

4 Miladunnabi celebrates the birthday of the Prophet Muhammad in 570 CE.

5 Lailatul Miraj celebrates the Prophet's Night Journey and ascension into heaven.

6 Lailatul Qadr celebrates the first time the Angel Jibril revealed the Qur'an to Muhammad. This festival takes place during Ramadan.

7 During Lailatul Bara'at many Muslims pray all night while their destiny for the year ahead is determined by Allah.

Festivals in Judaism

Rosh Hashanah

The festival of Rosh Hashanah (Hebrew for 'Head of the Year') marks the beginning of a new year for Jews. This is a day of complete rest. During this day, Jews examine their lives, motives and spiritual state. Jews believe that there are 10 days for Jews to repent of their sin and put right any wrongs. On the tenth day following Rosh Hashanah, God judges each person and decides whether or not they will remain in the Book of Life.

On the day of Rosh Hashanah, the shofar (ram's horn) is blown 100 times by a rabbi in the synagogue. This follows instructions given in the Torah and reminds Jews to repent of their sins.

During Rosh Hashanah Jews eat sweet food, including bread dipped in honey and bread sprinkled with sugar, as a symbol of hope for the year ahead. While eating, Jews say to each other:

'May it be the Lord's will to renew us for a year that will be good and sweet.'

In particular, during Rosh Hashanah, Jews remember:

- God's creation of the world in six days and his resting on the seventh
- God's judgement of every Jew according to their actions in the past year.

Yom Kippur

This Jewish festival takes place 10 days after Rosh Hashanah. Yom Kippur is known as the Day of Atonement and it is a solemn day for Jews.

- This is the day when God examines the Book of Life and decides whose name should remain.
- Jews hope that God will judge them favourably and that the coming year will bring them life and not death.
- Jews also use this quiet day of reflection to re-examine their lives and spiritual state. Many prayers are said and many Jews fast for the full 25 hours to show their **penitence** and faith.
- The Day of Atonement is also a day for Jews to say sorry to each other for any wrongs they have committed.
- During Yom Kippur, Jews also remember people in need and give to charities.
- Most of the day (which lasts for 25 hours) is spent in the synagogue. Jews listen to the story of Jonah from the Tenakh/Book of Prophets, which reminds them of the senselessness of disobeying God.

During Yom Kippur, Jews remember what happened to Jonah as a result of him disobeying God

Jonah and the Big Fish

Jonah was a prophet in Old Testament times who was told by God to warn the wicked people in the city of Nineveh that they would be destroyed unless they repented of their sins. Jonah ran away, was thrown overboard the ship in which he was travelling and was swallowed by a great fish. He was in its belly for three days before it spat him out on to dry land. Jonah discovered that he could not escape the responsibility that God have given to him, no matter how hard he tried.

Sukkoth

This seven-day festival takes place five days after Yom Kippur. During this festival, Jews 'live' in booths to commemorate the Israelites living in tabernacles (or booths) during their time in the wilderness. Jews remember God's provision during this time through supplying manna for the Jews to eat and water for them to drink. Sukkoth is a joyful time and importance is placed on the unity of the body and soul, the worship of God and the blessings and responsibilities of community life – including charity towards those who are in need.

Simchath Torah

This day is celebrated at the end of Sukkoth. It is the day when public reading of the Torah ends for the current year and begins for the next. During a special service, the Torah scrolls are distributed and paraded around the synagogue seven times.

Chanukah

Chanukah, or the Festival of Lights, is an eight-day festival that celebrates the victory of the Jews over the evil Antiochus Epiphanes, who occupied Jerusalem around 170 BCE. This leader tried to destroy Judaism and tried to force Jews to worship Greek gods and eat pork. A Jew named Mattathias, and later his son Judas, led a rebellion against Antiochus. Judas and his followers took occupation of the Temple in 164 BCE and, on 25 Kislev (December), Judas proclaimed the rededication of the temple to God. Although there was only enough oil to keep the perpetual lamp in the temple burning for one day, the lamp burned for eight days, signifying God's provision.

Case study	Pancakes, presents and people

Benjamin and Jacob have a menorah burning in the window of their home. Tonight, the last night of Chanukah, the final candle will be lit. Benjamin and Jacob are sad that the festival of Chanukah is coming to an end. They have enjoyed the family gatherings where they have eaten doughnuts and latkes (potato pancakes) and played games together. And they have really enjoyed receiving a gift for each of the eight days of Chanukah! But Benjamin and Jacob know that the most important part of the festival is respecting and celebrating the uniqueness of all people and remembering the importance of standing up for your beliefs and for truth and goodness.

Sukkoth prayer

May it be Your will, O my God and God of my fathers, that You cause Your divine presence to live among us, and may You spread a covering of peace over us.

DID YOU KNOW?

The Judas who led the rebellion against Antiochus had the nickname Maccabeus (meaning 'the hammerer'). From this, his family and descendents came to be known as the Maccabees.

The menorah is an eight-branched lamp used during Chanukah to mark the eight days of the festival and the eight days that the perpetual lamp in the temple burned, despite only having enough oil to burn for one day

Read the book of Esther in the Bible/Tenakh.

1 What do Esther 4:11 and 4:16 tell us?

2 What risk did Esther take in approaching the king?

3 Why do you think Esther commanded the Jews to fast?

4 List the benefits to Esther, Mordecai and the Jews as a result of Esther's actions.

Purim

This festival is known as the Festival of Lots and celebrates the victory of Esther over the wicked Haman. Esther became King Ahasuerus' wife while the Jews were exiled in Persia. Following Haman's plot to destroy all Jews in the kingdom, Esther approached the king to ask for mercy. The festival celebrates Esther's bravery and the Jew's escape from destruction. Jews fast the day before Purim to remember Esther's three-day fast before she approached the king. On the day of Purim, there is great feasting and festivity. Jews exchange presents and the story of Esther is read out to boos and hisses when the name of Haman is mentioned.

Pesach

The Jewish festival of Pesach (Passover) is very important for Jews. It remembers God's rescue of the Jews from Egypt where they were oppressed and abused. The festival of Pesach has been celebrated by Jews for thousands of years. It was the Pesach feast that Jesus would have shared in with his disciples during the Last Supper, the night before he was crucified. Pesach (Passover) gets its name from the final plague on Egypt 'passing over' Jewish homes marked with blood. This plague killed every firstborn Egyptian son and caused Pharaoh to finally release the Jews from slavery.

Families share in a Pesach meal called Seder and eat traditional symbolic foods such as bitter herbs and roasted eggs. The festival is a sombre time when Jews remember their persecution in many lands throughout history and also to pray for people trapped in slavery today.

CASE STUDY	The hunt

Hunting for leaven is the final preparation before Pesach

It is the night before Pesach in Jamaica and Benjamin and Jacob are hunting for leaven (yeast) and leavened bread in their home. For weeks, the whole family have helped to clean the house ready for the Pesach festival. Hunting for leaven is the final stage in preparing the house. It reminds Jews that, during the Exodus, when Moses led the Jews out of slavery in Egypt, there was no time to let dough rise, so bread was made without yeast. For Benjamin and Jacob, searching for leaven is just for fun, but thousands of years ago when Jews were preparing to leave Egypt – not knowing whether they would be attacked and having so little time to prepare – the atmosphere would have been very different.

A family sharing a Seder meal

Shavuot/Feast of weeks

This festival takes place seven weeks after Pesach. On this day, Jews remember Moses receiving the Ten Commandments from God on Mount Sinai. This festival is also the time that Jews thank God for their land and their harvest. Jews believe King David was born and died on Shavuot and, to mark this, Psalms written by King David are read out.

LINK

The Jewish festivals are covered in more depth in Option D, Judaism, starting on page 160.

KEY POINTS

1 Rosh Hashanah is a time when Jews remember responsibilities and examine their spiritual and moral state.

2 Yom Kippur is a solemn day of fasting and prayer to seek forgiveness for sins.

3 Sukkoth celebrates God's provision. Jews remember the tabernacles that Jews lived in during their wanderings.

4 Simchath Torah marks the end of one year's public reading of the Torah and the start of the next.

5 Channukah reminds Jews of the triumph of good over evil.

6 Purim remembers the evil of Haman, and Esther's victory over him.

7 During Pesach, Jews remember God bringing the Israelites out of slavery in Egypt.

8 Shavuot commemorates Moses receiving the Ten Commandments on Mount Sinai.

Festivals in Caribbean indigenous religions

7 Jan Rastafari follow the Ethiopian calendar, which celebrates Christmas on 7 January. Rastafari adopt the Ethiopian Orthodox traditions of Christmas, including burning incense, singing carols and feasting, followed by a Nyabhingi (a musical meeting).

21 April Haile Selassie's visit to Jamaica in 1966 is commemorated on this day with music, drums and chanting.

25 May Rastafari celebrate African Liberation Day (a public holiday in many African countries). This day celebrates the independence Africa gained from foreign rule.

23 July The birthday of Haile Selassie in 1892 is marked with Nyabhingi celebrations of singing, drumming and chanting.

2 Nov The coronation of Emperor Haile Selassie is one of the most important events in the Rastafari calendar. Haile Selassie was proclaimed Ethiopia's new leader on 2 November 1930. Rastafari mark this day with reasonings (based on teachings from the Bible and from Selassie), chanting and music.

Figure 7.5.1 Rastafari festivals throughout the year

Rastafari

Nyabhingi is a celebration of Rastafari. It is an orthodox interpretation of the religion and is heavily influenced by Ethiopian Orthodox Christianity. Music and drumming is an important part of this celebration of Rastafari. Annual Nyabhingi celebrations take place across the Caribbean and key features of the celebrations are drumming and chanting. Today, Rastafari meetings that involve lots of music are often referred to as Nyabhingi celebrations.

Revivalism

Revivalist Convention

Every year on the first Thursday in March there is a Revivalist Convention in Watt Town, St Ann in Jamaica – the place where Revivalism began. Revivalist worshippers come from across the Caribbean, and some even further, to pray and worship together. Worshippers often wear elaborate dress, and singing and dancing take place all day.

Table

The most important Revivalist service is called the Table. During this service, a table is decorated with fruit, flowers and candles and laid with foods such as bread and fruit, as well as glasses of water. Worshippers dance anticlockwise around the table to encourage spirit possession. These services can last several days and often mark special occasions such as thanksgiving, burial or healing.

Vodun

The main purpose of Vodun worship is to honour and summon a loa (spiritual ancestor). Ceremonies may also take place to honour or summon a particular spirit.

Following the death of someone with special abilities, a series of Vodun ceremonies take place to remove these abilities from the dead person (degradation) and transmit them to a successor. Alternatively, a relative of the dead can choose to undergo a Ceremony of Renunciation if they do not wish to receive the gift/ability. Another Vodun ceremony is a Ceremony of Dismissal, which takes place if a person wishes to be released from obligation to a loa (spirit).

Orisha

Oshun festival: The Oshun festival (also known as Osun) originated in Osun state, Nigeria. It celebrates the river goddess Osun, known for her sensuality and beauty. During the festival, offerings are made to Orisha gods and there is dancing, drumming and singing.

Rain festival: This festival marks the beginning of the rain cycle. It is an opportunity for refreshment, thanksgiving and cultivation – spiritually and physically. Orisha followers thank Shango, the god of thunder, for the rain that brings fertility to the earth. During this celebration, Orisha followers remember their responsibilities to the environment and recall lessons about the land learnt from their ancestors.

Earth festival: This festival, also called the Oduduwa festival, takes place on 21 March. It is a celebration of the orisha (god) of the earth. It also marks the start of the Yoruba New Year.

Spiritual Baptist

Candles are very important in the Spiritual Baptist tradition. Often, when worshippers meet, they light candles as part of their worship. The wax of the candles represents the spiritual darkness and primitiveness of humans. The wick represents enlightenment and release from the darkness.

Thanksgiving services are also important to Spiritual Baptists. During these services, offerings of food including bread, cake and fruit are made and this may be followed by a time of feasting. Spiritual Baptists believe that, by giving food as an offering to share with others, those who give will be blessed for their generosity.

Santeria

Abakua dance of the Ireme (diablito)

The Abakua is a secret society for men that originated in Nigeria. When African slaves were transported to Cuba, African traditions fused with Cuban culture. Today, Abakua is a fusion of Afro-Cuban religion, culture and practices. As part of the Abakua tradition, a special dance is performed during initiation ceremonies and at funeral gatherings. During these performances, an Abakua dancer, dressed in a tight-fitting suit and hood, dances with a stick and broom. The broom is believed to cleanse faithful members of the Abakua, while the stick chastises enemies and traitors. The dancer in these ceremonies is called the Ireme. These dancers are also known as diablito (Spanish for 'little devils').

Güiro

Güiro is a Santeria ceremony that takes place to honour and entertain the gods, in particular the orisha Eleggui. This orisha is responsible for opening and closing doors or new paths in life. The güiro instrument, from which the ceremony gets its name, is played, along with a bell and a conga drum. While music is played, Santeros (followers of Santeria) dance.

Bembe feasts

Bembe feasts take place to honour particular saints. As well as the feast, which will normally include the meat from a sacrificed animal, bembes involve singing, dancing and drumming to evoke the orishas. Dancers who have been possessed by orishas often perform strange and jerky movement – the orishas will use them to pass on messages from the spirit world.

ACTIVITY

As a revision exercise, draw up a table and label six columns with the Caribbean indigenous religions looked at in this topic. In each column, write in your own words, a short description of the festivals that each religion celebrates.

Dancing is a part of the bembe feast

KEY POINTS

1 Rastafari has a number of festivals including many honouring Haile Selassie.

2 Revivalism holds an annual convention in Watt Town, St Ann as well as holding Tables for specific occasions.

3 Vodun holds ceremonies in honour of spirits and ancestors, and following the death of a houngan or priest.

4 Orisha holds Oshun, rain and earth festivals.

5 Spiritual Baptists hold ceremonies of thanksgiving using lights and food.

6 Santeros use drumming, singing and dance in their ceremonies to honour and communicate with orishas.

8 Religious practices and rites of passage

8.1 Practices and rites in Christianity

Responsibilities of a parent and godparent

Parents and godparents, the Church receives these children with joy.

Today we are trusting God for their growth in faith.

Will you pray for them, draw them by your example into the community of faith and walk with them in the way of Christ?

Book of Common Worship, Baptism service, Church House Publishing, 2006

Rites of passage

Birth

CASE STUDY	A christening

'Do you reject the devil and all rebellion against God?'

Winston and Patricia are at the christening of their eight-month-old cousin, Ruth. The vicar has just asked Ruth's parents and godparents this question. They will be asked other questions too and they will be required to make a series of professions about their faith and beliefs. The answers to these questions, and the statements that the parents and godparents make, must be spoken out in public. The congregation are witnesses to the fact that the parents and godparents, who are responsible for the spiritual upbringing of Ruth, believe in God, Jesus and the Holy Spirit. Parents and godparents must promise to pray for Ruth and to nurture her in the Christian faith. When she is older, Ruth will have to make a choice about whether she wants to confirm these vows for herself in a ceremony called a confirmation.

At a christening, friends and family of a baby gather to witness the promises of parents and godparents to bring a baby up as a Christian. A christening, or infant baptism, is also the time that a baby is officially and publicly given its Christian name.

Ruth's family and friends are gathered around a type of big bowl called a font, which is filled with water. Now that Ruth's parents and godparents have made their promises, the vicar is pouring some of the water over Ruth's head. Patricia is worried that Ruth will cry but thankfully the water is not cold and Ruth just looks a bit surprised! The vicar marks Ruth's forehead with the sign of the cross. This symbolises that Ruth is a child of God and is part of the worldwide Christian family.

A christening, or infant baptism, is a time to celebrate and to thank God for the life of a child. Once the service is finished, Winston and Patricia will attend a party to celebrate the occasion.

Marriage

Christians believe that God designed a man and woman to live together faithfully in marriage. Many churches run counselling sessions to help couples prepare for married life.

During the wedding ceremony, the man and woman publicly make vows promising to love and care for each other and to be faithful to one another for life. It is the responsibility of the bride and groom's family and friends to support the couple and pray for them. In some traditions, including Anglican ceremonies, the woman promises to obey the man. This is based on Paul's teaching in Colossians 3. However, many women today choose not to include this vow.

Once vows have been made, the bride and groom exchange rings as a symbol of their everlasting love and faithfulness. These symbolic acts and the promises made are the same in all denominations of Christianity, although the words may differ.

Weddings are nearly always followed by a celebration, called a wedding reception. Nearly every Caribbean wedding party includes fruitcake, which is shared among the guests. Along with eating and drinking, wedding receptions usually include speeches.

Another important tradition of weddings is the tossing of the bouquet. All unmarried females have a chance to catch the bride's bouquet when she throws it. Whoever catches it is said to be next in line to get married.

Death

When a Christian dies, it is the end of their life on earth. However, Christianity teaches that their soul lives with God following resurrection. For this reason, although Christians are sad to say goodbye when a Christian friend or family member dies, they know that their goodbye is temporary – they will see their loved ones again in heaven. Many Christians hold a memorial or thanksgiving service instead of a funeral to celebrate the person's life rather than focus on their death. Even within a Christian funeral, thanks for the person's life plays a large part in the service. Some people choose to wear cheerful colours rather than black. During the service there is a sermon and songs, as well as a speech (called a eulogy) about the person who has died. Favourite songs for thanksgiving services in the Caribbean are 'Meet me by the River' and 'Some day I'll go where Jesus is'.

During a funeral or memorial service, people are reminded of the words Jesus said to his followers:

> I am the resurrection and the life. The one who believes in me will live, even though they die.

John 11:25

These words bring comfort by reminding Christians that their bodies are temporary but that their spirit never dies.

A favourite hymn sung at funerals is 'The Lord is my Shepherd', based on Psalm 23. Following a funeral service, bodies are either buried or **cremated**, as they are no longer needed since the person's spirit has now left their body.

Christianity teaches that marriage is a gift from God and it is the right context in which to enjoy sexual relations and to raise a family

Traditional Anglican wedding vows

To have and to hold,

From this day forward.

For better, for worse

For richer, for poorer

In sickness and in health

To love and to cherish

'til death do us part.

ACTIVITY

Look at the wedding vows on this page. Briefly summarise what they mean.

1 Is there anything you would want to add if you were making these vows?

2 Why do you think a bride and groom make promises to each other during their wedding service?

3 Why do you think couples make their vows publicly in front of friends and family?

DID YOU KNOW?

Couples who go away on holiday at the start of their marriage are said to be on a 'honeymoon'.

Rituals

Holy Communion

Holy Communion (also called the Eucharist, Mass, Breaking of Bread or Lord's Supper) is a special service in which bread and wine are eaten and drunk as a symbolic reminder of Christ's sacrifice. Holy Communion is a **sacrament** that Jesus instructed his followers to carry out. During the Last Supper, the night before his crucifixion, Jesus took bread and wine, blessed it and gave it to his disciples. Jesus explained that, by eating the bread, which represented his body, and drinking the wine, which represented his blood, his followers would share in his death and resurrection until he returned to earth. In this way, Christians accept Jesus as God's new covenant – a covenant based on love rather than the law, which brings freedom and forgiveness.

Prayer

Prayer is an integral part of Christianity. It is the means by which humans communicate with God. Prayer in Christianity can be personal, communal and informal, or it can be public and formalised. In some traditions, written prayers that congregations read together are called **liturgy**. Liturgy is important in the service of Holy Communion and in rites of passage such as weddings and funerals. In Anglican, Roman Catholic, Evangelical and Pentecostal churches, for example, there is also liturgy to help prepare for Holy Communion. In more informal churches, prayers are usually more personal and spontaneous.

Many Christians pray before eating a meal in recognition that all of their provision comes from God, and to thank God for His care. Praying before a meal is known as grace. Some Christians use a formal grace, while others use their own words.

A well-known grace

For what we are about to receive, may the Lord make us truly grateful. Amen.

Church service for Missionaries of the Poor, a religious order based in Kingston, Jamaica that works to help the disadvantaged

Initiation ceremonies

Baptism

Anglican and Roman Catholic Christians believe that baptising babies (christening) commits a baby to God when they are too young to do this for themselves. This is particularly important to Roman Catholics who believe that baptism cleanses babies from original sin.

Other denominations, such as Evangelicals, Pentecostals and independent churches, believe that baptism should only occur when a person can make a decision for themselves to follow Christ. These Christians practise adult baptism. During adult baptism, a person publicly declares that they have made a decision to follow Christ. Jesus himself instructed his followers to be baptised in water as well as by the Holy Spirit. During baptism, adults are submerged under water, symbolising their old, sinful self dying with Christ. Their re-emergence from the water symbolises the new, eternal life that they now live because of Christ's resurrection.

> Now when the apostles in Jerusalem heard that Samaria had accepted the word of God, they sent them Peter and John, who went down and prayed for them, that they might receive the Holy Spirit, for it had not yet fallen upon any of them; they had only been baptised in the name of the Lord Jesus. Then they laid hands on them and they received the Holy Spirit.
>
> Acts 8:14–17

LINK

Revivalists also practise adult baptism. There is information about this on page 87.

Confirmation

Confirmation occurs in Anglican, Methodist and Roman Catholic traditions. It allows people who have been baptised as babies to confirm their faith for themselves. In most cases, people are confirmed in their early teens, although adults converting to Christianity can also be confirmed.

The practice of confirmation originates from followers of Christ being prayed for to receive the Holy Spirit. Today, a bishop prays that those being confirmed will be strengthened and guided by the Holy Spirit. Following confirmation, participants become full members of the Christian community. In some churches, people cannot participate in Holy Communion until they are confirmed.

Symbols and worship

The most important Christian symbol is the cross. Some churches often have a statue of the empty cross – showing that Jesus is risen. Roman Catholics generally use a **crucifix** to remember Jesus' sacrifice. Today the cross has become a fashion accessory, but for many Christians, wearing a cross is an outward show of their acceptance of Jesus' sacrifice.

The sign of the fish is also symbolic in Christianity. During persecution, early Christians would draw a fish on the ground as a code to encourage fellow Christians. Today, the fish is used as a symbol of commitment to Christianity. Many Christians have fish stickers on their cars or wear a necklace or pin badge representing a fish.

KEY POINTS

1. During a christening/baptism/dedication, parents and godparents promise to bring a baby up in the Christian faith.

2. In Christian wedding services, a couple make their vows in front of God and others.

3. Some Christians hold funerals and memorial services to celebrate a person's life. Christianity teaches that Christians will be reunited in heaven.

4. The sacrament of Holy Communion recognises Christ's death and resurrection, and the new covenant this brings.

5. Written prayers, called liturgy, are used mainly in Anglican and Roman Catholic services.

6. Confirmation and baptism are ways for an individual to profess faith for themselves.

7. The cross and the fish are important symbols in Christianity.

Practices and rites in Hinduism

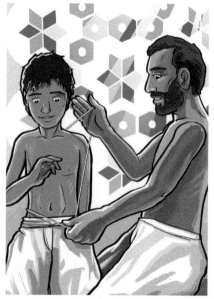

During the sacred thread ceremony, the holy thread is hung from a boy's left shoulder to his right hip. This signifies that the boy is old enough to begin his spiritual learning.

ACTIVITY

In ancient India, girls also used to perform the sacred thread ceremony. This is starting to happen again in many parts of the world, including the Caribbean. Do some research to find out where in the Caribbean girls have taken their sacred thread ceremony. Are there other differences between how the sacred thread ceremony is performed in India and in the Caribbean? Use your findings to create a short presentation for your family or a study partner.

Rites of passage (samskaras)

Birth

Hindus believe that children are a gift from the gods and that all life is sacred. The name of a child in Hinduism is extremely important. Hindus believe that the child's name will play an important role in their life. For this reason, many Hindus will consult a priest regarding the name. The priest draws up a horoscope based on the date and time of the birth, the place the child was born, the parents' names, and the positions of the stars and planets when the baby was conceived and born. This horoscope will produce certain syllables that should be included in the child's name. Once the name has been decided, the baby's name is announced at a samskara called Name-giving or Namkaran.

CASE STUDY	Sacred thread

Almost grown up!

Twelve-year-old Ramesh is preparing for his sacred thread ceremony. This is a major samskara in Ramesh's life. It symbolises that Ramesh is considered old enough to begin his spiritual learning.

During the sacred ceremony, a priest will hang a loop of thread over Ramesh's left shoulder. It will descend to his right hip. The thread will remain across Ramesh's chest for the rest of his life as a reminder that he has been born once physically and again spiritually.

Ramesh is thankful that he does not have to leave his family and go to live and study with his guru, as boys did in the past. Ramesh will stay with his family, but life will change. From now on, Ramesh has entered the brahmacharya stage of life where discipline, studying hard and respect for elders becomes more important than ever. Ramesh will also be expected to participate in daily prayers, like the rest of his family, carry out the necessary Hindu ceremonies and study Hindu scriptures.

Ramesh is about to become spiritually responsible, and he is taking the responsibility seriously. He feels proud that he is considered mature enough to undertake his sacred thread ceremony.

Marriage

Marriage is very important in Hinduism. It is believed to be the context in which children should be born and raised to be ideal citizens of a nation.

Like all samskaras, Hindu wedding ceremonies take place in front of a holy fire (agni). As a sign of the couple being joined together, the end of the bride's sari is tied to the end of the groom's kurta. During the ceremony, the bride and groom walk around the sacred fire seven (or four) times. Following this, they take seven (or four) steps north-eastward (called sapta-padi). After each step, they declare promises to each other and pray for health and prosperity, for mutual love and respect, for children, and for a lifetime of friendship. Friends and family shower flower petals over the couple. After the ceremony there is a vegetarian feast with friends and family or an evening reception before the couple go on their honeymoon.

The appearance of the bride is very important in a Hindu wedding. The bride wears a red and gold sari and wears intricate make-up and henna patterns on her hands and feet. She also wears lots of gold jewellery.

Death

Traditionally, when a Hindu person died, their body was burned within hours on a **funeral pyre**. These days, the time of cremation is determined by when relatives can come together. It is the responsibility of the eldest child to ensure that the cremation of the body is carried out properly. Traditionally the eldest son lights the pyre (although female relations can do this too). When the flames reach the body, it is his responsibility to pour ghee onto the flames (ghee is already on the body as part of the preparation), while mantras are recited by the pandit (priest). Three days after the cremation, the son returns to gather up the ashes. Following this, most Hindus perform ceremonies to assist the soul to find its new resting place. These ceremonies occur on the tenth, eleventh and thirteenth days following the cremation.

Rituals

Rituals are very important in Hinduism and feature in daily life. Each day, a Hindu performs puja (prayer and worship) at the family shrine. There are also special rituals that only priests can perform. These are often performed to ask the gods for a blessing such as a child or rain.

There are domestic rites that are taught by priests to be performed in the home. They celebrate new and full moons, changing of the seasons, first fruits of the harvest, the building of a new house, birth of a child and rites of passage.

Initiation ceremonies

Although young females do not have a coming-of-age ceremony, some Hindu girls follow the annual Monsoon Austerity Ritual of Purification by not eating cooked food for one or two weeks. This practice is known as Goriyo. During this time they cultivate wheat and mung beans from seed.

Symbols and worship

Symbols are significant in Hinduism. Hindus believe that every Hindu symbol points the worshipper to Brahman, the Ultimate Reality. Each god has its own statues, known as murti, that are worshipped. Rivers are also symbolic – they symbolise life and cleansing. Most Hindus believe that bathing in one of Hinduism's seven holy rivers will wash away wrong actions and bring a person closer to moksha. The sacred syllable Aum, which represents the characteristics of Brahman, is used in Hindu chants, mantras and prayers.

A Hindu marriage declaration

With utmost love to each other may we walk together … May we make our minds united, of the same vows and of the same thoughts. I am the wind and you are the melody. I am the melody and you are the words.

KEY POINTS

1 The naming of a baby is very important in Hinduism. A priest is consulted when deciding on a name.

2 The Sacred Thread ceremony marks the beginning of a child's spiritual learning.

3 The most important part of a Hindu wedding ceremony is the seven steps (or four) that a couple take around a holy fire (Agni) while making promises to each other.

4 Following the death and cremation of a person, Hindus perform ceremonies to help the soul to find its new resting place.

5 There are many rituals in Hinduism, some that can be performed by anyone and others that can only be performed by priests or Brahmin.

Practices and rites in Islam

Rites of passage

Birth

As soon as a Muslim baby is born it is washed and welcomed into the family by the father whispering the Shahadah into its ear. This is followed by the **adhan** being spoken to the baby. Muslims believe that these words mark the beginning of the child's spiritual learning. Soon after this, an older member of the child's family puts a small piece of date into the baby's mouth and prayers are said that the child will grow up to have a sweet nature. This is called the tahnik ceremony.

Seven days after birth, Aqiqah takes place. Great care is taken in choosing the baby's name and often older family members, particularly the child's grandfather, will advise. During Aqiqah, the baby's hair is shaved off and its weight in silver is given to charity. The Aqiqah ceremony is followed by a feast. Many Muslims also perform **circumcision** during Aqiqah as it is recommended that this practice be carried out during infancy.

Marriage

Islam teaches that marriage is the context in which sexual relations should be enjoyed and children raised. Traditionally, in a Muslim marriage the groom gives the bride money or property known as a mohrar or dowry.

During the wedding, verses from the Qur'an are read out (often Surah 4). The bride and groom are asked three times if they accept each other in marriage according to the terms of their traditional marriage contract or nikah. Then they sign the contract, the marriage is sealed, and the congregation may bless them.

Following the marriage there is feasting.

Death

> **Traditional Muslim wedding vows**
>
> Bride: 'I, _____, offer you myself in marriage and in accordance with the instructions of the holy Qur'an and the holy prophet, peace and blessing be upon him. I pledge, in honesty and with sincerity, to be for you an obedient and faithful wife.'
>
> Groom: 'I pledge, in honesty and sincerity, to be for you a faithful and helpful husband.'

> **An Islamic funeral prayer**
>
> O Allah, forgive our dead and alive, our present and absent, our young and old, our male and female [Muslims]. O Allah, whomever among us You gave life, let him live with Islam. Whomever among us You took life from, let him die with Iman (Faith).

CASE STUDY	Funerals

Death is not the end

Maryam, Muhammad and Aadam are at the funeral of their grandfather. Just before he died, the children and the rest of the family gathered around his bed. Their grandfather asked for forgiveness from his friends and family as well as from Allah for any wrongs he had committed and then he recited the Shahadah. Maryam, Muhammad and Aadam are pleased that their grandfather was able to do this before he died. Just as the Shahadah is the first thing a person should hear when they are born, if possible it should be the last thing they say before they die.

After their grandfather died, the children's father washed his body in scented water and placed his hands at his side. He was wrapped in three plain sheets to show that all are equal in death.

Maryam, Muhammad and Aadam are joining in the prayers for their grandfather. After this, their grandfather will be lowered into the grave with the right-hand side of his body and his head facing Makkah. Muslims believe that the body should be in contact with the earth when it is buried.

Maryam, Muhammad and Aadam are sad that their grandfather has died. But they are happy that he is at peace and that they will see him again one day when all the dead are raised to life and Muslims who have sought Allah's forgiveness will live together in Paradise.

After death, Muslims are washed, wrapped in simple sheets and their arms are placed at their sides as in worship, before they are buried facing the direction of Makkah

Rituals and initiation

The main rituals in Islam are the acts that make up the Five Pillars (declaration of faith, prayer, almsgiving, fasting and pilgrimage).

Muslim children are considered Muslim from birth. Although there is acknowledgement that individuals must make their own conscious decision to follow Islam, there is no specific initiation ceremony to mark a young Muslim's progression into adulthood.

Symbols and worship

In Islam, symbols representing Allah or Muhammad are forbidden as they are thought to encourage idol worship, which is condemned by the Qur'an. However, symbols are used in masjids. Circles and stars are often used to decorate the inside of masjids. The circle is thought to symbolise eternity and the points of the stars symbolise the influence of Islam spreading across the world.

The following acts, which take place during Hajj, are also symbolic and are important acts of worship:

- Sacrificing an animal: this is symbolic of Ibrahim's willingness to sacrifice Ismail.
- Iblis (stoning of Satan when he was trying to prevent Ibrahim carrying out the sacrifice of his son): the throwing of pebbles at a rock symbolises a person's commitment to fight evil.
- Running between Safa and Marwah: this symbolises Hajar searching for water in the desert and being saved by Allah, revealing Allah's mercy.

DID YOU KNOW?

The star and crescent moon may feature on the flags of Muslim countries, but they are not considered symbols of Islam by many Muslims. Many believe them to be political rather than religious symbols.

KEY POINTS

1 Muslims believe it is very important that the first words a baby hears are the declaration of faith. These should also be a person's last words before they die.

2 The Five Pillars are the most important rituals in Islam.

3 Symbols representing aspects of Allah or Muhammad are forbidden in Islam.

Practices and rites in Judaism

During a Jewish wedding ceremony, the groom crushes a wine glass under his foot to symbolise times of pain, as well as blessings, in their marriage

Rites of passage

Birth

When a Jewish girl is born, the father announces the baby's name and reads from the Torah in the synagogue. If the baby is a boy, his birth is marked by circumcision eight days after he is born. The Hebrew name for the circumcision ceremony is brit milah. In Genesis, God commanded Abraham to circumcise all of the males in his family to show their special relationship with God. Today, circumcision is still practised as a sign of the covenant and it is an important symbol that men belong to the Jewish faith.

During the procedure, the boy's grandfather holds him. After the procedure, the father says: 'God has commanded me to introduce my son in to the covenant of our father, Abraham.' To which everyone present responds: 'As he has entered into the covenant, so may he enter into the study of the Torah, marriage and a life of good deeds.'

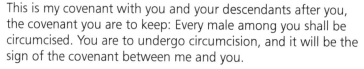

Circumcision – a sign of the covenant

This is my covenant with you and your descendants after you, the covenant you are to keep: Every male among you shall be circumcised. You are to undergo circumcision, and it will be the sign of the covenant between me and you.

Genesis 17:1011

Marriage

Judaism teaches that man and woman should be united within marriage. The completion of the marriage is the gift of children.

Before a Jewish marriage, the groom signs a wedding document (called a ketubah) in which he promises to provide for and care for his wife. During the wedding service, seven blessings called Sheva Brachot are read out. After each blessing the bride and groom sip wine. After this, the groom crushes the wine glass under his foot to symbolise that there will be hard times in the marriage as well as blessings. During the ceremony, the ketubah is read aloud and blessings are pronounced over the couple. The groom then places a ring on the bride's finger to symbolise their everlasting love.

The wedding ceremony is followed by a party where guests will feast, drink and dance. Food may include spicy chicken jerky, rice and vegetables, curried goat and dark, fried plantain and black cake.

Death

There is no firm teaching in Jewish scriptures about life after death and Jews hold mixed views on the subject. Most Jews believe in resurrection following death. All Jews agree that a person should focus on their earthly conduct rather than on what might happen after death.

If a Jew is close to death, they speak out a prayer confirming their belief in God, asking for His healing and confessing their sins. If the person dies, burial takes place as soon as possible. Since the body cannot be left alone, appointed helpers called chevra kadisha stay with the body and prepare it for burial.

During burial, those attending the service say a prayer before using a spade to scatter earth on the coffin.

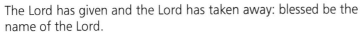

Scripture spoken at Jewish funerals

The Lord has given and the Lord has taken away: blessed be the name of the Lord.

Job 1:21

ACTIVITY

Choose from either birth, marriage or death and compile a table to show the similarities and differences between these rites of passage within the four main religions.

Jewish symbols

As with Islam, Judaism also forbids the use of images or statues to depict God. However, Jews do use objects and symbols to represent their faith.

The mezuzah

This is a decorated box that strict Jewish households place in the doorways of their homes. The box contains paper on which the Shema is written. Jews use their right hand to touch the mezuzah whenever they go through the doorway to remind them of their belief in one god. This practice dates back to the teaching in Deuteronomy that the Jews should write God's laws on the doorframes of their houses.

The mezuzah

The menorah

The menorah is a seven-branched candlestick that reminds Jews of their responsibility to be a light to the world.

At Chanukah, Jews use a nine-branched menorah to remind them of the eight days during the uprising against Antiochus when a menorah burned in the Temple with only one day's supply of oil. The middle candle is used to light the other eight.

The menorah

The Star of David

The Ark of the Covenant

The Star of David

Opinions differ, but many believe that the six points on the Star of David symbolise God, the world, man, creation, revelation and redemption. Others believe that the 12 sides of the star represent the 12 tribes of Israel.

The Ark of the Covenant

The Ark in synagogues symbolises the original Ark of the Covenant that the Israelites built as a physical sign of God's presence.

ACTIVITY

Numbers are significant in Judaism. In particular, the numbers three and seven are symbolic.

1 Who are the three patriarchs and what are the three pilgrimage festivals?

2 What happens on the seventh day of the week in Judaism?

3 What has the number seven got to do with creation?

Initiation ceremonies and rituals

Bar mitzvah

CASE STUDY | Two celebrations in one week!

Today is Benjamin's thirteenth birthday. Benjamin is excited to be having a birthday and to finally become a teenager. But Benjamin's birthday is particularly important this year because, when a Jewish boy reaches 13 years of age he is considered old enough to be responsible for his own spirituality. This is the beginning of Benjamin's entry into the adult world.

Benjamin is looking forward to the next Sabbath, in three days' time, when his bar mitzvah will take place. But he is a bit nervous about reading from the Torah in public for the first time – what if he stumbles over his words or, even worse, drops the yad (pointer) that he will use to follow the passage he is reading? Benjamin is going to make sure he has had plenty of practice before Saturday. During the bar mitzvah ceremony, Benjamin will also receive his tallit (prayer shawl) and tefillin (boxes containing the Shema).

Tonight, Benjamin will have a special birthday dinner and cake with his family and on Saturday, after his bar mitzvah, there will be another party to celebrate. It is not often you get the chance to have two celebrations in a week – Benjamin is going to make the most of it!

When a boy reaches 13 years of age he celebrates his bar mitzvah. He reads from the Torah scroll and from then on he is considered responsible for his own spiritual welfare

Bat mitzvah and bat chayil

A bat mitzvah is the equivalent coming-of-age ceremony for a girl. Not all synagogues hold these ceremonies and they are becoming less and less common. If they occur, they are held after the girl's twelfth birthday. As in a bar mitzvah, the girl reads from the Torah or another part of the Jewish scriptures. More common is a bat chayil ('daughter of worth') ceremony. During this ceremony, a girl's achievements are celebrated and prayers are said for her. The girl may read from the Tenakh, but usually not from the Torah as this is considered a responsibility of men.

DID YOU KNOW?

The Hebrew words 'bar mitzvah' mean 'Son of the Commandment'. So what do you think the words 'bat mitzvah' might mean?

Kosher

Many ceremonies are marked with a celebration that often includes food. As with Shariah in Islam, Jews are only permitted to eat food that is considered kosher (the Hebrew word for 'fit'). This refers to the type of food Jews are permitted to eat (they cannot eat pork or certain types of seafood, for example) as well as the way in which animals must be slaughtered.

KEY POINTS

1 Jewish boys are circumcised eight days after birth, as a sign of the covenant between God and the Jewish people.

2 At a Jewish wedding, the groom will crush a wine glass under his feet to symbolise that the marriage will contain difficult times as well as good.

3 Most Jews believe in resurrection following death. However, all Jews believe that their conduct on earth is more important than what will happen to them after they die.

4 Judaism forbids symbols or images that depict God. However, Jews use various symbols, such as a menorah, in their worship.

Practices of Caribbean indigenous religions

Spiritual Baptist

Mourning ceremony

The mourning ceremony is a reminder to Spiritual Baptists of their frailty and it is a time for them to focus on their spiritual rather than physical needs. In the past, the mourning ceremony lasted for three weeks, during which time worshippers would fast, go without any comforts and spend long amounts of time lying on an earthen floor or in a coffin in the dark.

These days the mourning ceremony only lasts for three days and most people only fast for part of this time or they may simply reduce their food intake or eat simple foods. By focusing on their spiritual state, it is hoped that participants can heighten their psychic powers. Many people also look for a cure for an illness during the ceremony or hope to receive a message from a dead relative.

Nation dance

Dance has always been important in Caribbean traditions, no matter what religion you follow. Spiritual Baptists use dance extensively in their worship. At significant times, such as the night before a wedding or on the anniversary of a family member dying, Spiritual Baptists perform a special dance called a nation dance.

Vodun

Degradation ceremony

In Vodun, when a person with special abilities dies, such as a houngan (male high priest) or mambo (female high priest), their abilities must be removed and passed on to a successor. Voduns believe that if degradation does not take place, the dead person will torment their living relatives until the abilities are transferred.

Ceremony of transmission

Once the special abilities have been removed from the deceased person they must be transferred to the successor. A ceremony of transmission takes place. During this ceremony the person to take on the special abilities, usually an heir or relative of the houngan, is appointed and the deceased person's abilities are transmitted to that person.

Ceremony of renunciation

For heirs or relatives of the deceased houngan who do not wish to receive the special abilities, there is a ceremony of renunciation. During this ceremony the heir renounces their claim on any special abilities from the deceased.

Ceremony of dismissal

Vodun teaches that family loas (spirits) are passed down through family members. If an inheritor does not wish to receive a loa, a ceremony of dismissal takes place. During this ceremony, the person is released from any obligation to the family loa.

Revivalism

Baptism

Like many denominations of Christianity, Revivalists practise adult baptism. Baptism symbolises that a person wants to share in Jesus Christ's death and resurrection and accept God's new covenant through Jesus. During a Revivalist baptism, which often takes place in a river or the sea, the person being baptised will declare their belief and trust in Jesus before being submerged briefly under the water.

A baptism in the Revivalist congregation is a very joyful occasion. The service will contain prayers for the person or people being baptised, and singing and dancing.

Santeria

Initiation ceremonies

A person being initiated into Santeria is known as an iyawó, which means 'bride'. Initiation into Santeria involves a series of four ceremonies:

- Receiving your eleke (beaded necklace) matching the colours of your parent orisha. The eleke is ritually bathed in a mixture of herbs and other potent substances. Elekes are thought to give protection to the wearer.
- Creation of an elegguá. The iyawó collects stones and brings them to the initiator, who chooses one to create an image around using clay and shells. This elegguá is kept at home and offerings are made to it. Again, the elegguá protects the initiate.
- Receiving implements of warrior orishas (gods). These include iron implements, a bow and arrow, and a cup and rooster. These all represent different warrior gods in Santeria.
- The Asiento — possession of the iyawó by the parent orisha. This can only be performed after the first three ceremonies.

Completing the four initiation ceremonies takes a few days and, in the months following initiation, the iyawó returns to the Santeria priest for further purifications.

Funerals

Santeros (followers of Santeria) believe that funerals are controlled by the orishas, although the ceremonies are overseen by priests. Death rituals include music, dancing and sometimes animal sacrifice. The special dress worn by santeros during their initiation into the religion is also worn by them for their burial.

Santeria funeral ceremonies include music and dancing

KEY POINTS

1. During mourning ceremonies, Spiritual Baptists focus on their spirit by denying their body its usual comforts and seeking guidance through prayer.

2. When a houngan or mambo dies in the Vodun tradition, their special abilities are removed. The special abilities are passed on to the person's heir or relation, who can choose whether to accept or reject them.

3. Revivalists practice adult baptism as a sign of acceptance of Jesus.

4. Anyone wishing to become initiated into Santeria must take part in a series of four ceremonies, which culminate in orisha possession.

9.1 Comparing religions

Table 1: God

	Christianity	Hinduism	Islam	Judaism	CIR
Monotheism (belief in one god)	Yes	No – although some branches of Hinduism hold the view that different Hindu deities are incarnations or names of the one god Brahman and therefore Hinduism does teach monotheism	Yes	Yes	Rastafari, Revivalism and Spiritual Baptist: yes Vodun, Santeria and Orisha: no. These religions believe in many smaller gods or orishas
God as creator	Yes	Yes	Yes	Yes	Yes
Believe God appeared in human form	Yes – as Jesus	Yes, e.g. Krishna and Rama (only Vaishnava Hindus)	No	No	Rastafari: yes, as Haile Selassie Revivalism and Spiritual Baptist: yes, as Jesus Orisha, Santeria and Vodun: no

Table 2: Origins of religion

	Christianity	Hinduism	Islam	Judaism	CIR
Religion built on teaching of prophets	No. Christians believe that Jesus was God and not a prophet	No	Yes. Islam was established by the Prophet Muhammad	Yes. Judaism was established by the Prophet Abraham	No. Rastafari believe that Haile Selassie was God, not a prophet
Religions grew from the same root (Adam and Abraham)	Yes	No	Yes	Yes	No
Religion originated in the Middle East	Yes	No – Asia	Yes	Yes	No – blend of African religions and Christianity
Religion introduced to the Caribbean through slave trade and/or indentured workers	No – through missionaries 1700–1800s	Yes	No – there were some Muslims before	No – through Jews escaping persecution in Europe	Yes. African slave religions combined with Christianity, except Rastafari

Notes on Table 1

- All of the religions believe that God created the world, although different religions, and even different denominations within the religions, have different beliefs about how God did this.
- Christianity is the only major religion to teach that Jesus was God. Vaishnava Hindus believe that many incarnations of Vishnu take human form. Rastafari, Revivalism and Spiritual Baptists take this belief from Christianity. Islam believes that Muhammad was God's final prophet but was not God incarnate (God in human form). Rastafari believe that, after Jesus, Haile Selassie was the final incarnation of God on earth.

Notes on Table 2

There are many similarities in the origins of Judaism, Christianity and Islam.

- All three religions are founded on Adam (the first prophet), and Abraham's covenant with God in Mesopotamia (modern-day Iraq).
- The Qur'an, Tenakh and Bible share much of their content.
- Christianity broke away from Judaism with the coming of Jesus.
- Jews did not accept that Jesus was God's Messiah as Christians did.
- Christians stopped trying to follow the strict Jewish laws and instead followed Jesus' teachings of love and forgiveness.
- Islam broke away from Judaism and Christianity through its belief that Muhammad was the final prophet.

The Middle East is an area of the world with a rich religious heritage. Judaism, Christianity and Islam all originated in the Middle East and have strong ties with Jerusalem.

Table 3: Sources of authority

	Christianity	Hinduism	Islam	Judaism	CIR
Follow the biblical Old Testament	Yes, but the New Testament takes precedence	No	Yes, but the Qur'an takes precedence	Yes – this is called the Tenakh	Yes, except Santeria, which is based on oral tradition
Sacred writings contain stories and guidelines for moral living	Yes	Yes	Yes	Yes	Yes. Santeria uses stories passed on orally
Sacred writings attempt to explain the origin of the world and man's purpose in it	Yes	Yes	Yes	Yes	Yes
Sacred writings are believed to have been inspired or revealed by God	Yes	Yes	Yes	Yes	Yes – Rastafari, Revivalism and Spiritual Baptist

Table 4: Places of worship

	Christianity	Hinduism	Islam	Judaism	CIR
Have shrines	Yes – mainly Roman Catholic Christians. Some shrines are pilgrimage sites	Yes – for worship of gods and goddesses in homes and temples	Some, although worship does not usually take place at shrines	Yes – mainly graves or sites of historic interest. Worship does not usually take place at shrines	Yes
Worshippers sit on floor	No	Yes	Yes	No	Sometimes – more to do with style of building than a religious practice
Use a specific building for regular worship	Yes	No	Yes	Yes	Yes, although some CIRs (e.g. Spiritual Baptist, Revivalism) use buildings more than others
Have pilgrimage sites	Yes, e.g. Lourdes	Yes, many, including River Ganges and Allahabad (city of God)	Yes	Yes – the Western/ Wailing Wall	Yes. Revivalism – Watt Town, Jamaica
Worship often takes place in homes	Yes	Yes – home worship is more common than temple worship	Yes – especially tahajjud (night prayer) usually prayed around 3–4am	Yes – Friday evening	Yes

Table 5: Religious practices

	Christianity	Hinduism	Islam	Judaism	CIR
Practise initiation ceremonies	Yes	Yes	No	Yes	Yes – Santeria Rastafari hold up a baby to dedicate it to Jah
Celebrate festivals	Yes	Yes	Yes	Yes	Yes
Hold ceremonies for birth, death and marriage	Yes	Yes	Yes	Yes	All practise death ceremonies; some practise marriage ceremonies
Use of symbols in worship	Yes	Yes – but not all	No	No	Yes – tables, altars, seal, poles, colours, candles, etc.
Practice baptism using water and in the Holy Spirit	Yes	No	No	No	Yes – Revivalism and Spiritual Baptist
Follow rules concerning what food is permitted	Yes – Seventh-Day Adventists cannot eat pork	Yes – beef is forbidden. Many Hindus are vegetarian	Yes – only halal food allowed	Yes – only kosher food can be eaten	Yes – Rastafari – certain food is not permitted, generally vegan

Table 6: Major teachings

	Christianity	Hinduism	Islam	Judaism	CIR
Concept of sin and salvation	Yes	Yes. The Hindu concept of sin is paap (moving away from dharma). The concept of salvation is moksha	Yes	Yes	Yes – Rastafari, Revivalism and Spiritual Baptist
Concept of judgement and punishment or reward	Yes	Yes – through reincarnation according to karma. Moksha as the ultimate reward	Yes	Yes	Yes – Rastafari, Revivalism and Spiritual Baptist
Concept of a Judgement Day/ End of the World	Yes	No – a concept of the end of one cycle of creation followed by the dawn of another	Yes	Yes	Yes – Rastafari, Revivalism and Spiritual Baptist
Belief in reincarnation	No	Yes	No	No	No, although Vodun teaches that a person's gifts/abilities can be passed on to the living. Yes. Rastafari – Haile Selassie was a reincarnation of Jesus
Belief in life after death	Yes	Yes – through reincarnation of the soul	Yes	Yes	Yes – although most CIRs do not have a concept of heaven or hell
Religion provides a moral code to live by	Yes	Yes	Yes	Yes	Yes
Communicate with ancestral spirits	No – spirits lie dormant, awaiting resurrection	No	No – spirits lie dormant, awaiting resurrection	No – spirits lie dormant, awaiting resurrection	Yes – many CIRs practice communication with spirits No – Rastafari

Notes on Table 6

- Most Christians believe that Jesus will come to earth again and that, at this time, all people, alive and dead, will be judged.
- Hindus believe that at the end of one cycle of creation all beings lie dormant waiting for the next cycle of creation to begin when souls will be reincarnated.
- Muslims believe that there will be a day when Allah will cease life on earth and all people will be judged.
- Jews believe that judgement will take place after the Messiah has come to earth. Some Jews believe that the Messiah will be an era, rather than a person, during which time there will be peace and prosperity on earth.

ACTIVITY

Try drawing concept maps or flowcharts, arranging key words around different topic headings to help you remember the similarities and differences between the different religions.

Option A: Christianity

A.1

Human life issues

LEARNING OUTCOMES

In this section you will learn to:

- discuss the meaning and purpose of life as reflected in the Bible

- explain the concept of stewardship and its application to daily living

- assess issues related to justice and peace and the value and dignity of human life as reflected in the Bible

- discuss the responsibilities and rights of individuals in areas of family life and work as reflected in the Bible

- illustrate how the biblical concept of love applies to different areas of life and relationships

- describe the Old Testament background to the concept of the reign of God

- describe the New Testament background to the concept of the reign of God.

LINK

For an introduction to Christianity, see Section 1, Essentials of religion, starting on page 2.

Meaning and purpose of life

The Bible has much to say about the meaning and purpose of life and it gives guidance about how to live. Christians often regard the Bible as a handbook for living as well as an insight into the nature of God. The creation story in particular, from the book of Genesis, explains who made humans and why.

Christians believe that each person is unique and special and that human beings are different from all other animals and the highest form of creation. Look at others around you – our bodies and our personalities are unique, and humans have a spiritual side too.

Made in God's image

The Bible says that we have been created in God's image and likeness (Genesis 1:26–27). Does this mean that we physically look a bit like God or are aspects of our personality similar to God's? Christians believe that each person has qualities that God also has – for example, the ability to be loving, creative and forgiving. If each person is made in God's image, then we are all of value.

Part of God's family

Aside from our families here on earth, the Bible teaches that humans are made and created by God (Ephesians 3:15, Acts 17:27–29) to be part of God's family (Genesis 22:20, Acts 3:25, Ephesians 3:15). The Bible says that when God was creating the earth He made both men and women (Mark 10:6–9) and blessed them with intelligence and **free will** (Genesis 3:7–14, John 14, 15 and 16). In Genesis 3, Adam and Eve – the first humans – are guided by God but given the freedom to make decisions of their own – though they then have to live with the consequences of their choices.

God as the source of life and human values

The Bible points to God as the Creator of all life (Genesis 2:3, Ezekiel 37:5, Acts 17:25) and states that God's love for each person began before they were even born. Christians believe that having faith in God is the best way to receive direction and purpose in their lives.

Concept of stewardship

Through the creation story, the Bible teaches that each person has a responsibility as a 'steward' to take care of the world that God has made and everything in it. This is part of each person's purpose.

The Bible does not just talk about humans' responsibility for taking care of the planet (Genesis 1:28–30), it also has instructions for how humans should conduct themselves in everyday life, including:

- guidance about how to be good stewards of the things we have
  (2 Corinthians 9:6–9)
- how to treat the sick (Mark 3:1–6, Matthew 20:30–34)
- how to treat those who are suffering (Mark 5:1–42, Luke 17:12–19)
- the care and treatment of children (Luke 8:40–56; 18:15–17, Psalm 131:1–2, Proverbs 22:6, 1 Corinthians 13:11, Ephesians 6:1–4)
- caring for people who have been rejected or outcast by society (John 8:1–11, Luke 17:11–19, Luke 19:1–10).

In other words, **stewardship** is integral to living life as a Christian.

CASE STUDY | Being special

Seventeen-year-old Rachel goes to the same church as Patricia and Winston's family. Last week at church she spoke about what the Bible means to her. She has learnt that the Bible is God's word and a guidebook for her life. She was honest with the congregation and admitted that she tries to read it every day, but that there are parts that are difficult to understand and it is not always easy to work out what God might be saying to her through some of the passages. Lots of people in church, including Patricia and Winston, agreed. However, Rachel spoke about how she knows that the Bible says that she was made by God and that God knows all about her – the Bible even says that God knows exactly how many hairs Rachel has on her head! Through the Bible, Rachel knows that she is special and unique and loved by God. And that makes her feel good.

Despite some parts being easier to read than others, Rachel has come to understand that, whatever situation she finds herself in, the Bible has some words of advice for her. So when she has decisions to make about her future or wants advice on the best way to act, then she will read her Bible and pray that God will help her to understand.

Rachel finds that the teachings in the Bible guide her to make the right decisions in life, as well as encouraging her that she is special to God

---

Value and dignity of human life

The expectation of Christians to be good stewards influences their attitude towards different issues, such as those outlined below.

Child abuse

The Bible teaches that children are a gift from God (Psalm 127:3) and there are many stories in the Bible that show children as a blessing from the Lord to their parents (Genesis 13:6, Ruth 4:13–16, 1 Samuel 1:11). Therefore, Christians would say that abuse of children in any form is never acceptable or part of God's plan for relationships. Many charities exist to help children who are being abused, physically, mentally or sexually. Some of these charities were originally set up by Christians who were inspired by their faith to help the many abused or neglected children in society.

1 Find more verses in the Bible that could both support and argue against the death penalty (e.g. Exodus 21:12–14, Romans 13:1–5, Exodus 20:13 and John 8:7–11).

2 Do you feel the teachings of the Bible support one view more than another?

3 What is the significance of most of the verses that seem to support the death penalty appearing in the Old Testament?

4 What is your view on the issue?

Capital punishment in the Old Testament

Show no pity: life for life, eye for eye, tooth for tooth, hand for hand, foot for foot.

Deuteronomy 19:21

Capital punishment in the New Testament

Do not judge, or you too will be judged. For in the same way as you judge others, you will be judged, and with the measure you use, it will be measured to you.

Matthew 7:1–2

Segregation between whites and blacks in the US in the 1950s and 1960s was an example of extreme prejudice and discrimination. Today this period in history is universally recognised as wrong, although at the time many Christians supported the segregation.

Substance abuse

The Bible tells us that our bodies are 'temples of the Holy Spirit' and that we should be honouring God by treating our bodies well (1 Corinthians 6:19–20). Therefore, Christians believe that anything that causes harm to the body – such as abusing drugs or alcohol – is wrong. This does not mean that all Christians are against alcohol or prescription medicine – it is about whether the substance is damaging or helping our bodies. Drugs and alcohol in particular can be highly dangerous and could potentially end life by human hands and not by God's will.

Capital punishment

Capital punishment is also known as the death penalty. This is when someone is killed as punishment for the crimes they have committed such as murder or treason. The Bible does not give direct guidance as to whether capital punishment is acceptable or not. However, it does teach that God is loving and forgiving and that, therefore, Christians should try and love and forgive everyone. This does not mean that criminals should go unpunished though. The Bible teaches that murder is wrong, but Christians have differing views about capital punishment.

Poverty

The Bible teaches that although poverty will always be with us, it is not something that we should ignore or do nothing to change. The Bible teaches that Christians should show justice, love and kindness and help others in need. In particular, the book of James, in the New Testament, speaks about the uselessness of faith without actions.

Unemployment

As discussed at the start of this section, Christians believe that we have each been born for a reason and that God has a purpose for our lives. Presumably then God has roles and jobs for us to do. In Jeremiah 29:11–14 we can read that God has good plans for our lives. Paul, the writer of many New Testament books, gave this advice to the people of Thessalonica in 2 Thessalonians 3:10–11: 'If anyone is not willing to work, let him not eat'. However, the majority of unemployed people want to work, of course, and cannot help their lack of employment. The Bible urges people not to be anxious (Philippians 4:6) but to trust in God. The Bible also urges others to help their brothers (in God's family) when they find themselves without food or money (Deuteronomy 15:7–8).

Prejudice and discrimination

People can be discriminated against for different reasons – because of race, religion, gender, age, etc. Prejudice is an attitude not based on fact and therefore it cannot be made illegal. Discrimination as an action, however, is generally against the law, but it can still happen. The Bible teaches that all people are equal in the eyes of God (Galatians 3:28) and every individual should be treated fairly and with respect.

Male and female roles and relationships

Christians have different ideas about the roles of men and women within relationships. The Bible was written in a patriarchal society where males dominated public life. When Jesus was on earth, society was very **patriarchal**. However, the Bible also clearly states that men and women are equal in Christ Jesus (Galatians 3:28) so most Christians believe that it is not about who is in charge of who but about using the skills that God has given in the best possible way. In Jesus' time, women were elevated and set free to learn under a rabbi and do things other than keeping the home, as shown in the story of Mary and Martha.

Violence, vandalism and war

The Bible sometimes suggests that some wars are instructed by God, but it also clearly states that Christians should love their enemies (Matthew 5:44). This leads to Christians being divided over whether fighting in a war is justified or not. Some Christians believe there are times that fighting is acceptable – such as to ensure that good will overcome evil. Some Christians are **pacifists**. Some people say that there is a lot of fighting and war in the Old Testament but that the New Testament promotes peace and love. Jesus' teaching in the Sermon on the Mount (Matthew 5) certainly suggests that Christians should be peaceful, not violent.

The Bible does not directly mention vandalism but it does call on people to discern what is right and wrong and to only do what is pleasing to God (Matthew 7:12).

Treatment of the mentally and physically challenged

There are many stories in the Bible of Jesus and the disciples treating with love and kindness people who were physically challenged and those struggling mentally and, in many situations, healing their disabilities. As we have mentioned, Christians believe that each person is special and that we are all equal. Therefore, the mentally and physically challenged should be treated with love and respect, in the same way that all fellow humans should be treated. There are many Christian organisations, such as the Barbados Children's Trust and the Leonard Cheshire Foundation Home in Trinidad, that exist to support people with mental and physical challenges.

Dealing with Human Immunodeficiency Virus/Acquired Immune Deficiency Syndrome (HIV/AIDS)

As the first case of HIV/AIDS was not recognised until the early 1980s, there is no direct mention of HIV/AIDS in the Bible. However, in biblical times, an equivalent disease was leprosy. People with leprosy were treated as outcasts, but Jesus ate with lepers (Mark 14:3) and touched them (Matthew 8:2–4). Jesus' actions teach Christians that they should show love and compassion to all. Therefore, the Christian response to HIV/AIDS and those suffering with it should always be one of grace and mercy.

ACTIVITY

Do you think that people still show prejudice and discrimination in day-to-day life? How might these attitudes be shown through both words and actions?

There is neither Jew nor Gentile, neither slave nor free, nor is there male and female, for you are all one in Christ Jesus.

Galatians 3:28

ACTIVITY

Research the issue of pacifists in the First and Second World Wars. Did pacifists face any discrimination? Were there other ways in which pacifists contributed to the war effort? What are your views on pacifism?

The Bible contains teaching and advice for children, parents, husbands and wives to encourage good family relationships

Roles, responsibilities and rights in family life and work

Family

Although the Bible was written thousands of years ago, there are many similarities between the situations of Bible characters to situations that people are in today. This is because, although times may change, human issues have not changed much from biblical times. Therefore, Christians can look to the Bible and use it as a guide for how to live now. For example, family life in biblical times faced many of the same issues that families deal with today – arguments, favouritism, deep love, etc. The story of Joseph and his brothers in Genesis 42 shows how an arguing family can be reunited. The Bible teaches that family units are important and that relationships in families should be loving, respectful and positive.

Marriage

The Christian church teaches that marriage is a gift from God and that marriage should be for life, until one person dies. Direction is also given in the Bible for how a husband and wife should treat each other and the role that each person should take within a marriage (Ephesians 5:21–33).

Such passages (see also 1 Peter 3:1–7) tend to cause much debate as to their meaning, as initial reading seems to suggest that the wife is less important than the husband. It is important to remember that relationships and society in general was very male-dominated in biblical times and that these passages were written within that context. However, it is generally accepted that Christian marriage is about mutual love and respect for each other and about loving the other person as much as God loves us.

The Bible teaches that sex is a gift from God but that it should be confined to **monogamous** marriage. God intended men and women to live together, but not to live together outside marriage.

Children

The Bible also has advice within family life for the relationships between children and their parents. Children should honour and obey their parents (Ephesians 6:1–2, Colossians 3:20) and parents should not irritate their children but bring them up showing a good example (Ephesians 6:4, Colossians 3:21). In all areas of family life, each person has the responsibility to love and respect those within the family.

Work

In work situations, the Bible expects a positive work attitude (Deuteronomy 5:13) and views work as a necessity to living (2 Thessalonians 3:10). God and Jesus have set the example for working hard (John 5:17). There are also expectations about how a master treats their slave (or an employer treats their employee) and how a slave treats their master (or an employee treats their employer). Employees should work with all their heart, all of the time and not just when they think they are being watched (Colossians 3:22–23). The Bible also calls upon employers to ensure they pay their employees (1 Timothy 5:18)!

Implications of biblical teaching of love in human relationships

The Bible teaches that life is to be enjoyed and lived to the full, and most Christians integrate into society fully. However, the Bible teaches that God should be a Christian's number one priority and that trying to follow His guidelines is the best and safest way for a person to enjoy their life. This means that, in some areas, Christians take a different view to society at large.

The Bible, particularly in the New Testament, talks a great deal about love and about loving others. This type of love is called 'agape', a Greek word for the kind of love that God shows for humankind. It is different from the kind of love a husband might feel for his wife or a mother might feel for her child. Christians are called to show agape love to all those around them regardless of their race or social status. This kind of love is respectful, caring and kind.

The concept of the reign of God

The Old Testament: background

The Old Testament is very much about God creating the world and the whole world belonging to God. Psalm 8 is a song glorifying God and celebrating the world that He has made.

After the creation, it tells of the relationship that God had with his people (the Jews). God reigned over the people he had created as a nation, although they still had their free will and chose to disobey God on many occasions. Israel was shown as a light to the rest of the world. God promised the people of Israel a kingdom to live in, and the Old Testament tells the story of their journey to that kingdom of God.

> When I consider your heavens,
> the work of your fingers,
> the moon and stars
> which you have set is place,
> what is man that you are mindful of him?
>
> Psalm 8:3–4

The New Testament: background

The New Testament is about the life and ministry of Jesus, whom Christians believe was God's son. The message is about how God can reign in each individual. Instead of searching for God's kingdom in this lifetime, the New Testament's message is that God's kingdom is something that people work towards by having faith in God and living in the way God wants people to.

According to the New Testament, many people had lost their relationship with God. In Acts 17:22–31, a follower of Jesus, called Paul, gave a speech calling on people to turn from their beliefs in other gods and allow God to be their Lord.

Christians believe that through faith in Jesus, people are offered another chance to follow God and that this faith will result in living with God for ever, even after our deaths, in heaven (1 Peter 1:3–5). The New Testament talks of belief in God and Jesus as something that people must choose individually if they wish to dwell (or live) with God in the future (Revelation 21:1–3).

The Bible

LEARNING OUTCOMES

In this section you will learn to:

- describe how the books of the Bible were transmitted and selected
- identify the different types of writing in the Bible
- explain how biblical passages may be applied to areas of daily life
- relate biblical teachings to personal and social experiences.

DID YOU KNOW?

Of the 27 books in the New Testament 14 were written by the apostle Paul.

How the Bible came into being

Christians believe that the Bible is the most important and holiest book. They consider the Bible to be the word of God and, through it, God communicates with people. It was written over many centuries by many different people and Christians believe that God chose its writers and inspired them to write so that their words showed the character and plans of God (2 Timothy 3:16).

Some Christians believe that the Bible is literally true and that everything in it happened as described. Others think that the Bible needs to be interpreted in order to work out what it means for us today. Either way, Christians try to follow the Bible's teachings.

The Bible is made up of two parts – the Old Testament and the New Testament. The Old Testament was written before Jesus came to earth. The New Testament was written following Jesus' death. The Old Testament contains 39 books that tell the story of God's relationship with his people from creation through to the time before Jesus was born. The New Testament contains 27 books and tells the story of the life and death of Jesus and what it means to be a Christian. Together, it is a bit like a library of books that tell God's story from the beginning of time and still gives guidance for life today.

How the books of the Bible were selected

The stories in the Bible would have initially been passed on from generation to generation orally, but then, as writing developed, they were written down and copies were made. The books of the Old Testament were used by the Jews and early Christians as part of their worship. At first, the apostles and disciples would have spoken about Jesus and his teaching during these services. These stories and teachings began to be written down and copies were made. Christians collected these writings and the letters that had been written by Jesus' followers and they were used in the teaching and worship of the early church.

The first official list of such writings was produced by Marcion in 140 CE, but different Christians had different views regarding what writings about the life of Jesus should be accepted and given authority. Finally, church leaders met together in 367 CE, 393 CE and 397 CE to decide which writings would become the Bible as we know it today.

The Dead Sea Scrolls

In 1947 shepherds entering a cave on the shores of the Dead Sea, in what is now the West Bank, discovered manuscripts and other books dating back to before the time of Jesus. It is thought that the people from the nearby community of Qumran must have hidden their library of scrolls in the caves because of the impending Roman invasion. The Dead Sea Scrolls are thought to have been produced between approximately 150 BCE and 70 CE.

The Dead Sea Scrolls are the earliest known copies of Hebrew scriptures, thought to have been written between approximately 150 BCE and 70 CE

Scholars were able to compare these scrolls with the later manuscripts in existence and found them to be virtually the same text, which is a testimony to the remarkable care taken by scribes who copied out the Hebrew text by hand before printing came into being. The fact that the Jews preserved their scriptures so accurately over many centuries says much about the reliability of the text.

Different types of writing in the Bible

The word 'testament' means 'agreement'. The Old Testament was an agreement that God made with the people of Israel. The New Testament is about the agreement that God has made with all people who believe in Jesus.

Both the Old and the New Testament are made up of books, each book being broken down further into chapters and verses. As you would expect from different books on a bookshelf, there are different types of books in the Bible and different styles of writing. This is sometimes because the books were written by a number of different people and sometimes the different styles are because of the content of that particular book. For example, the book of Leviticus contains information about laws so it is written in a very factual way. The book of Psalms, however, is a book of songs so it reads more like a poetry book. On the following page is an outline of some of the different styles of writing found in the Bible.

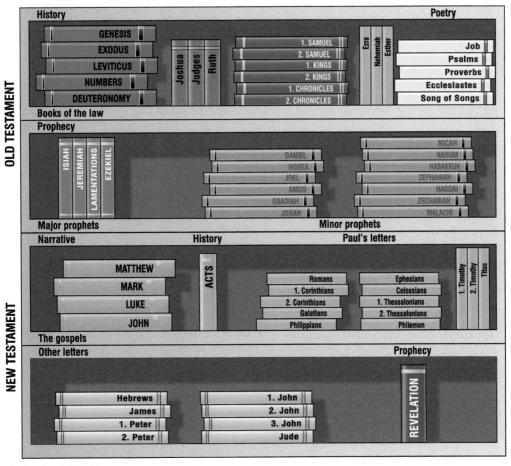

The books of the Bible

Narrative

Much of the Bible is written in a narrative style – telling the story or giving an account of something that happened. In the first five books of the Bible (often known as the Pentateuch), the account is the beginning of God's relationship with people and what happened to them (the Jews) after that.

Laws and instructions

The first five books of the Bible from Genesis to Deuteronomy are known as Books of the Law. The best known of the laws are the Ten Commandments in Exodus 20. Laws and instructions are also given in the New Testament – see especially Matthew 5–7 and John 14–16. Laws and instructions set out God's rules for his people about living a happy life and the right way to worship.

Prophecy

The books in the Old Testament from Isaiah to Malachi are known as the Books of Prophecy. In these books, the **prophets** (men called by God to speak to his people) explain to the people where they are making mistakes and how God will act in the future. Christians believe that these books also talk about the coming of Jesus.

Apocalyptic writing

Apocalyptic writing gives detail about the future and what might happen at the end of the world (Matthew 24, Mark 13, Luke 21). The last book of the Bible, Revelation, outlines a vision of the future when Christians believe Jesus will return to earth again.

Parables

The first four books of the New Testament – Matthew, Mark, Luke and John – tell the life story of Jesus. When Jesus was talking to people, he liked to illustrate what he was saying by telling parables – stories with a meaning. There are many parables in these books, such as the Parable of the Sower (Matthew 13) and the Parable of the Tenants (Luke 20:9–19).

Wisdom sayings

The Book of Proverbs in the Old Testament is full of down-to-earth advice and wise sayings about life and God (Mark 1:23–28).

Miracle stories

Throughout the Bible there are stories of miracles that have taken place. These include accounts of miracles that Jesus performed, such as driving out evil spirits, Jesus calling the first disciples, Jesus healing people and even bringing people back to life (John 11:1–44).

Biblical teachings applied to personal and social experiences

We have acknowledged that Christians view the Bible as a handbook for living and, therefore, there is much in the Bible about personal feelings and situations that most people experience. Christians use these as an example of how the Bible is relevant to today.

Words of wisdom from the Bible

A fool finds pleasure in evil conduct, but a man of understanding delights in wisdom.

Proverbs 10:23

The Bible to Christians

Your word is a lamp to my feet and a light for my path.

Psalm 119:105

The Bible is not merely a book; it is a Living Being, with an action, a power, which invades everything that opposes its extension, behold! It is upon this table: This Book, surpassing all others; I never omit to read it, and every day with some pleasure.

Napoleon Bonaparte

Passages about personal and social experience include:

- examples of relationships with family and peers – arguing brothers Cain and Abel (Genesis 4), devoted but different sisters Mary and Martha (Luke 10:38–42)
- comfort in times of sorrow (2 Corinthians 3–5, Romans 8:26–28)
- relief in times of suffering (2 Corinthians 12:8, Hebrews 12:3–13)
- courage in time of fear (Hebrews 13:5–6, 2 Timothy 1:7)
- protection in time of danger (Psalms 91, 121)
- how to behave in professional and business matters (Psalms 15)
- dealing with material wealth (Luke 12:16–21).

| CASE STUDY | Getting braver |

Winston is being bullied at school. Some boys in his year are ridiculing him for working hard and for not messing around in class like they do. They have also been making fun of his beliefs and telling Winston that he is boring and that his religion stops him from having any fun. Winston knows this isn't true, but it is hurtful to be rejected and ridiculed by his peers.

Winston has spoken to his dad about his problems. His dad has said that there will always be difficult people to deal with in life – even as adults. These people have to be stood up to.

Winston's dad also showed Winston that the Bible has something to say about being strong and courageous. 2 Timothy 1:7 says 'For the Spirit God gave us does not make us timid, but gives us power, love and self-discipline.' If we bring our troubles to God and ask him to make us strong, He will be with us and will give us courage to face our difficulties. The Bible also promises in Isaiah 41:10 that God will always be with us. Winston is praying each day for God to make him strong and courageous to stand up to the bullies. And he is grateful for the reassurance that God is with him.

Winston is finding courage to face his bullies through reading God's promises that He will be with him

Applying biblical passages to daily life

As previously mentioned, Christians believe that even though the Bible was written many years ago, the guidance it gives can still be applied to daily life today. There are some key passages that Christians see as giving clear guidelines for living. These include:

- the Ten Commandments (Exodus 20:1–17)
- the Sermon on the Mount (Matthew 5–7)
- the Golden Rule (Matthew 7:12)
- the Greatest Commandment (Matthew 22:36–4)
- Christ's New Commandment (John 13:34–35)
- Christian Love (1 Corinthians 13)
- the way of salvation (John 14:6, Acts 16:31, Romans 10:9)
- marriage and divorce (Matthew 19:3–9).

God

In this section you will learn to:

- describe the roles of God
- explain the significance of the names of God
- describe the idea of God as Father, Son and Holy Spirit
- explain the attributes of God.

God as provider

Then Jesus said to his disciples: 'Therefore I tell you, do not worry about your life, what you will eat; or about your body, what you will wear. For life is more than food, and the body more than clothes. Consider the ravens: They do not sow or reap, they have no storeroom or barn; yet God feeds them. And how much more valuable you are than birds!'

Luke 12:22–24

Roles of God

When you think of God, what idea comes to mind? Some people see God as a rescuer – someone they can call out to in times of difficulty. Other people see God almost like a policeman watching over them to check how they behave. The Bible says much about who God is and what He is like. God can be described as multifaceted or having many different aspects or roles:

- Creator: throughout the Bible God is recognised as creator and Lord of all. He rules over the earth, heaven, animals, fish, plants, humans, and social and political systems (Genesis 1:2, Psalm 8, Acts 17:16–31).
- Provider: God provides for the needs of all living things (Psalm 23, Luke 12:22–34).
- Protector and liberator of systems and people (Joshua 23, Psalm 91, Luke 13:34).
- **Sovereign** ruler over all (Psalm 6, 47, 97, Luke 10:21–22).
- The source and sustainer of life: God not only created all life forms, but it is God who sustains life on earth. For example, the earth is the only planet in our solar system that is exactly the right distance from the sun to sustain life. Christians believe this is God's design. And that, at any time, God can choose to end life on earth or the life of individuals. Similarly, He can choose to give life back, even to people who have already died (Genesis 1–2, John 5:19–24, Romans 8:18–23).
- Revealer and teacher: the Bible talks about how we can know God and understand His teachings through the Holy Spirit, who speaks to our human spirit (John 14:15–17, 16:7–15, 1 Corinthians 2:9–16).

Significance of the names of God

The original Hebrew and Greek text of the Bible is very descriptive about God. It uses different words for the name of God, all of them emphasising a different aspect of His character. It also describes God and Jesus in many different ways. In the same way a person can have many words linked to them that describes something of who they are – a man could be a son, brother, doctor, husband, etc. – God and Jesus are given names that reflect

Name	Meaning	Bible reference
Yahweh	Yahweh is the main name for God in the Bible. It is thought to mean 'He brings into existence whatever exists' or 'I am'	Psalm 90:2
King, Redeemer, Shepherd	Showing God as a ruler, saviour and also a protector	Job Psalm 23:1
Adonai	Master or my Lord	Exodus 4:10–12 Joshua 7:8–11
Elohim	Plural terms for God – Authority, Plenitude	Genesis 31:3 Deuteronomy 5:9
El-Shaddai	Almighty	Genesis 17:1–20
Jehovah-Jireh	The Lord will provide	Genesis 22:8–14
Jehovah-Rapha	The God who heals	Exodus 15:26
Jehovah-Shalom	God is peace	Judges 6:24
Christos	Anointed one Refers to Jesus	John 1:41
Yeshua	God is salvation	Matthew 16:13–16 John 6:42
Father, Advocate, Lord	Someone who appeals on our behalf Refers to Jesus	Matthew 6:26, 1 John 2:1 Deuteronomy 10:17

something of their attributes. In English there is really only one word for God so it is helpful to look at the Hebrew and Greek in order to understand more of what God is like.

God as Father, Son and Holy Spirit

The Bible teaches that there is only one God but that He can be understood in three different ways – as God the Father, God the Son and God the Holy Spirit. These three ways or different personalities are known as the Trinity.

God is sometimes referred to in the Bible as Father of humankind (Isaiah 9:6, 64:8), reflecting a loving and close relationship and also an element of dependence on Him. People today sometimes talk about God being a mother as well as a father.

God the Son refers to Jesus. Christians believe that Jesus was God in human form (Matthew 8:29). Jesus was also referred to in different ways. In John 1:19–31, John the Baptist called Jesus the Lamb of God, suggesting gentleness. Jesus is also referred to as the Bread of Life (John 6:32–35), meaning he is the nourishment we need.

The third aspect of God is as Spirit – the way in which God lives in the hearts and lives of believers. God the spirit was at work in the creation of the world (Genesis 1:1–2) and individuals (Psalm 139:7). God the spirit is also an advocate, someone who will speak to God on our behalf (John 14:15–17, Acts 2:2–4, 11–12).

Attributes of God

We have discovered that studying the different names given to God can tell us more about what God is like. Further passages tell us even more about the attributes of God:

- Unity – God is one (Deuteronomy 6:4, 1 Corinthians 8:6).
- Eternal – God transcends time (Genesis 21:33, Psalm 90:2).
- Omnipresent – God is present everywhere (Psalm 139:1–4).
- Omniscient – God knows all things (Psalm 139:1–4, 147:4–5).
- Omnipotent – God is all-powerful (Matthew 19:26, Revelation 19:6).
- Love – God's love is limitless (Psalm 103:17, John 3:16, 1 John 8:10).
- Justice – God is fair and does not show favourites (Acts 10:34–35).
- Holy – God is righteous, perfect and set apart from all sin or evil (1 Peter 1:16).
- Righteous – living according to the laws of God (Psalm 19:7–9).
- Merciful – God shows undeserved compassion to all (Exodus 3:7).

ACTIVITY

Think back to the image of God that you had in your mind at the start of this section. How do you view God now? Has your opinion changed?

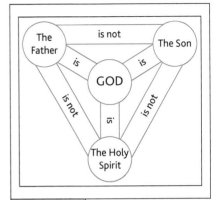

Figure A.3.1 The concept of the Trinity can be hard to explain, but this illustration, called the Shield of the Trinity, can help us to understand how three things can be part of one whole

We eat to satisfy our hunger, but then grow hungry again. Jesus compares himself to food when he describes himself as the Bread of Life. He states that those who believe in him will never hunger spiritually again.

The Serenity Prayer
The Serenity Prayer has been used by many people (not just Christians) for over seventy years. It highlights three of the attributes of God that He passes on to those who ask: serenity (peace), courage and wisdom.

God, grant me the serenity
to accept the things I cannot change,
Courage to change the things I can,
And wisdom to know the difference.

Reinhold Niebuhr, theologian

Concept of sin and salvation

In this section you will learn to:

- explain the basic concept of sin
- explain how sin affects the quality of life for the individual, the society and the environment
- describe biblical examples that state the consequences of sin
- explain the basic concept of salvation
- discuss the involvement of God in the work of salvation through Jesus Christ
- show that salvation is available for all through faith in Christ
- explain essential factors in the process of salvation using biblical illustrations.

DID YOU KNOW?

Hosea was an Old Testament prophet whose life played out God's relationship with the nation of Israel. God told Hosea to marry a prostitute, Gomer (who represented Israel). Hosea loved Gomer deeply and cared for her, but Gomer was unfaithful (just as Israel had been unfaithful by worshipping other gods). Gomer's children were given names that reflected God's feelings towards Israel at that time, for example Lo-Ruhamah meaning 'not loved'.

Sin

Sin is the breaking of God's law (Romans 1). In Genesis, we read that God created humans to have free will and, therefore, the ability to make good and bad choices. The first sin in the Bible (sometimes known as the original sin) can be found in Genesis 3 when Adam and Eve eat fruit from a tree that God had forbidden them to touch.

The Bible has harsh words to say about sin. It describes sin as the state and condition of humankind (Romans 5:12):

> When Adam sinned, sin entered the entire human race. His sin spread death throughout the world, so everything began to grow old and die, for all sinned.
>
> Romans 5:12, see also Psalm 51:5

Committing a sin is moving away from God's plan for your life and shows rebellion against God (Genesis 3, Matthew 23:37–39, Romans 1:18–32). The Bible also describes sin as a personal failure to be responsible (Genesis 3, Luke 12:41–48) and also a joint failure, alongside others, to do the right thing (Luke 11:39–52, 17:1–3).

How sin affects the quality of life

Christians believe that committing sin moves people away from the best plans that God has for each individual's life. It can affect individuals (Mark 7:11–13, Luke 16:20–21) and can lead to further sin (see Kofi's story on the following page). The Bible gives examples of how sin can also affect society. In Genesis 6, there is so much sin in the world following Adam and Eve's initial sin, that disobeying God's laws had become a way of life and it angered God. So God decided to flood the earth, saving only one family who had strived to keep God's law.

Sin can also affect the environment and, therefore, the quality of life for everyone in the world (Genesis 3:17–25; Romans 1:24–25). The message of the Bible is that while small, individual sins may seem insignificant, they can have knock-on effects that cause much bigger problems.

The consequences of sin

The Bible says that there are consequences to sin. If people sin they risk:

- alienation from God and others (Luke 15:11–32, Romans 1:24–25)
- suffering and degeneration (Genesis 2–3, Luke 15:11–19, Romans 1:18–32, 2:9)
- feelings of guilt and shame (Genesis 3:1–10, Luke 15:1–19)
- death (Genesis 2–3, Joshua 7, Luke 19:12–27, Romans 6:20–22).

Concept of salvation

Salvation is a spiritual term describing a way to restore your relationship with God through the forgiveness of sin. It can be described as the deliverance, freedom and liberation from all of the consequences of sin (Galatians 4:1–7, 5:1, Romans 8:19–23). The Bible's teaching on sin is harsh, but that salvation is easily available to all.

God in salvation

Christians believe that the message of the New Testament is all about salvation. It tells the life story of Jesus, who was God in human form, come to earth to pay the price for all sin and restore humankind's relationship with God. Jesus was put to death on a cross but came back to life (also known as the resurrection) three days later, showing that God is more powerful than death.

The Bible teaches that Jesus was God's special gift to the world (John 3:16) and, through Jesus, God shows His love for humankind (John 15:12–17).

Salvation and faith

The Bible teaches that salvation is available for all people, regardless of race, age or gender. The only requirement is that a person believes that Jesus was the son of God who died and was resurrected (Acts 4:1–12, John 3:6).

Essential factors in the process of salvation

The Bible explains that there are factors or stages in the process of salvation:

1 Repentance – in order to be forgiven for sin, a person must be sorry for what they have done (Luke 7:35–50, 5:11–14, 19:1).

2 Justification by faith – having the knowledge that if people are truly sorry and acknowledge what Jesus did for them by dying on the cross they will be forgiven (Acts 16:30–32, Romans 3:21–26, Romans 10:11–17, James 2:14–17, Romans 5:1–21).

3 Reconciliation or atonement – this is about renewing a person's relationship with God, knowing that they are loved and forgiven (Luke 15:11–24, 19:1–10, Ephesians 2:11–22).

4 Regeneration or new birth – Christians believe that to be able to live life in the way that God intends, a person must start anew. This is sometimes referred to as being born again (Colossians 3:12–17, Ephesians 4:23–24).

5 Sanctification – a daily growing in godliness as a consequence of striving to live according to God's guidelines (Ephesians 2:1–10).

Christians do not believe that once they have salvation they will never sin again. But they believe that they have been forgiven, that they can continue to say sorry to God for things they do wrong and that they can continue to live a life pleasing to God.

CASE STUDY | Kofi's story

Kofi is a classmate of Winston. He recently confided in Winston about shoplifting.

Some of Kofi's friends had stolen items from a clothes shop and dared Kofi to steal a cap. Kofi did not want to seem weak and he wanted his friends to respect him, so he stole too.

When his parents asked him where he got the cap, Kofi lied and said that one of his friends had given it to him. He felt horrible lying to his parents and his mood has been irritable and gloomy ever since. To make things worse, the shopkeeper has now banned children from entering the shop due to too much theft.

Kofi feels terrible about what he has done and the consequences of his actions for his peers, as well as the tense atmosphere he has created at home because of his moods. He is worried that if he tells his parents what he did they will never trust him again. But he does not feel he can live with the guilt. He has also felt very far away from God and he feels too ashamed to pray.

ACTIVITY

Imagine you are Winston. What advice would you give to Kofi based on teaching in the Bible?

Christians believe that Jesus' death pays the price for human sin and that, through believing in Jesus' death and resurrection, people's relationship with God can be restored

Adam's one sin brought the penalty of death to many, while Christ freely takes away many sins and gives glorious life instead.

Romans 5:16

Option B: Hinduism

B.1 Human life issues

LEARNING OUTCOMES

In this section you will learn to:

- discuss the meaning and purpose of life as reflected in the Bhagavad Gita
- explain the concept of 'guruhood' and 'discipleship' and its application to daily living
- assess issues related to justice and peace and the value and dignity of human life as reflected in the Gita
- illustrate how the Hindu concept of love applies to different areas of life and relationships
- discuss the roles and responsibilities of individuals in areas of family and relationships
- describe the scriptural teachings on the nature of human beings
- describe the sanctity of life from the Hindu perspective.

LINK

For an introduction to Hinduism, see Section 1, Essentials of religion, starting on page 2.

Meaning and purpose of life

In Hinduism, life is about attaining moksha (liberation) by breaking the cycle of rebirth (samsara). The path to moksha is to live a good life according to the requirements of Hindu dharma, thereby building up good karma. Hindus believe that rebirth is determined by past and current karma, created by how they live their current life. Therefore, as well as having a moral obligation to live well, Hindus have a personal reason to gain good karma in this life.

However, Hinduism is not just about improving your status in the life to come. Hindu scriptures, such as the Bhagavad Gita, help to give meaning and purpose to life today. In the Gita, Krishna explains that it is Bhakti Yog (devotional service), Karma Yog (action), Raj Yog (meditation) and Jnana Yog (knowledge) that lead to enlightenment, fulfilment and happiness in this life. Krishna teaches that although we are in this world, we should also look beyond it and connect with our immortal self or atman.

Hinduism teaches that followers should worship God, respect others, help those in need, love their family and care for the environment. As with all religions, belief in higher beings brings perspective to life. Knowing that all of creation, including the people we share the earth with, are made by God encourages respect for others.

> ### The purpose of life according to Gandhi
>
> God demands nothing less than complete self-surrender as the price for the only real freedom that is worth having. And when a man thus loses himself, he immediately finds himself in the service of all that lives. It becomes his delight and his recreation. He is a new man, never weary of spending himself in the service of God's creation.
>
> Mahatma Gandhi

Concept of guruhood: the spiritual guide and the disciple

Traditionally, between the ages of eight and 12 years, a boy would leave his family and spend his adolescent years (until his manhood) as the **disciple** of a guru. Today this rarely happens, but gurus are still revered and sought out for spiritual teaching by Hindus. In modern times, both boys and girls in the Caribbean have gurus as personal spiritual guides.

The role of a guru is to provide guidance and build wisdom in their followers so that devotees can eventually recognise and respond to their own divine nature. Ekalavya and Gandhi, whom you will read about on the next page, are both men from whom we can learn powerful lessons.

ACTIVITY

Do you have any personal experience of having somebody you look up to who can offer you spiritual and other advice? What does this person mean to you?

Ekalavya in the Upanishads and the *Mahabharata*

In the Hindu epic the *Mahabharata*, the story is told of Ekalavya. Ekalavya is a tribal prince of low caste, but he is determined to study archery under the guidance of the great Guru Drona. When Drona rejects him because of his caste, Ekalavya makes a clay statue of Guru Drona, considering this to be his guru, and he studies archery by himself in front of the statue. Eventually he becomes a highly skilled archer – more skilled even than Arjuna, Drona's star pupil. When Drona discovers this, he demands that Ekalavya give his right thumb as Dakshina (a gift given by a student to the guru at the end of learning) for learning from him. Ekalavya obeys, crippling himself and ruining his archery skills in the process. However, he continues practising his skills using four fingers, and eventually becomes renowned for his archery skills.

This story highlights the determination of a young man to learn and the importance of respecting the knowledge of others, as well as showing complete loyalty to a guru.

Mahatma Gandhi

Mahatma Gandhi (real name Mohandas Karamchand Gandhi) lived between 1869 and 1948. Gandhi was a great teacher and politician. His teachings on the principles of love, self-sacrifice, acceptance and peace demonstrate the universal values in Hinduism. Gandhi did not just teach though, he lived out his beliefs and values through his actions.

Gandhi spent his life peacefully protesting against the British occupation of India. Thousands of people were motivated and inspired by Gandhi's words and by his determined but peaceful campaigning. In 1931 Gandhi was invited to speak to the British government about Indian independence and finally, in 1947, India's independence was granted.

Gandhi is known as the Father of the Indian nation, as he led the struggle for independence. This led to the partition of India and the emergence of Pakistan. Not long after this, in January 1948, Gandhi was assassinated. Gandhi's model of non-violent protest inspired oppressed people around the world, including Martin Luther King, who protested in the US against racism and discrimination towards African-Americans.

DID YOU KNOW?

The word 'guru' comes from the Sanskrit words 'gu' meaning darkness and 'ru' meaning 'remover'. A guru, therefore, brings their disciples spiritual light or guidance.

Through his words and actions, Gandhi showed the importance of courage and peace

DID YOU KNOW?

Every year Gandhi is honoured on 2 October, his birthday. Worldwide, the day has been declared International Day of Non-violence. In some parts of the Caribbean, the day is marked by ritual observations about Gandhi's life, contribution and the importance of peaceful protest.

Brooding about sensuous objects
makes attachment to them grow;
from attachment desire arises,
from desire anger is born.

From anger comes confusion;
from confusion memory lapses;
from broken memory under-
standing is lost;
from loss of understanding, he
is ruined.

Bhagavad Gita 2:62–63

The fall and rise of man

The Bhagavad Gita teaches that focusing on and chasing after worldly wealth brings spiritual death. The Hindu devotional text, Bhaja Govindam, encourages followers to rise above the pursuit of wealth in order to achieve spiritual freedom. Hindu disciples use yoga, meditation and worship to focus on their spirituality and to break their attachment to worldly things.

The company of the good weans one away from false attachments;
When attachment is lost, delusion ends;
When delusion ends, the mind becomes unwavering and steady.
An unwavering and steady mind is merited for Jeevan Mukti (liberation even in this life).

Bhaja Govindam, verse 9

Value and dignity of human life

Hinduism has a lot to say about the way people behave, deal with difficult issues and relate to each other. A summary of Hindu teaching on various life issues is outlined below.

Child abuse and abortion

Hinduism teaches that children are a blessing from God. Hinduism also teaches that all living things are sacred and should be treated with respect and care. Abuse of children mentally, physically or sexually is unacceptable to Hindus.

Bhagavad Gita teaching on the eternal soul
Why do you worry without cause? Whom do you fear without reason? Who can kill you? The soul is neither born, nor does it die.

The Gita teaches that the soul carries life rather than the body. Hindu teachings do not approve of abortions or the illegitimate taking of life. However, if a baby needs to be aborted in a life-and-death situation for the mother, most Hindus would support this.

Substance abuse

Hindus believe that the body should be respected and cared for as the carrier of the soul. Substance abuse damages the body and mind, prevents a person from spiritual progress and brings pain and suffering to family and friends. Therefore, Hindus are strongly against any illicit drug taking.

Capital punishment

Capital punishment in the Bhagavad Gita
Taking as equal pleasure and pain, gain and loss, victory and defeat, gird thyself for the battle; thus thou shalt not incur sin.

Bhagavad Gita, 2:38

Arguments, based on Hindu teachings, can both support and dispute capital punishment. In the Gita, righteous punishment is promoted to maintain the moral and social order of the universe. However, Hinduism also teaches ahimsa – the principle of non-violence, as Gandhi famously demonstrated. One thing is true – that the Hindu teaching of reincarnation means that, although death destroys the body, it cannot destroy the soul.

ACTIVITY

Based on what you have learnt, give an example of when a Hindu may justify capital punishment.

Poverty and unemployment

Hinduism teaches that every Hindu should work hard, within the discipline of their dharma, in order to accumulate wealth (this is one of the four **purushartas**). However, this should not be done out of greed but out of a desire to provide for the family. Hindu scriptures teach that wealth that is not shared with those in need will not bring happiness or good karma.

Hinduism teaches that people should work hard to provide for their family and in order to give to those in need

Prejudice and discrimination

Hinduism is a very open religion and Hindus are taught not to show prejudice against anyone, even other Hindus who have beliefs different to their own. All people should be respected as Brahman's creation. Hinduism also teaches respect for the elderly. Most Hindus live with elderly relatives in their homes and care for them.

Male and female roles and relationships

Traditionally, Hinduism teaches that males and females have different roles to play in the family and society. In a traditional Hindu home, sons were treated preferentially as they were thought to bring prosperity and respect to the family through their wage. Sons also carried out the important job of performing funeral rites for their parents. Daughters were expensive, as dowries were paid when they married. Also, daughters joined their husband's family after marriage and cared for their parents-in-law.

However, these roles within Hinduism are changing. Many Hindu women today are in employment and, in most modern Hindu homes, girls are considered equal to boys and are given the same care and opportunities. In modern times in the Caribbean, dowries are no longer paid and, generally, a husband and wife will live in their own home and care for each set of parents equally.

> An eye for an eye ends up making the whole world blind.
>
> Mahatma Gandhi

ACTIVITY

Compare and contrast different views within Hinduism towards disability. Express both the positive and negative attitudes that Hindus may have towards disability.

Violence, vandalism and war

Hinduism teaches peace and respect for all living things since Brahman is in all. Despite this, the Bhagavad Gita does teach that fighting in a righteous war is a Hindu duty. The pacifist Gandhi understood this to mean that all Hindus should fight the holy internal war against evil, temptation and selfishness, and many Hindus share this view. Of course, Hindus, like every other group of people, agree that mindless violence and vandalism (attacking people or property for no reason) is always wrong.

Treatment of the mentally and physically challenged

Hinduism explains disability as a result of negative karma. Disability can be avoided in the next life by following good dharma in this life. However, Hinduism teaches that every Hindu should minimise suffering where possible. Therefore, rather than judging, many Hindus believe it is their duty to show care and respect to those with disabilities.

Roles, responsibilities and rights in family life and work

CASE STUDY	Getting on

Kamala and Ramesh live with their mother, father and grandfather. Their grandfather has lived with them ever since their grandmother died. Even before this, their grandparents lived close by. Every day, a member of the family would visit and take them meals.

Kamala and Ramesh enjoy having their grandfather living with them. He tells them stories of the Hindu deities, jokes and gives them money for sweets. However, there have had to be changes since their grandfather came. Ramesh now shares his bedroom with his grandfather. Lately, their grandfather has been getting more forgetful and confused and more of their mother's time is spent looking after him. This means Kamala is helping more around the house.

The children are glad that their family is fulfilling dharma through caring for their grandfather. It seems strange to think this, but they know that one day they will depend on their own children for their needs too.

Recently, they heard the story of Shravan Kumar from the *Ramayana*. Shravan was the perfect son who was dedicated to his parents. Kamala and Ramesh look to Shravan's example but hope that they will not suffer his fate!

The *Ramayana* tells the story of Shravan Kumar, the perfect son who was shot while carrying his blind parents on a pilgrimage around the Hindu holy sites of India

Other responsibilities of Hindus

- Children, particularly sons and daughters-in-law who live with their parents, are expected to honour and care for the parents in old age.

- Husbands should love and protect their wives; wives should love and honour their husbands. Rama and Sita give a good example of love, harmony and devotion within marriage.
- Parents should love their children and provide for them spiritually, physically and emotionally. The *Ramayana* tells about the conflict between Dasharatha and his wife Kaikeyi over their son Rama being crowned king. Despite the tensions, the love that Rama's parents have for their sons is highlighted.
- Hindus should work hard, while not becoming attached to worldly achievement or reward. Each person should follow their own path and not compare themselves to others.
- The Manusmriti teaches that mutual respect should be shown between employer and employee.

Implications of Hindu teaching of love in human relationships

Hindus should integrate into society, earn money, enjoy life and build up spiritual merits. However, Hinduism teaches that worldly pleasures should always come second to spiritual commitment, and that Hindus should not become distracted from spiritual devotion.

Hindus view sex positively. However, Hindu practice is that sex should only be enjoyed within marriage. Also, young people in the brahmacharya stage of life should abstain from sex in order to focus on their education and to be disciplined.

Social status

Hinduism teaches that all people are created by Brahman. Therefore, all races and religions carry aspects of the Supreme Being and are to be respected. Hinduism is a tolerant religion. Over the years, it has even incorporated other beliefs and customs. However, the caste system privileges one group of people above another based purely on the group they are born into. In the Caribbean the caste system only has ritual status. It is not generally acknowledged in day-to-day life and inter-caste marriage is not an issue, though it can be in India. Social status in Caribbean Hindu families is represented by economic standing, political affiliations and family.

Scriptural teaching on the nature of human beings

In Chapter 15 of the Gita, Lord Krishna explains the purpose and value of knowing God and outlines how God can be found. The Bal Kand of the *Ramayana* illustrates how everyday actions in the lives of human beings symbolise the eternal journey of our soul.

Sanctity of life

Hinduism teaches that Brahman is in all and that life is a gift of God. Therefore, all life is sacred. Through our connection to Brahman, we are also all connected to each other. Hinduism teaches respect for the sacredness of every living thing. Hindus live so as to cause as little distress to any living being as possible.

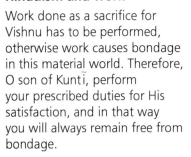

Hinduism and work

Work done as a sacrifice for Vishnu has to be performed, otherwise work causes bondage in this material world. Therefore, O son of Kuntī, perform your prescribed duties for His satisfaction, and in that way you will always remain free from bondage.

Bhagavad Gita 3:9

DID YOU KNOW?

The Vedas speak of society being classified according to the skills and nature of human beings. This was called the varna system and was divided into four levels:

1. The Brahmins – the priestly caste.
2. The Kshatriyas – the warrior caste.
3. The Vaishyas – the merchants
4. The Shudras – servants or labourers.

However, many Hindus use the varna system as an example of an ideal society where people are respected for their skills and their nature and all can work together in harmony for the greater good of society.

Devoid of false ego and illusion, free from degraded association, perceptive of the eternal and the transitory, disassociated from lust, completely liberated from the dualities identified as happiness and distress; the wise reach the imperishable shelter of the Supreme Lord.

Bhagavad Gita 15:5

The *Ramayana* and Bhagavad Gita

The Bhagavad Gita records the words of the avatar Krishna to Arjuna as he prepares for battle. It is thought to have been written around the 4th–3rd century BCE.

The Supreme Law
This is the summit of the dharma (duty); Do naught to others which, if done to thee, could cause thee pain.

Mahabharata 5:1517

How the *Ramayana* and Bhagavad Gita came into being

The epic Hindu poem of the *Ramayana* was originally written in Sanskrit, sometime between the 2nd century BCE and the 2nd century CE by the poet Valmiki. In order for the message of the text to reach the mass population, it was translated into Avadhi, which is part of the Hindi language group, in the 16th century CE by Tulsidas in India.

The Bhagavad Gita, also known as 'The Song of the Lord', forms two chapters of the *Mahabharata*, the world's longest and oldest poem. It records the **avatar** Krishna's words to Arjuna as they sit in his chariot preparing for battle. It is thought that the Gita was written around the 4th–3rd century BCE by Vyasa, although other writers and thinkers may have added to his words.

Different types of writing in Hindu scripture

Two types of writing are used in Hindu scriptures: prose and poetry.

Prose

Prose is the ordinary form of written or spoken language. It is simple communication without rhythm applied to it. Prose is often the technique used in written instructions, conversations and teaching. Many of the Hindu scriptures are written in prose, including many of the Vedas.

Poetry

Poetry is written or spoken language organised into a rhythm or pattern and often rhyming. Poetry often conveys feelings and emotion. Couplet poetry is commonly used in Hindu writings. Couplets are a pair of lines that have the same rhythm (or metre) and often rhyme. Other forms of Indian poetry include doha, sortha, choupai, shloka and chhanda. The most famous poems in Hinduism are the *Mahabharata* and the *Ramayana*.

Choupai is used particularly in medieval Hindi poetry. It uses a rhythm of four syllables. Chhanda poetry is used particularly in northern India and Pakistan, where it is recited at weddings. Shlokas are vedic chants used during worship. These chants bring enlightenment and knowledge and encourage good actions in both the speaker and the listener.

Scriptural teaching as it relates to daily life

The Hindu scriptures teach that promoting the welfare of all living beings, particularly humanity, is one of Hinduism's highest duties. Needlessly causing harm or distress to another person is considered a great sin (or paap) in Hinduism.

Hindu teachings applied to personal and social experiences

- Honesty – in Chapter 16:1–3 of the Gita, Krishna describes honesty as one of the virtues of a divine nature.
- Righteousness – the *Ramayana* describes Bharat, the brother of Rama, as being righteous. Knowing that his appointment as king in place of his brother was wrong, he refused the throne and acted only as Rama's representative until Rama returned to rule.
- Faith – the story of Shabari in the *Ramayana* tells of a woman who showed great faith. On the instruction of her guru, Shabari cleaned the ashram and collected fruit every day in the hope that Rama would pass by. Although it took many years, Shabari never gave up believing that Rama would come. Finally, when the woman was old, her faith was rewarded with Rama's arrival.
- Forgiveness – the *Ramayana* tells the story of Jayant seeking forgiveness from Lord Rama. Lord Rama shows mercy and forgiveness through not killing Jayant, but, as a consequence of karma, he destroys one of his eyes instead.
- Mercy and love for your enemy – Shri Rama is known as the protector of the Hindu devotees. The *Ramayana* tells of the great mercy he showed to his enemy Rawana. Hindus are encouraged to show similar mercy.
- Faithfulness – Lakshman and Bharat show faithfulness to Rama through their support for him while he is in exile.
- Justice – the story is told in the *Ramayana* of Bali who tries to kill his brother, Sugriva, and expel him from the kingdom after Sugriva mistakenly traps Bali in a cave. The story goes on to tell how justice is done through Rama's killing of Bali. The message of the story is that justice will prevail.
- Love for God and prayerfulness – Prahlada, the king's son, showed utter devotion to the god Vishnu. When his father asked him who was greater – the king or God – Prahlada answered God, even though this resulted in his father and then his aunt trying to kill him. The story shows the importance of love and devotion to God.
- Dealing with material wealth – Hinduism teaches that material wealth is secondary to spiritual riches and, though a certain amount of money is necessary, chasing money and possessions is a path to destruction. Bharata gave up his status as king and all of the material wealth that would accompany that in order to support his brother Rama as the rightful king.
- Protection in danger and courage in fear – Hinduism shows how the deities can protect us in times of danger. When Lakshman's life was threatened, Hanuman (the monkey deity) protected and preserved it by finding the plant that could heal him. We can also be inspired by Hanuman to show courage in difficult times. During his journey to rescue Sita from Sri Lanka, Hanuman nobly and bravely carried out his duty, showing courage and quick thinking when obstacles were put in his path.

ACTIVITY

Write out the Supreme Law of Hinduism in your own words.

Which Hindu teaching appeals to you the most and why?

Prayerfulness

Hiranyakasipu ordered that rocks be tied to Prahlada so that he and the rocks would sink to the bottom of the ocean. Prahlada started praying: 'Glory to thee, O Supreme Being. You as Brahma created this world; as Vishnu, You preserve this world; and as Rudra, You destroy it. Thou art everything, all things are only Your forms. Thou art everywhere, here at the bottom of the ocean as also in the sky high above. I am everlasting, imperishable and unchangeable because I am one with Thee.' Thus meditating, Prahlada was lost in prayer and became one with the object of his meditations. At once, the bonds which bound him were burst asunder, the piles of rock crumbled into sand and he came up floating on the waves.

Bhagavata Purana

The *Ramayana* tells the story of Shabari, a woman who showed great faith. Shabari cleaned the ashram and replaced the fruit in it each day in faith that, one day, Rama would visit.

The Absolute and avatars

Roles of God

Hinduism teaches that the Supreme Being, Brahman, encompasses all of life. Brahman can be all things to Hindus. He can fill the role of mother, father, companion and friend. In the words of the Twameva Maataa mantra, Brahman provides a Hindu with all that they need.

Twameva Maataa prayer

Twameva Maataa, Cha Pitaa Twameva.
Twameva Bandhu, Cha Sakha Twameva.
Twameva Vidya, Dravinum Twameva.
Twameva Sarvam Mama Deva Deva.

O God,
You are my mother, you are my father, you are my brother, you are my friend,
You are my wisdom, you are my wealth.
Oh! God you are all in all for me.

Significance of the names of God

The Hindu God Brahman has manifested himself as many different deities. The most significant of these are the three gods that make up the Brahman Trinity. These avatars or incarnations of God are:

- Vishnu – the all-prevailing one who sustains and protects life on earth
- Brahma – the creator god who made the world
- Mahesh or Shiva – the destroyer or transformer who brings destruction to the earth in order to make way for a new cycle of creation. This is not negative, as rebirth and new beginnings come out of destruction.

The Brahman Trinity is made up of Vishnu, Brahma and Mahesh (Shiva)

God as Nirgun and Sagun Brahma

These are two ways of viewing God in Hinduism. Nirgun Brahma (literally meaning 'the Absolute without qualities') is God **unmanifest** – that is, God devoid of any form, qualities or attributes. Nirgun Brahma is seen as an impersonal, indescribable force. He is absolute, all-encompassing, all-powerful and eternal, but without any physical or tángible qualities. Nirgun Brahma is considered the Absolute Truth and Hindus constantly seek to connect with this infinite, indescribable force that lives within all living things. However, it was felt that Hindus also needed to understand God on a personal level.

Therefore, the Upanishads put forward the view of God as Sagun Brahma (literally meaning 'the Absolute with qualities'). This describes Brahman as a personal god made **manifest**, with attributes and form. Sagun Brahma is the creator, sustainer and controller of the universe. In male form, Sagun Brahma is known by many names, including Ishvara and Parameshvara. In its female form, Sagun Brahma is known as Durga or Kali. Most Hindus choose to worship Brahman in physical form as one of the avatars, such as Krishna or Rama. This is because it is easier to connect with and worship a personal and physical being than a concept. Being able to know God in physical form enables Hindus to learn lessons from the attitudes, actions and teachings of these manifestations of God.

DID YOU KNOW?

Qualities or attitudes are called gunas in Sanskrit.

Nirgun Brahma in the Gita
This whole world is pervaded by me in My Unmanifest form.
Bhagavad Gita 9:4

The Parmatma

The **Parmatma** is believed by Hindus to be the super soul that lives within the souls of all living beings and directs them to the truth. While the soul of a person can become distracted by wealth and material desires, the Parmatma simply observes. If the soul, through meditation, can focus away from worldly pleasures and remove itself from the strains and pressures of daily life, a person will discover that the super soul residing within them can bring fulfilment and peace. Connecting with the Parmatma brings equality as everyone has a super soul and, in this sense, everyone is on the same level.

The Rig Veda illustrates the roles of atman (the individual self or soul) and Parmatma (the super soul) by describing two birds on the tree of life. One bird looks on and is detached (this illustrates the role of the Parmatma) while the other bird eats the fruit (this illustrates the role of atman). The Parmatma is the ruler, atman is the ruled and they are friends.

Concept of sin and liberation

In this section you will learn to:

- explain the basic concept of sin
- discuss how sin affects the quality of life for the individual, the society and the environment
- describe how sin affects survival in the present-day situation
- explain the concept of liberation
- explain how the freedom of choice and liberation is the birth right of all
- explain the way out of bondage through liberation, for example Valmiki.

Sin

The concept of sin refers to carrying out actions that hinder the soul's progress towards moksha. Such actions are called paap or adharma.

Dharma, the divine law, stems from Brahman and governs the natural and supernatural world. All people move away from this divine law at times, since humans are imperfect and life is a spiritual struggle. This moving away from dharma is called adharma. However, there is no mortal sin that destroys a soul forever and condemns it to hell. Hindus can find atonement (forgiveness) from their sins through tapasya.

Tapasya

Tapasya, also spelled tapas, is the Sanskrit word for heat and refers to a person adopting strict morals and undergoing spiritual suffering in order to achieve a goal. Tapasya often involves a person fasting and denying themselves worldly pleasures. While undergoing tapasya, a person will seek to connect with Brahman through meditation and yoga. Through tapasya a person can 'burn off' negative karma that they have accumulated and eventually move closer to moksha.

How sin affects the individual, society and the environment

CASE STUDY | Paying the price

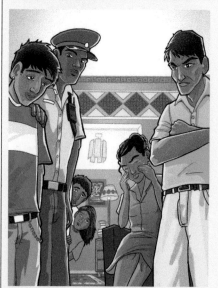

Paap or adharma can bring distress for the person who has committed the sin as well as their friends and family

Ramesh has been comforting his friend, Ranjit. Ranjit's older brother, Sunil, is in trouble with the police for a small-scale robbery. He got involved with the wrong crowd and allowed himself to be influenced by them. He is very sorry and regrets what he has done. Nevertheless, he and his family now have to face the consequences of his actions.

Sunil feels lonely. He feels his paap has separated him from God as well as affecting his relationship with his family. Sunil is also scared about what may happen to him now. Since it is his first offence, his family hope that his punishment will be lenient.

Sunil's mother is very upset. She is ashamed to go out and be seen in the community because of the shame that her son has brought on the family. Sunil's father is angry and disappointed, and the atmosphere at home is very tense. Ranjit and his sister feel that they cannot relax at home and that the happiness and fun there once was in their family is gone, at least for now.

Not only is Sunil suffering but, because of his paap, the whole family is paying the price.

In the case study, Sunil is sorry for what he has done. The repercussions of his actions are affecting the whole family, but if Sunil seeks forgiveness through tapasya and meditation, and if he follows the right path in the future, he can lead a fulfilling and full life once again. Sunil needs to connect his soul (atman) back with God.

However, the *Ramayana* describes how an individual who continually sins without repentance may eventually have their humanity destroyed. This is highlighted in the Bal Kand section of the *Adhyatma Ramayana*, in which Rama takes on human form and comes to earth in order to deal with the many asuras (demons) who have sprung up as a result of adharma on the earth. Ravana in particular shows asuric (demon-like) qualities as a result of his sin.

This degeneration spreads to the whole of society. The Lanka Kand shows how the whole society in which Ravana lives has become influenced and polluted by his sinful actions. Finally, the Ayodhya Kand describes how even an environment can become depressed and lifeless as a result of sin. The account is given of the once vibrant and active community of Ayodhya and the royal palace becoming grey and despondent as a result of Rama's unjust exile into the forest.

Consequences of sin

On the individual

On an individual level, sin brings alienation from God and man. Depending on the seriousness of the sin, friends and family may reject the person who has committed it or, even if they try to support the person, the relationship may become strained. Until the person has repented and sought liberation from their sin, they cannot enjoy peace either within themselves or with God.

> **ACTIVITY**
>
> What advice would you give to someone, such as Sunil in the case study, who had sinned and felt lonely, regretful and isolated from God and other people? What advice, from Hindu teachings, could you give to this person?

On the community

When individual sin spreads, and sin within a family or community becomes commonplace, that community suffers. Boundaries of acceptable and unacceptable behaviour become blurred and the framework on which a society is built begins to collapse. When people no longer have a moral or religious code to follow in terms of how to treat other people and the environment, suffering soon follows. A healthy society depends on people thinking of the needs of others. Social programmes such as youth clubs and family support groups depend on volunteers. When people think only of themselves such programmes cannot run and all of society suffers. Also, when people no longer nurture their spirit, spiritual fulfilment and guidance is lost.

On society

Sinfulness can also lead to an unhealthy environment as people no longer abide by or care about laws that protect the environment, such as not dropping litter and controlling pollution levels. When sinfulness takes hold of a society, people think only about that day rather than protecting the environment for future generations. When a society degenerates and an environment suffers, disease increases. Pollution, lack of respect for the environment, dirty living conditions and disrespect for the well-being of others all contribute to the spread of disease.

Dropping one piece of litter may not seem like a sin, but it can become a problem if everybody does it

Concept of liberation (moksha)

The concept of ultimate liberation in Hinduism is known as moksha. The Indian Hindu leader Swami Vivekenanda has said that in Hinduism, the greatest error is to let sin defeat you. In order to be liberated from the sin that holds a person back, the individual must find oneness with God in all that they think, feel, say and do. They must fulfil their duties and connect with God's spirit. This connection is achieved through meditation. This oneness with God brings liberation from earthly restraints, temptations and influences that can bind the spirit.

> The Vedanta recognises no sin it only recognises error. And the greatest error, says the Vedanta is to say that you are weak, that you are a sinner, a miserable creature, and that you have no power and you cannot do this and that.
>
> Swami Vivekenanda, Indian Hindu leader, 1863–1902

Bondage and liberation

- Bondage is being tied to the cycle of birth and death. Liberation is escape from this cycle through moksha.

- Bondage is viewed as the type of thinking that causes a person to put limits on themselves. They think that they cannot accomplish something or cope with a situation. Therefore, because of the negativity of their mind, they do not achieve their goals or have the strength to face difficult times.

- Liberation begins with retuning the mind to think differently, to believe that you can achieve a goal, that you are strong and that you do not have to be controlled by sin or negative thinking. This kind of attitude enables a person to achieve. There is a state of consciousness called Sat-Chit-Aanand-Svaroop (blissful consciousness that cannot be destroyed) that all Hindus try to achieve through meditation. This is union with God.

- Free will – every person has a choice over how they live and every person must face the consequences of what they think, feel and do.

- Through aligning one's mind and spirit with God, a person will make the right choices and achieve liberation from bondage. This is illustrated in the story of Valmiki, the author of the *Ramayana*. Valmiki, originally called Valya Koli, transformed himself from a highway robber into a saint through the power of thought and meditation. He meditated for so long that anthills literally grew around him, earning him the name Valmiki, which means 'anthill'.

Hinduism teaches that the power of the mind can lead to bondage or liberation. If you think negatively this will affect your performance, but if you use meditation and positive thought you are far more likely to achieve your goals. This kind of positive thinking can help performance in exams.

> **DID YOU KNOW?**
>
> The word for meditation in Hindi is dhyana. 'Dhya' means 'focus' and 'na' means 'no'. The aim of meditation is therefore to free your mind of any focus and be free of any thought. This is called a 'no mind state'.

Option C: Islam

C.1 Human life issues

LEARNING OUTCOMES

In this section you will learn to:

- discuss the Islamic teaching of the meaning and purpose of life
- discuss the concept of khilaafah (vicegerency) and its application to daily life
- examine issues related to justice, peace and human dignity as represented in Islam
- discuss the responsibilities and rights of individuals in areas of family life and work as reflected in Islam
- describe the concept of Ibaadah (worship) and its impact on daily life
- analyse the Islamic response to the social ills and inadequacies of society
- assess the Islamic answer to the socio-economic problems of society.

The meaning and purpose of life

Islam teaches that knowing (worshipping) God and attaining closeness to Him is the highest purpose of life. Muslims also believe that, on the earth, they have a duty to represent Allah to others. They are the means by which Allah can carry out His will and show His love. Muslims believe that humankind is also appointed by God to care for the world. The Qur'an records the angels objecting to God's decision to make men and women His representatives on earth due to their failings. However, Allah reassures the angels that He knows what they do not.

Muslims believe that Allah has trusted life to them. This does not mean that people will not make mistakes and get things wrong. However, Muslims have a duty to live their life well and in line with Allah's commands. When mistakes are made, the Qur'an teaches that Allah is merciful.

> Allah the Almighty has said: 'Whosoever shows enmity to a friend of Mine, I shall be at war with him. My servant does not draw near to Me with anything more loved by Me than the religious duties I have imposed upon him, and My servant continues to draw near to Me with supererogatory works so that I shall love him. When I love him I am his hearing with which he hears, his seeing with which he sees, his hand with which he strikes, and his foot with which he walks. Were he to ask [something] of Me, I would surely give it to him and were he to ask Me for refuge, I would surely grant him it'.
>
> Hadith 38

LINK 🔗

For an introduction to Islam, see Section 1, Essentials of religion, starting on page 2.

ACTIVITY

List three ways the Muslim faith helps to give purpose and meaning to life.

The purpose of life

And I have not created jinns and mean, except that they should serve (worship) Me.

Qur'an 51:56

Vicegerency of man

Islam teaches that people are God's representatives (or **vicegerents**) on the earth. Muslims are responsible for carrying out God's will on the earth and showing His rule, love and mercy to others. The Islamic term for this is khilaafah. Allah's first vicegerents on the earth were Adam and Eve.

Adam and Eve in the Qur'an

Allah created Adam and Eve and gave them knowledge so that they could act as His vicegerents on the earth. Adam and Eve were

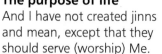

120

tested by Allah through being told not to approach a particular tree. However, Adam and Eve were persuaded by Satan to approach the tree. When Adam and Eve repented, Allah forgave them. He promised that He would guide Adam and Eve and that they would enjoy His blessing. Their responsibility was to obey and worship Him.

The Islamic understanding of Adam and Eve presents two important points in Islam:

- Adam and Eve are equal vicegerents (representatives) of Allah on earth. Therefore, both men and women are equally important, although they have different roles to play in society.
- All humankind is descended from Adam and Eve. This should lead to a shared humanity and respect for each other, regardless of colour of skin, language or ethnicity. This point is emphasised in 49:13 of the Qur'an, which declares that different nations were created to know each other and that it is a person's righteousness that matters to God.

> Behold your Lord said to the angels: 'I will create a vicegerent on earth.' They said: 'Will You place therein one who will make mischief therein and shed blood? – while we do celebrate Your praises and glorify Your holy (name)?' He said: 'I know what you do not know.'
>
> Qur'an 2:30

Issues related to value and dignity of human life

The Qur'an contains much teaching on how a Muslim should conduct themselves. Some of these teachings are considered below.

Justice

Qur'an 4:135 teaches the importance of upholding justice – even if this means speaking out against family members or friends who have done wrong, or admitting your own faults. The Qur'an also stresses the importance of following divine law rather than your own feelings and desires.

The heavenly and earthly balance

The Qur'an speaks of God's creation of the heavens and the earth, as well as his control over it. Qur'an 55:7–9 and 57:4 describe the balance of justice that God has set and his observance of people's actions.

The value of human life

> On that account: We ordained for the Children of Israel that if any one slew a person – unless it be for murder or for spreading mischief in the land – it would be as if he slew the whole people: and if any one saved a life, it would be as if he saved the life of the whole people. Then although there came to them Our Messengers with Clear Signs, yet, even after that, many of them continued to commit excesses in the land.
>
> Qur'an 5:32

This verse highlights the value of a human life through comparing the death of one person to the death of a whole nation.

Peace is integral to Islam and references to it can be found throughout the religion. A name of Allah is As-Salaam-Peace. The Muslim greeting As Salaamu Alaikum means 'peace be upon you' and one of the names of paradise means 'the Abode of Peace'. However, most importantly, the word 'Islam' means 'peace and submission' and the word 'Muslim' means 'one who is peaceful and submissive'.

The goals of Shariah

Muslims believe that Shariah law provides all that a person needs in order to live a righteous life. The goals of Shariah are the preservation of: human life, dignity, intellect, property, religion and progeny (offspring). The importance and role of Shariah is outlined in Qur'an 45:18 and 57:25.

The concept of peace

> Do no mischief on the earth, after it has been set in order, but call on Him with fear and longing (in your hearts): for the mercy of God is (always) near to those who do good.
>
> Qur'an 7:56

Nobility and brotherhood of man

At many points the Qur'an reminds readers that they are all created from a single source and that all people share the same nobility and rights (see Qur'an 4:1).

Mercy to the young

The Qur'an demands that a Muslim show mercy to the young, in particular orphans, who should be cared for until they reach an age where they can care for themselves. Commands regarding children and orphans can be found in Qur'an 4:6 and 6:151–152.

The Qur'an teaches that Muslims should show mercy to orphans. These orphans are being cared for at an Islamic orphanage.

Care for the aged

Your Lord has decreed that you worship none but Him, and that you be kind to parents. Whether one or both of them attain old age with thee, say not to them a word of contempt, nor repel them, but address them in terms of honour. And, out of kindness, lower to them the wing of humility and say: 'My Lord! Bestow on them Your mercy even as they cherished me in childhood.'

Qur'an 17:23–24

Care for the sick

Charity is an important concept in Islam and, through the Hadith, Muhammad teaches that everyone is able to give something, regardless of their wealth or position in life: visiting the sick is charity, worshipping Allah is charity, caring for those in need is charity, speaking out against wrongdoing is charity. In these ways, every Muslim can carry out charitable work.

Care for animals and the environment

CASE STUDY	Looking to the future

Aadam, aged 14, is involved in a school project to clean up the local area. He and his classmates have been split into groups to carry out tasks such as clearing litter, planting shrubs and vegetables, and setting up water butts to collect rainwater.

Aadam knows that caring for the environment is something that his faith requires. Allah has appointed humans as his vicegerents on the earth to care for the environment, plants and animals. One of the Hadith declares that 'Whoever plants a tree and diligently looks after it until it matures and bears fruit is rewarded.' And the Qur'an commands Muslims not to damage or alter Allah's creation (Qur'an 30:30). Aadam is proud of the importance his faith places on caring for the environment. But he knows that all religions teach that caring for the environment is important. This is one way that different faiths can work together.

Some of Aadam's classmates have put together a presentation for the local community about the importance of caring for the environment. The class have invited parents and leaders from the local community to come along. During the presentation, Aadam's classmates will give examples of how everyone can care for the environment and they will explain that it is everyone's responsibility to protect the earth, whatever religion they follow, or even if they follow no religion at all.

Aadam and his classmates know that if the world is not looked after today, then future generations will suffer.

Aadam and his classmates are acting on the Islamic teaching to care for the environment

Care for animals

The Prophet was asked if acts of charity even to the animals were rewarded by the Almighty. He replied: 'Yes, there is a reward for acts of charity to every beast alive.'

Hadith

Roles, responsibilities and rights in family life and work

Family

Family is central to Islamic teaching. When the human race began, Allah told Adam to procreate (produce children) and Muslims still regard having children as an important responsibility in order to continue the

Guidelines for husbands and wives

Men are the protectors and maintainers of women, because God has given the one more (strength) than the other, and because they support them from their means. Therefore the righteous women are devoutly obedient, and guard in (the husband's) absence what God would have them guard. As to those women on whose part you fear disloyalty and ill-conduct, admonish them (first), (next) refuse to share their beds, (and last) beat them (lightly); but if they return to obedience, do not seek against them means (of annoyance): for God is Most High, Great (above you all).

Qur'an 4:34

human race and grow the Islam faith. In Islam, each member of the family has a role to play. It is important for everyone to fulfil their role in order for the family to function peacefully. Respect of and care for the vulnerable – including children and the elderly – is required by Islam.

Husband and wife

Islam teaches that husbands should protect and support their wives and that women should obey their husbands. The Qur'an contains guidelines for disciplining women for wrong behaviour. However, this should always be done kindly and in the best interests of the woman. The first action should always be to speak to the woman about her behaviour and give her a chance to change her ways before any other discipline is used (4:34).

Parents and children

The Qur'an teaches that children should respect and honour their parents and care for them in their old age. Islamic teaching recognises the important role that parents play in their children's development and advises that this care is repaid by children when their parents need them (17:23–25).

Extended family, relatives and neighbours

The Qur'an teaches that Muslims should be kind with their wealth and their time. A Muslim's first responsibility is to provide for their parents and family. In addition though, Muslims should care for others in need such as orphans, travellers and widows, particularly if these people are fellow Muslims.

Employers and employees

Islam promotes hard work and employment and teaches that all people should be treated with respect. Employers should respect the rights of their employees and employees should work hard for their employers. At all times, contractual agreements should be met. Al-Tirmidhi Hadith 2987 says: 'Give the hireling his wages before his sweat dries'.

The dignity of labour

Muhammad is recorded as saying: 'It is better for any of you to take your rope and bring a bundle of wood and sell it (in which case Allah will guard your honour), than to beg of people, who may give Him or reject Him'. In other words, a Muslim should always aim to work for their living.

The Qur'an teaches that Muslims should work hard in honest employment to earn their living

Ibaadah and its impact on daily life

Pervasiveness of worship

The Qur'an teaches that the single most important purpose of humankind is to worship Allah. Serving and worshipping Allah should influence everything that a Muslim does.

Social ethics and interaction

Islam teaches that people should get along with each other, respecting one another as fellow human beings and treating each other in the way in which they would wish to be treated. In particular, the Qur'an teaches that people should not:

- gossip about each other
- be sarcastic to one another
- be suspicious of each other
- spy or eavesdrop on each other
- criticise one another or put each other down.

The Qur'an often reminds readers that all humankind comes from the same single source and has equal rights.

Social responsibilities

It is not righteousness that you turn your faces toward East or West; but it is righteousness – to believe in God and the Last Day, and the Angels, and the Book, and the Messengers; to spend of your substance, out of love for Him, for your kin, for orphans, for the needy, for the wayfarer, for those who ask, and for the ransom of slaves; to be steadfast in prayer, and practice regular charity; to fulfil the contracts which you have made; and to be firm and patient, in pain (or suffering) and adversity and throughout all periods of panic. Such are the people of truth, those who fear God.

Qur'an 2:177

Moral behaviour and decency

God commands justice, the doing of good, and liberality to kith and kin, and He forbids all shameful deeds, and injustice and rebellion: He instructs you, that you may receive **admonition**.

Qur'an 16:90

ACTIVITY

Write out this verse in your own words, to explain what it teaches about moral behaviour and decency.

Salah and its relationship with human activities

The Qur'an outlines the importance of being humble and of praying regularly. However, the Qur'an also teaches that prayer on its own is not enough. Prayer must be accompanied by moral living and righteous actions in order for Muslims to gain favour with Allah.

Zikr (constant remembrance of God)

One of the teachings of Islam is that Muslims should constantly remember God and 'celebrate His praises' wherever they may be and whatever they may be doing. Praying five times each day is one practical way that Muslims follow this teaching.

Response to social ills and inadequacies

Child abuse

Islam forbids any abuse of power and it has particular guidance on how parents should treat their children. The Qur'an forbids parents from killing their children. This may seem extreme but, in the time in which the Qur'an was written, human sacrifice did occur. This teaching also applies to the forbidding of abortion. The Qur'an teaches that parents should provide for their children, love them and treat them fairly.

Substance abuse and gambling

The Qur'an makes it clear that Muslims should not drink alcohol or gamble. Such things are considered to be created by Satan to distract Muslims from the worship of God and to cause disharmony.

These Muslim volunteers are working through the charity Islamic Relief to prepare food for families in need

Poverty

The Qur'an contains much teaching on the responsibility of Muslims to give generously to those in need. In 2:268 Allah reminds his followers that, although Satan threatens poverty and tries to convince people not to show generosity, Allah promises his followers forgiveness and bounties (rewards). This verse reminds Muslims that God cares for them so they can care for others, trusting Allah to provide for their needs.

Prejudice and discrimination

A Muslim should not speak badly of others, gossip, defame (attack somebody's reputation), be suspicious towards each other or speak sarcastically to another. Instead, the Qur'an encourages Muslims to deal fairly with one another and to practise justice. Muslims are warned not to let hatred of others lead them to sin.

Spousal abuse

Muslims are forbidden to force women to marry, or to treat their wives harshly. The Qur'an instructs men to treat their wives fairly and with kindness. It is rare in the Caribbean for a Muslim to take a second wife, but for Muslims that do, they should not take anything away from the first wife. Wives are expected to respect and obey their husbands. Lewdness or disobedience is a form of spousal abuse.

Violence and crime

Islam teaches that violence and killing is not acceptable unless this is a punishment for murder or another serious criminal act. The Qur'an likens killing one person to killing all of humanity, and saving one person to saving all of humanity.

The Qur'an promotes decent, lawful conduct and Shariah law allows for harsh punishments for those who commit crime and wage war against Islam. However, the Qur'an also points out that if a person repents, Muslims should remember that God is forgiving and merciful, and they should show these same qualities.

Islamic answers to socio-economic problems

Islam holds important lessons to enable society to function effectively. Some of these are described below.

Zakah

Zakah (compulsory charity) is one of the Five Pillars of Islam. The importance of Muslims giving to charity has already been outlined in Topic 6.3, Major teachings of Islam. The Qur'an teaches that Muslims should give alms to those in need as well as being willing to accept alms themselves if they are in need. Qur'an 9:103 describes how taking alms, even from sinful people, can help to purify and sanctify the giver. Charitable giving does not just have to involve money. The Qur'an also outlines the importance of praying for others, and of giving time and energy to build a good society.

Charity and support for the destitute

Qur'an 2:261 describes how those who give of themselves (through wealth, time and energy) will receive back from Allah. This concept of God blessing those who are willing to give is also present in many other religions, including Christianity.

Interest-free banking

The Qur'an forbids the lending or borrowing of money with interest being charged. Islam promotes trade but not **usury.**

Exploitation of labour

Muslims believe that Allah knows all things and decrees what happens to us in our life on earth. This means that no one can boast about what they have achieved or despair over opportunities they have missed as it is God who controls all things. Muslims should work hard but not exploit others or allow themselves to be exploited – achievement lies in God's hands.

Islam teaches that a Muslim should show charity to those in need

The Holy Qur'an

In this section you will learn to:

- explain the preservation, transmission and compilation of the Qur'an
- discuss the importance of the Arabic language in understanding the message of the Qur'an
- discuss the miraculous nature of the Qur'an revealed to Prophet Muhammad
- discuss the main tenets presented in the Qur'an
- explain the role of the Hadith as the second source of guidance along with the Qur'an
- discuss the teachings of the Qur'an and Hadith on daily life.

ACTIVITY

Memorisation is not just a Muslim practice. Jews and Christians often memorise favourite or significant parts of their scriptures too. Have a go yourself. Try memorising some of the verses from the Qur'an that are given in this guide – it may be useful to quote these in your exam.

Can you think of some benefits of having the Qur'an written down as well as it being transmitted and preserved orally?

The Qur'an was revealed to Muhammad by the Angel Jibril. It was revealed in stages over 23 years of Muhammad's life. The Qur'an is the ultimate authority for Muslims on Islamic doctrine (belief) and law.

Preservation, transmission and compilation of the Qur'an

Muhammad received his first revelation in the cave of Hira outside Makkah while meditating. During this revelation, the Angel Jibril instructed Muhammad to read. In 96:1–5 the Qur'an echoes this command where it instructs people to read and credits Allah with giving man knowledge, including the knowledge to write. The words that were revealed from Allah to Muhammad through the Angel Jibril began to be memorised, recorded and compiled during the lifetime of Muhammad by his companions. The students of Muhammad's companions then memorised the Qur'an from the companions. In this way, the Qur'an was transmitted and preserved. Care was taken to ensure that the words memorised and recorded were the exact words of Allah, as received from Muhammad.

Preservation of the Qur'an

It is vitally important to Muslims that the Qur'an is preserved and protected.

- Many Muslims read the entire Qur'an each month in order to memorise its words.
- Usually from around the age of six Muslim children begin learning the Qur'an.
- Some Muslim children have memorised the Qur'an by age seven.
- The Qur'an is memorised in Arabic since this is the original language it was transmitted in.
- **Oral transmission** is the most important mode of transmission and preservation of the Qur'an. The Qur'an in written form is an additional means of preservation and comes second to oral transmission.
- Memorisation means that, even if the printed Qur'an disappears, the words of the Qur'an can never be lost. Putting the words of the Qur'an into practice is another way of preserving its teachings.
- Ultimately, whatever human efforts are made, Allah gives assurance that He Himself will preserve and protect the Qur'an. For this reason, Muslims believe its words are indestructible.

Transmission and compilation of the Qur'an

During Muhammad's life the Prophet recited new sections of the Qur'an as they were revealed to him. His followers then learnt these revelations and wrote them down. Records show that 29 scribes wrote down Muhammad's revelations throughout his life. By the time

Muhammad died (632 CE) the entire Qur'an had been written down, although not collated together. As time passed, and many of the people who had memorised the Qur'an died, Muhammad's successor (Khalifah), Abu Bakr, decided that the teachings of the Qur'an needed to be preserved. The Khalifah ordered that all of Muhammad's revelations be compiled into one complete work. Years later, the third Khalifah, Uthman, ordered that copies be made of the Qur'an and distributed around the Muslim world. This official copy of the Qur'an became known as the Uthmani manuscript. This is considered the authentic reference point for all future copies.

The Qur'an was originally written in Arabic. Muslims believe that all other language versions reveal only the Qur'an's meaning rather than being the Qur'an itself.

Names, attributes and structure of the Qur'an

The Qur'an is described in many different ways, which help to describe its attributes (qualities) including:

- the Criterion (a principle or standard that something is judged by)
- the Message
- a healing or a mercy.

Although not a name or attribute of the Qur'an, the initials ALM appear frequently in the Qur'an. Their meaning is known only to Allah.

The Qur'an is organised into chapters (called surahs) and verses (called ayahs). This enables people to easily refer to particular sections or teachings in the Qur'an.

The Arabic language as the language of the Qur'an

Muslims believe that the Qur'an remains exactly as it was revealed to Muhammad. It is forbidden to add to, change or take away anything from the recorded revelation of Allah that forms the Qur'an.

The Qur'an has been translated into many different languages, often with commentaries to help explain its meaning. These versions are considered to be interpretations of the Qur'an rather than being the Qur'an itself. In 43:2–3 the Qur'an describes itself as a 'book that makes things clear – written in Arabic.' For Muslims, only the Arabic manuscript is the Holy Qur'an itself.

The Qur'an as the Permanent Miracle revealed to Muhammad

Muslims believe that Allah has performed miracles through all of the prophets (e.g. parting the Red Sea through Moses and healing those who were ill through Jesus), but the Qur'an, revealed to Prophet Muhammad, is considered by Muslims to be the greatest miracle.

The Qur'an responds to those who doubt that it is **kalaamullah** (the Perfect Words of Allah) by challenging them to compose even one ayah (verse) to compare to the Qur'an's words. It highlights the fact that the Qur'an is perfectly composed and does not contain discrepancies as proof that its words come from God. The Qur'an is sometimes referred to as the Permanent Miracle as Muslims believe it to be Allah's final revelation. Muslims claim that its profound teachings and guidance remain as relevant today as they were when they were first revealed and will still be in the future.

> And we have indeed made the Qur'an easy to understand and remember: then is there any that will receive admonition?
>
> Qur'an 54:40

> The true and well-formulated message of your Lord has now been completed, and none is able to change it.
>
> Qur'an 6:115

DID YOU KNOW?

There are different types of Arabic writing in the Qur'an including:

- Faseeha and Fusha – pure Arabic language. Fusha is the classical (purer) form of Arabic language and Faseeha is the modern standard Arabic language (used in newspapers etc.). The Qur'an is written in Fusha Arabic.
- Balaga – rhetoric or poetic expression in the Arabic language.

Uloomul Qur'an is a science of the Qur'an itself.

Writings recorded in the Qur'an

The revelations recorded in the Qur'an contain direct teaching, for example 4:163–165, as well as historical accounts of conversations and incidents. An example is the conversation between Moses and Pharaoh recorded in Qur'an 26. Archaeological and historical discoveries are also recorded in the Qur'an:

• In the first verses of Qur'an 30 the defeat of the Roman Empire is recorded – a prediction that later came true.
• In Qur'an 10 the account is given of Pharaoh's life being saved as a sign of Allah's power.
• Qur'an 11 records Noah and the flood.

Finally, the Qur'an contains scientific writing and facts that point to Allah's creation, power and control of the universe. Examples include:

• an accurate description of the foetus in a time when there was no scientific knowledge of this
• wind being used as a means of pollination.

The Qur'an points out that animals and plants are made by God and provide humankind with food and drink. The Qur'an also illustrates Allah's rule by pointing out the details of creation.

Main tenets of the Qur'an

The Qur'an contains some tenets or principles on which its teachings stand, which are outlined below.

Views of Allah

The Qur'an depicts Allah as the one eternal God – all-knowing and all-powerful – who guards and directs his creation, particularly humankind. Qur'an 2:255 describes Allah:

> God! There is no god but He, the Living, the Self-subsisting, Eternal. No slumber can seize Him, nor sleep. His are all things in the heavens and on earth.

Qur'an 2:255

Views of man

The Qur'an states that mankind's origins come from God, who created man from a clot of blood and created a mate for him so as to populate the earth. Muslims believe that all human beings are descendants of Adam. The purpose of humankind is to worship God so that all nations and people will live in peace and harmony (Qur'an 49:13). The creation of different races, different-coloured skin and different languages is seen as a sign of Allah's power and creativity. Finally, and arguably the tenet that all of the Islamic faith is based on, is that humankind is made to worship God.

Views of life

The Qur'an contains teachings and laws for all aspects of life, to enable people to live peacefully with God and with each other. Some of the areas that the Qur'an contains clear instructions on are:

- what a Muslim can and cannot eat (Qur'an 5:3)
- that a person should follow the religion of Islam (Qur'an 3:19, 85)
- that humankind should follow the regulations and teachings of the Qur'an and not their own vain desires (Qur'an 5:47–49)
- to abstain from using drugs or alcohol (Qur'an 5:90–91)
- to deal fairly in trade and business (Qur'an 83:1–3).

The Hadith: the second source of guidance

The relationship between the Qur'an and the Hadith

The Hadith is a record of the sayings, actions and approvals of Muhammad. It is the second most important reference point for Islamic doctrine and guidance after the Qur'an. Although the words of the Hadith are not viewed as part of Muhammad's revelation from Allah, the Qur'an states that all of Muhammad's words are influenced by God. Therefore, whatever Muhammad says or does can be used for instruction and guidance. Qur'an 4:64 states that Muhammad is God's messenger and that both God and Muhammad should be obeyed.

The Hadith as a source of Islamic law

Along with the Qur'an, the Hadith is used as a source of Islamic law. In Qur'an 59:7 Muslims are instructed to 'take what the Messenger assigns to you, and deny yourselves that which he withholds from you'. In other words, Muslims are expected to look to Muhammad's teachings and example as their guide in life. Qur'an 4:58–59 encourages Muslims to look to Muhammad's teaching to solve disputes and for guidance on matters of justice.

The collection and classification of the Hadith

The actions and teachings of Muhammad chosen to form the Hadith went through a selection procedure to discern genuine recordings from those that were false. Two genuine collections of Hadith resulted. These are known as the Bukhari collection and the Muslim collection.

In order to be genuine, a Hadith was required to meet three criteria:

- The narrators must have met each other.
- The narrators must not be known to be liars or evil doers.
- The narrators must be known to have strong memories.

The authenticity of the Hadith is decided by looking mainly at its chain of narrators (sanad). Once it can be ascertained that what the narrators are reporting is truthful, without any breakage in the chain, then that Hadith is considered genuine.

All of Muhammad's words, practices, habits and approvals that regulate Islamic belief and practice can be considered to make up the Sunnah. The Sunnah contains the Hadith (narrations of the sayings and actions of Muhammad) as well as an account of Muhammad's way of life. The Hadith are graded by scholars according to their reliability into the following classifications:

The Qur'an contains clear instructions about what Muslims may and may not eat. Many Caribbean islands contain halal shops selling food permitted for Muslims to eat.

DID YOU KNOW?

Many people have compiled Hadith, but An-Nawawi's 40 Hadith is the most well known. It is a selection of 42 Hadith that the scholar An-Nawawi chose, considering them the most important Hadith in Islam. He believed that, together, these Hadith give guidance on a broad spectrum of important issues in life.

- Sahih – sound
- Hasan – good
- Da'if – weak or infirm

ACTIVITY

How do you think the Hadith were recorded and kept alive?

Teachings of the Qur'an and the Hadith for daily life

Daily conduct

The Hadith have a lot to say about good conduct and righteous living. Hadith 20 instructs that our conscience play a part in controlling our deeds. Hadith 24 goes on to say that we can all show acts of charity through the things we say and do and the way we treat others. Hadith 34 contains specific instructions for how a Muslim should respond to evil and wrongdoing.

Good will wipe out bad
Fear Allah wherever you are, and follow up a bad deed with a good one and it will wipe it out, and behave well towards people.
Hadith 18

Prayer and worship

Islam, like all other religions, requires its followers to have faith in what cannot be seen. The Qur'an teaches that those who exercise such faith through prayer are rewarded and that Allah hears all prayers uttered. The Hadith contain teaching on how a Muslim should pray, and the Qur'an explains how to prepare for prayer in unusual circumstances, such as when travelling (4:43). The overall message on prayer and worship, from the Qur'an and Hadith, is that Muslims should constantly remember God (zikr), pray often (salah) and come to Allah with their needs (dua).

CASE STUDY | Broken promises

Maryam has been mean to her best friend Sarah. Now Sarah will not speak to her and both girls are feeling sad.

Maryam's mother reminded Maryam of the lesson that Hadith 18 teaches – that wrong deeds should always be followed up by good deeds. Maryam also remembers the verses she read in the Qur'an last week about speaking well (17:53). Maryam is sorry that she was mean to Sarah, but she is grateful for the guidance of the Qur'an. She is doing what she can to put things right.

Maryam has written Sarah a letter to apologise and has invited her over for dinner. Maryam has also used some of the money she has been saving to buy Sarah a friendship bracelet. All Maryam can do now is wait – and hope that Sarah will remember the Qur'an and Hadith teachings on forgiveness!

Hadith 18 teaches that a wrong deed should be followed up by a good deed

Social responsibility

Respecting and taking seriously your social responsibility creates harmony in society. Where people do not practise social responsibility, disharmony and chaos can quickly build. The Qur'an has much to say about how to act with social responsibility (17:22–37). It also contains guidance for how to respond to wrong behaviour (49:6–13). Hadith 14 teaches that there are three instances of antisocial behaviour where a Muslim can be punished. These are:

- adultery
- murder
- stealing.

Punishment helps a person to take their sin seriously and think twice before committing the act again. It also acts as a deterrent to others. Muslims are required to follow the law of the land in which they live in relation to forms of punishments.

The Qur'an speaks much more about what Muslims should do in order to live a righteous life and create a harmonious society, than about how the unrighteous should be punished. Below are two examples of Hadith on social responsibility.

> Righteousness is good morality, and wrongdoing is that which wavers in your soul and which you dislike people finding out about.
>
> Hadith 26

> None of you [truly] believes until he wishes for his brother what he wishes for himself.
>
> Hadith 13

Day-to-day life

The Qur'an and Hadith contain much guidance on day-to-day issues such as diet, dress, sexuality, homes, art and entertainment:

- Qur'an 5:3–5 instructs Muslims on what they are permitted to eat. Hunted animals may be eaten, but they must still be halal. Pork, meat that contains blood, or animals slaughtered by non-halal means are not permitted.
- Muslims are only permitted to marry other Muslims or 'People of the Book' (Jews and Christians).
- The Qur'an requires modest dress and commands that at certain times of day members of a household should seek permission before approaching their elders (as they may be in a state of undress).
- The Qur'an encourages dining in each other's homes.
- The Qur'an states that there is no shame in disability (Qur'an 24:61).

Hadith 6 summarises the law for Muslims by stating that, if there is any doubt about whether something is lawful or not, a Muslim should avoid it.

ACTIVITY

Using some of the references from the Qur'an and Hadith in this topic, write up a brief instruction sheet for humanity based on Islamic teaching.

Teaching on responding to evil

Whosoever of you sees an evil action, let him change it with his hand; and if

he is not able to do so, then with his tongue; and if he is not able to do so,

then with his heart; and that is the weakest of faith.

Hadith 34

C.3

The concept of Allah (God)

LEARNING OUTCOMES

In this section you will learn to:

- discuss the concept of Tawhid
- explain belief in the angels
- explain belief in the divine scripture
- discuss the concept of prophethood
- explain belief in the hereafter
- explain belief in Al-Qadr (divine decree)
- examine the relationship between Allah and His servants.

ACTIVITY

Look up Qur'an 23:1–9 and 70:22–34. What are some of the specific actions and attitudes of Tawhid that God will honour and reward?

But verily over you (are appointed angels) to protect you – Kind and honourable – writing down (your deeds):
They know (and understand) all that you do.

Qur'an 82:10–12

Concept of Tawhid

The concept of Tawhid in Islam is the belief that there is just one God. This God (Allah) that Muslims worship is the same God that appeared before Abraham and is also the God of the Jews and the Christians (Qur'an 2:133). The Qur'an teaches that those Muslims who practice worship, prayer and righteousness will be honoured by God and inherit paradise after this life.

The following are the three aspects to Tawhid.

Tawhid al Rububiyyah (Unity of Lordship)

Say, He is God, the One and Only;
God, the Eternal, Absolute;
He begets not, nor is He begotten;
And there is none like unto Him.

Qur'an 112:1–4

Tawhid al Ulluhiyyah (Unity of worship)

Your Lord has decreed that you worship none but Him, and that you be kind to parents.

Qur'an 17:23

Tawhid al Asma wa al Sifaat (Unity of His names and attributes)

God! There is no god but He! To Him belong the Most Beautiful Names.

Qur'an 20:8

Belief in the angels

Islam teaches that angels were created by light. It was an angel (Jibril) who brought the message of the Qur'an to Muhammad. The Qur'an describes the angels as constantly worshipping Allah and having wings. In 4:97 the Qur'an describes how angels completely follow Allah's commands, including overseeing punishment of those who do not follow Allah's commands. It is also the duty of angels to take the souls of those who die (Qur'an 4:97) and to record the words and actions of humans. The Qur'an describes two angels watching over every person and writing down everything that person says or does (Qur'an 50:17–18).

Belief in divine scripture

The concept of revelation

The Qur'an repeatedly speaks of how Allah has given revelation (wahi) to God's messengers and prophets, including Nuh, Ibrahim,

Jacob, Solomon and Isa (Qur'an 4:163). These revelations are to guide Muslims and to confirm previous revelations. Since these scriptures are believed to be divine, it is important for Muslims to follow and obey the instructions contained in them. The Qur'an warns what will happen to anyone who fakes revelation from Allah (Qur'an 6:93).

The previous books and the Qur'an as the final revelation

Qur'an 6 describes how Allah gave messages and guidance to people other than Muhammad – prophets such as Ibrahim, Isaac, Nuh, Musa and Dawud. Muslims also believe that previous 'books', such as Exodus (containing the Ten Commandments) and the Psalms, are important and sacred. However, Muslims believe that the Qur'an is the final revelation and the only scripture that has not been altered from the original revelation. In 92:6, the Qur'an declares that its writings are a confirmation of all the revelations that have come before. The Qur'an describes itself as the final and 'most accurate' revelation from God (17:9).

The concept of prophethood

Islam believes in the same Old Testament prophets that Christianity and Judaism recognise. Muslims also believe that John the Baptist and Isa (Jesus), whose words and actions are recorded in the biblical New Testament, were prophets appointed by Allah. In Qur'an 6:82–90, prophets including Dawud, Solomon, Nuh, Ibrahim, Zechariah, John and Isa are recognised as having been given favour and guidance by Allah.

ACTIVITY

Which divine scriptures do Christianity, Judaism and Islam share? Make a table comparing them.

> And indeed, We sent Nuh and Ibrahim, and placed in their offspring prophethood and Scripture. And among them there are some who are guided; but many of them are rebellious.
>
> Qur'an 57:26 (Tafsir Ibn Kathir translation)

Attributes and qualities of prophets

- The prophets were normal people who walked, talked, ate and slept like anyone else (Qur'an 25:20).
- Prophets give glory and praise to Allah rather than seeking it for themselves (Qur'an 3:79–80).
- Prophets' words should be obeyed. Prophets have the right to ask for God's forgiveness on behalf of those who come to them in repentance (Qur'an 4:64).
- A prophet is always trustworthy (Qur'an 3:161).

The role of prophets

Allah called His prophets to bring both glad tidings and warnings to the nations of earth. The Qur'an also states that Allah gave the prophets revelation, which is the Qur'an and the Books that came before it, to reveal the truth and by which disputes could be settled and judgements made.

This is the cave in the mountains near Makkah where Muhammad is believed to have received his first revelation

The abbreviation PBUH, that Muslims write after Muhammad's name, stands for Peace Be upon Him, and shows recognition of Muhammad as a prophet.

Prophet Muhammad

Muslims believe that Muhammad is the final and most important prophet. He came to complete the revelation from God that had begun with the prophets before him. The Qur'an describes Muhammad's message as universal (Qur'an 34:28) and describes Muhammad as the Messenger of God and Seal of all the Prophets (Qur'an 33:40), a sanctifier and instructor (Qur'an 62:2), as having God and the angels' blessings (Qur'an 33:56) and as an example to follow (Qur'an 33:21). By studying Muhammad's life (known as his seerah or 'journey') Muslims believe that Muhammad's prophethood (divine role and purpose) is revealed.

Belief in the hereafter

Death and immortality of the soul

The Qur'an states that every human body and soul will die but be resurrected on the Day of Judgement. The Qur'an points out that a person only dies when God wills it (3:145). On the Day of Judgement, a person will be judged according to their actions. Through the mercy and compassion of Allah, those who have worshipped God and lived their life well will enter the garden of paradise. It is the purpose of a Muslim's life on earth to love God and fulfil the requirements to enter heaven. Those that have served God in their life on earth will be rewarded in the life to come.

Qur'an 102 warns of the dangers of being distracted by the riches and pleasures of this world, which lead to death. In 23:100, the Qur'an makes it clear that no one will be permitted to revisit the earth after their death to put right any wrongs they have committed. After death, a person remains in the grave until the time comes for them to be judged. This time is called the barzakh. Islam teaches that everyone will have to give an account of their actions in the hereafter – no one can escape the judgement of Allah.

The Last Days

There are a number of Hadith that describe what will happen on earth before the **Last Day** comes:

- Increased fighting: 'The world will not come to an end until a day would come to the people on which there will be general massacre and bloodshed.' (Muslim collection)
- Destruction: 'Great cities will be ruined and it will be as if they had not existed the day before.' (Al-Muttaqi al-Hindi, Al-Burhan fi Alamat al-Mahdi Akhir al-Zaman)
- Earthquakes: 'The hour (Last Day) will not be established until … earthquakes will be very frequent.' (Bukhari collection)

There are also more specific signs of the last days, such as the coming of the antichrist (Masih-ad-dajjaal), the dukhan (smoke) and the rising of the sun in the west. The verses opposite describe what will happen on earth in the Last Day. The Qur'an though also gives assurance that, although the world will seem in turmoil, Allah will remain in control:

The Last Days on earth

When the sky is cleft asunder;
When the stars are scattered;
When the oceans are suffered to burst forth;
And when the graves are turned upside down;
(Then) shall each soul know what it has sent forward and (what it has) kept back

Qur'an 82:1–5

the whole of the earth will be but His handful, and the heavens will be rolled up in His Right Hand

Qur'an 39:67

The Qur'an then goes on to describe two trumpet blasts when everything in heaven and on earth will swoon (faint) before God.

Muslims believe that more frequent natural disasters, along with increased fighting in the world over the last century, are signs that the Last Days are not far away

Reward and punishment

The Qur'an warns that, on the Day of Judgement, it will be too late for sinners to repent and plead for mercy. Qur'an 39:69–75 tells how prophets and witnesses will be allowed to make intercession for people to enable them to enter Paradise. Those who have rejected God and have ignored the signs and messages that He has sent will be punished for eternity in hell – a place of fierce fire (77:31). Those who have feared God and accepted His messages will be rewarded by entering the Gardens of heaven where they will

recline in the (Garden) on raised thrones, they will see neither the sun's (excessive heat) nor excessive cold. And the shades of the (Garden) will come low over them, and the bunches of (fruit) there will hang low in humility.

Qur'an 76:13–14

Belief in Al-Qadr (Divine Decree)

Muslims believe that Allah knows and wills all things – on the earth, in the sea and in the heavens no creature, plant or even grain exists without Allah's knowledge. The Qur'an speaks of God keeping a record of all things (22:70) and of no event occurring that God did not know about in advance (57:22).

However, God's involvement does not stop with Him simply knowing about what will happen on the earth. The Qur'an describes how Allah has a Divine Will that is played out on earth. Qur'an 2:253 speaks of God's plan being fulfilled through generations fighting over

ACTIVITY

Muslims believe that divine decree is not an excuse to commit wrong and blame God's will, since no one knows in advance what is ordained. A person simply chooses to take an action or not. However, the tension between predestination and divine or free will is something that many people struggle with.

To help you explore these tensions, draw up a table. On one side write all of the arguments you can think of to support an Islamic view of free will (e.g. if it was not for free will, surely Allah would make everyone Muslim) and on the other side write all of the reasons you can think of to support predestination (e.g. what is the point of Allah's power if he cannot control anything?).

their differing beliefs. The Qur'an declares that if God had so willed, He could have stopped the fighting. In 82:29 we learn that a person only has free will to make their own decisions because God gives that will. We are all ultimately subject to God's will over whether we live or die, whether the earth continues or ends, even our choice to do something or not, comes from God.

The Qur'an describes how God alone made the earth, without help from a partner or a begotten son (as is believed in Christianity). Not only did God create all things, including human beings, but He also sustains all things – choosing when life should come to an end. All is under God's divine decree.

Relationship between Allah and His servants

Ibaadah (worship)

As outlined at various points in this guide, Muslims believe that their purpose in life is to worship God – that is why they were made. This point is repeatedly made in the Qur'an. But the Qur'an is specific about the type of worship that people should bring to God. Muslims should be sincere in their devotion to God and should pray regularly. But it is not enough simply to show devotion to Allah through their words. Muslims should worship through their actions: giving regularly to charity and showing kindness to others.

Salah (prayers)

The Qur'an outlines the importance of regular prayer in maintaining a sure and strong faith. Frequently the Qur'an uses the word 'steadfast' when it speaks of prayer – encouraging people to pray patiently and with perseverance.

The Qur'an also gives practical guidance for how to approach prayer:

- A person's mind should be clear.
- A person's body should be pure (having undergone wudu).
- If a person is travelling or ill or has come from a place of impurity and is unable to find water, clean sand or earth can be rubbed on the face and hands to cleanse the person before prayer.

As well as telling a person that they should pray and giving guidance on how to pray, the Qur'an describes the benefits of prayer:

> for prayer restrains from shameful and unjust deeds; and remembrance of God is the greatest (thing in life) without doubt. And God knows the (deeds) that you do.

> Qur'an 29:45

> This is the Book; in it is guidance sure, without doubt, to those who fear Allah.

> Who believe in the Unseen, are steadfast in prayer, and spend out of what We have provided for them.

> Qur'an 2:2–3

How and when to pray

Celebrate (constantly) the praises of your Lord, before the rising of the sun, and before its setting; yes, celebrate them for part of the hours of the night, and at the sides of the day: that you may have (spiritual) joy.

> Qur'an 20:130

Zakah (charity)

Just as the Qur'an requires Muslims to practice regular prayer, so it also instructs followers to practice regular charity. The Qur'an goes on to promise that God sees all and that we will be rewarded for what we do for others (2:110). Muslims should not be choosy about who they show charity to. The Qur'an states that a person should show charity not just to their family and friends but to 'those who ask' (2:177) – in other words, anyone!

> And be steadfast in prayer and regular in charity: and whatever good you send forth for your souls before you, you shall find it with Allah, for Allah sees well all that you do.

> Qur'an 2:110

Sawm (fasting)

Although fasting during Ramadan is a requirement of the Qur'an for Muslims, it is not meant to cause undue suffering. If anyone is ill or travelling, pregnant or too young or old to complete the fast, they are excused. They may make up the fast at a later date or miss it altogether and feed a poor Muslim for every day of the fast that they miss instead. During Ramadan Muslims are permitted to eat and drink between nightfall and daybreak. Husbands and wives are also permitted to partake in sexual relations during this time, although not if they are taking part in retreats (I'tikaaf) in mosques, which last for the final 10 days of Ramadan (Qur'an 2:183–185, 187).

CASE STUDY	Trip of a lifetime

Next year, Muhammad will be celebrating Eid ul Adha during Hajj with his dad. Muhammad is already busy planning the trip and he is getting very excited!

Hajj is an opportunity to be part of a group of millions of pilgrims from all around the world who have come together to worship Allah and obey the Prophet's command. It is also an honour for Muhammad to know that he will have completed the Fifth Pillar of Islam.

In line with the Qur'an's instructions, Muhammad and his father will sacrifice a goat during Hajj. Muhammad is particularly looking forward to praying at the base of Mount Arafat (where the Prophet gave his farewell sermon) and to camping overnight at Muzdalifa.

Muhammad will use the time during Hajj to renew his commitment to Allah, to ask for forgiveness for his sins and to thank Allah for the privileges he enjoys. Muhammad knows that he is lucky. Not everyone will have the money or the opportunity in their lifetime to carry out Hajj.

During the Day of Arafat, Muslims spend all day at Mount Arafat seeking God's forgiveness and devoting themselves to Islam

Concept of sin, punishment and reward

In this section you will learn to:

- explain the concept of sin
- discuss the effects of sin on the individual, society and the environment
- describe the impact of taqwah (piety) and ihsan (excellence)
- analyse the progression of spirituality in attaining closeness to Allah.

Concept of sin

The Qur'an describes human beings as the best of Allah's creation. Although the Qur'an points out man's foolishness and injustice, man has been entrusted with God's blessing and with knowledge. Qur'an 33:72 describes how God's trust was offered first to the earth and the mountains, but they did not take it. Trust was then offered to man, who took it.

Muslims believe that human beings are born in a state of fitrah (natural purity), untainted by sin.

This is upheld by verses such as 7:29 in the Qur'an that states:

> Say: 'My Lord has commanded justice; and that you set your whole selves (to Him) at every time and place of prayer, and call upon Him, making your devotion sincere as in His sight: such as He created you in the beginning, so shall you return'

Qur'an 7:29

However, this sinless state is blemished by the sinful world that humans are born into, by learned behaviour from family and friends, and through the selfishness and spiritual darkness in society.

The two types of sin

The purpose of human beings, along with the rest of creation, is to submit to the creator, Allah. The word 'Islam' comes from the Arabic word 'aslama', which means 'submission to God'. However, the Qur'an gives account of how humans have deviated (turned away from) the divine purpose that Allah has given them. The Qur'an teaches that each person must answer for their own sin on the Day of Judgement. The Qur'an describes two types of sin:

- An omission – what a person has failed to do or has done without thinking. Sins of omission include speaking without knowledge about holy matters, losing your temper, failing to keep the Five Pillars (e.g. daily prayers, fasting during Ramadan) and gossiping about people.
- A commission – a planned sin, something wrong that a person has planned and purposefully done. Sins of commission include actions such as murder, stealing or adultery.

Major and minor sins

The Qur'an recognises that there are major and minor sins, and punishment is given out accordingly. Qur'an 53:32 declares that 'Those who avoid great sins and shameful deeds, only (falling into) small faults – verily your Lord is ample in forgiveness'. Qur'an 17:23–38 outlines various practices that Muslims should follow, including:

- being kind to parents
- showing humility

The Day of Judgement and personal responsibility

Every man's fate We have fastened on his own neck: On the Day of Judgement We shall bring out for him a scroll, which he will see spread open. (It will be said to him:) 'Read your (own) record: sufficient is your soul this day to make out an account against you.'

Who receives guidance, receives it for his own benefit: who goes astray does so to his own loss: no bearer of burdens can bear the burden of another: nor would We visit with Our Wrath until We had sent a Messenger (to give warning).

Qur'an 17:13–15

- being responsible with money
- showing fairness and justice in business dealings.

Actions such as adultery, murder and stealing are considered major sins – these things are described as 'hateful in the sight of your Lord' (17:38).

The effects of sin

On the individual

Muslims are instructed to avoid sin, not only to please Allah and escape punishment in the afterlife, but also to benefit their lives on earth. Islam teaches that sin leads to moral, spiritual and physical degradation. The Qur'an describes how 'Those who invent a lie against God will never prosper' (10:69) and describes the spiritual desolation, meaninglessness and lack of reward for those who do not follow Allah's signs and commands (6:125, 7:146–147).

On society

Islam teaches that the effects of sin go beyond affecting the individual. The moral code laid out in the Qur'an enables society to function effectively. When people respect each other, care for the poor, work hard, do not steal and act fairly, all of society benefits. Conversely, when many people sin and ignore Allah's commands, trouble filters through the whole of society, affecting its values and structure. In 30:41 the Qur'an describes the mischief that sin brings to the world, but describes how God uses this turmoil to show the painful results of sin. The hope is that this will encourage people to turn away from sinful acts.

Islam teaches that sin brings pain and trouble to the whole of society – breeding discontent, wrong behaviour and intolerance

On the environment

Islam teaches that Allah made the world and everything in it and that humankind are his vicegerents (his appointed representatives on the earth). Therefore, humans have a responsibility to show respect and care for the earth, its plants and animals, and for each other. When this does not happen, the environment suffers – for those living on the earth now and for future generations. God stresses the importance of creation in 40:57 of the Qur'an, which says, 'Assuredly, the creation of the Heavens and the Earth is a greater (matter) than the creation of men: yet most men do not understand.'

The consequences of sin

The Qur'an warns about the removal of Allah's mercy, guidance and protection for those people who are intent on doing wrong and who ignore the signs and instructions given in the Qur'an. In 2:257 the Qur'an describes how God will lead those with faith from darkness into light, but those who reject the faith will be led into darkness. Even if they see Allah's signs, they will not recognise or accept them but instead will follow the wrong path. They will follow their base, immoral passions and desires and will have little regard for the values and opinions of others (22:72).

Disease of the qalb

For those people who reject the teachings of Islam, the Qur'an speaks of a disease of the heart (**qalb**). The belief is that when a person sins their heart is affected, until eventually the heart becomes so laden down with sin that it weakens and dies. Thus a person's body becomes the grave of a dead heart – they are spiritually dead. The Qur'an describes these people's hearts as harder than rocks (2:74). Such people may feel that they believe in God and the Last Days but, according to the Qur'an, they deceive themselves since they believe in false religions. These people, the Qur'an says, actually cause trouble on earth while thinking they are doing good. Only when they face their eternal punishment of 'blazing fire' will these unbelievers regret their actions (8:50–51).

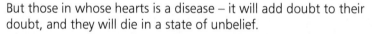

Disease of the soul

But those in whose hearts is a disease – it will add doubt to their doubt, and they will die in a state of unbelief.

Qur'an 9:125

The concept of taqwah (God consciousness)

Taqwah is the Islamic term for God-consciousness and fear of God – the permanent presence of God in a person's thoughts and actions. Without taqwah, the Qur'an describes the crumbling nature of life (9:109). But:

He provides for him from (sources) he never could imagine. And if anyone puts his trust in God, sufficient is (God) for him.

Qur'an 65:3a

Muslims believe that part of taqwah is being aware of one's moral responsibility as a vicegerent of God on the earth. In 30:30 of the Qur'an, Muslims are instructed to establish God's handiwork on the earth and not to cause any changes to God's design. The Qur'an describes those who have faith and do righteous deeds as the 'best of creatures' in 98:7.

DID YOU KNOW?

The Hadith says that for every sin that a person commits a black spot appears on the heart. For every good deed a person commits, a white spot appears on their heart. If the black spots overtake the white, the heart will eventually die.

Muslim, Mu'min and Muhsin

There are three levels or ranks of followers in Islam. These are outlined by Muhammad in Hadith 2, in which he describes Islam, Eman and Ehsan.

- A Muslim (Islam) follows the Five Pillars but is neglectful in other areas, such as showing humility and kindness. This is the minimum requirement to follow Islam.
- A Mu'min (Eman) has gone a step further and tries to follow all of the teachings of Islam for fear of Allah's judgement.
- A Muhsin (Ehsan) acts out of belief that Allah sees constantly. This person is dedicated to Islam purely out of love and devotion to Allah.

In 49:15 the Qur'an also cites a lack of doubt as being an important part of the level of faith that a person has.

The concept of ihsan

In a world damaged by hatred, ignorance, selfishness and sin, it is easy to lose faith in man's inherent goodness. However, Allah knows that man has the potential to achieve excellence and goodness – described as **ihsan** in Islam, which literally means 'perfection'. When faced with arguments against man's suitability as vicegerents from the angels, Allah declared, 'I know what you do not know' (2:30). And in 95:4, the Qur'an declares: 'We have indeed created man in the best of molds'. Hadith 38 describes how, when a person loves and obeys Allah, what they see, hear and do comes directly from Him. There can be no higher level of goodness or excellence than this.

The Qur'an promises beautiful gardens, flowing rivers and mansions for eternity for those who love Allah and follow the laws of Islam

Attaining closeness to Allah

The Qur'an's description of closeness to Allah

> For, Believers are those who, when God is mentioned, feel a tremor in their hearts, and when they hear His Signs rehearsed, find their faith strengthened, and put (all) their trust in their Lord.
>
> Qur'an 8:2

The Qur'an's description of the rewards of Allah

> He will forgive you your sins, and admit you to Gardens beneath which rivers flow, and to beautiful mansions in Gardens of Eternity: that is indeed the supreme achievement.
>
> Qur'an 61:12

Option D: Judaism

D.1 Human life issues

LEARNING OUTCOMES

In this section you will learn to:

- discuss the meaning and purpose of human life as reflected in the Tenakh

- explain the concept of stewardship and its application to daily living

- explain the concept of moral living and its application to daily living

- assess issues relating to justice, peace and the value and dignity of human life as reflected in the Tenakh

- discuss the roles, responsibilities and rights of individuals in areas of family life and work as reflected in the Tenakh

- describe the concept of the reign of God as displayed in the Tenakh

- discuss the teachings of Judaism on specific health and medical issues.

Humans made in God's image

So God created mankind in His own image, in the image of God He created them; male and female He created them.

Genesis 1:27

Meaning and purpose of human life

Created in the image of God

One of the main beliefs of Judaism is that humans are created 'in the image of God' (in Hebrew 'tzelem Elohim'). Since humans reflect the characteristics of God, they share the same dignity and value. This is the case whether a person is Jewish or not. Jews respect other people because of this shared human dignity and value, and they recognise the potential in everyone to do good in the world.

Tzelem Elohim brings with it responsibilities as well as rights. Humans have a role as God's representatives to carry out God's will on the earth. Jews believe that human beings should use their power, consciousness and free will to be wise stewards of creation.

Created male and female

The Tenakh states that both men and women were made in God's image. Therefore, both male and female characteristics equally reflect God's nature and are equally important and valid. Jewish people find meaning and purpose within their lives through the fact that they have been created male or female and have different but equally important roles to play. After creating Adam God says: 'It is not good for man to be alone; I will make him a helper' (Genesis 2:18). Men and women were made to help and complement each other.

Endowed with intelligence and free will

Jews believe that Yahweh created humans as free beings because He wants people to love and follow Him out of choice rather than force. Everyone has free will and intelligence. Jews believe that each person is therefore responsible for their own actions. Human intelligence is a tiny reflection of the knowledge and intelligence that God has. Part of human beings' responsibility is to use their intelligence to 'rule over the fish of the sea and the birds of the air ... over all the earth' (Genesis 1:26).

God is the source of life and human value

Genesis 2:7 states that: 'The Lord God ... breathed into his nostrils the breath of life, and the man became a living being'. Jews believe that it is God who gives us life and, through our intelligence, free will and conscience, He also gives us value. In Genesis 1:31, 'God saw all that He had made, and it was very good.'

Concept of stewardship

Co-workers with God

Judaism teaches that God controls and sustains the earth, but that the responsibility of a Jew (as one of God's chosen people) is to look after and nurture His creation. This is part of their covenantal relationship with God. God's side of this covenant agreement is to care for Israel (the Jews) as His chosen people.

Human responsibility to care for creation

Jews believe that God created the world and everything in it. All living things have an in-built value given from God. Genesis 2:15 instructs Jews to be good stewards of the earth: 'The Lord God took the man and put him in the Garden of Eden to work it and take care of it'. Jews therefore see it as their duty to protect and care for the earth, which belongs to God and which human beings are the stewards of.

Thanksgiving offerings

The concept of giving thanks is very important within a Jew's relationship with God. One way in which a Jew gives thanks to God is through tithing (giving a percentage of their money to those in need). The Torah instructs Jews to tithe in Leviticus 25:35 and Deuteronomy 15:7–8. In addition to tithing, many Jews make additional offerings. This shows gratitude to God and care for their fellow man, as well as recognising that all of their wealth comes from God. Through these acts of thanksgiving and generosity, Jews are being good stewards and taking care of God's creation.

ACTIVITY

What are your views on tithing? Do you think 10 per cent is a reasonable amount of a person's income to expect them to give away? Do you think it is right that there are laws for how much a person should give to charity, or should it be up to the individual to decide?

Care for the foreigner and less fortunate

The Torah is seen as God's guide to man for a good, moral life and it teaches the Jewish people to show respect and kindness for man and animals, particularly those who struggle. Leviticus 19:14 says: 'Do not curse the deaf or put a stumbling block in front of the blind', demonstrating how Jews are to respect and care for everyone.

Moral living in daily life

God is moral and the source of moral values

Judaism teaches that God is holy and **moral** and that the human conscience comes from the morality that God has placed in human beings. However, humans sometimes need guidance to recognise or apply these morals on the earth. Jews believe that the Ten Commandments were given directly by God so that people can live moral lives. It is considered a **mitzvah** (commandment) to study and understand the law.

Human responsibility to imitate God in moral rectitude

Within Judaism, some of the attributes of God include truth, justice, goodness, purity and holiness. Since Jews believe that they were

Teaching for Jews on caring for the less fortunate

When you reap the harvest of your land, do not reap to the very edges of your field or gather the gleanings of your harvest. Do not go over your vineyard a second time or pick up the grapes that have fallen. Leave them for the poor and the foreigner. I am the Lord your God.

Leviticus 19:9–10

The story in the Tenakh of Ruth gathering abandoned corn from Boaz's field illustrates the Jewish practice of leaving gleanings (scraps of corn) for the poor during harvesting, in obedience of God's teaching

made in God's image, they have a responsibility to be like God by showing these same qualities.

Human responsibility to love and serve God

Abram and his descendants made a covenant (promise) that they would always love and worship the one true God. The Jews therefore have a responsibility to keep this promise, although God wants the Jews to love Him out of desire rather than duty. In Deuteronomy 6:5 it states: 'you shall love Yahweh your God with all your heart, and with all your soul, and with all your might'. And the first of the Ten Commandments is: 'Do not worship any other gods'.

Sexual issues

Within the Jewish faith, sex outside of marriage is not allowed, but sex between a husband and wife is a mitzvah. Traditional Judaism views adultery, incest and homosexuality as sinful and immoral.

Race relationships

In Old Testament times, Jews and Gentiles (non-Jews) rarely mixed. However, in the modern world it is essential and expected that Jews mix with people of other faiths and those with no faith. Today, people of different racial backgrounds live in the same areas, attend the same schools, work together and relax in the same places. Regardless of their differences, the Torah teaches that Jews are to act morally and care for other races (Leviticus 19:9–10).

Social status

In the past, the Jewish community has been discriminated against, never more so than during the Second World War (1939–45), during which time six million Jews were killed. Today, there has been a breaking down of barriers between Jews and the outside world. Jews have intermarried and Jewish people are found throughout all levels of society and classes.

A Jew would say that working hard is a moral act, but to serve God is always more important than achieving social status.

Issues related to value and dignity of human life

Child abuse

Judaism teaches that all life comes from God and is sacred and valuable. In particular, children are considered to be special and a gift from God. It is the role of adults to respect, nurture and care for children. To abuse any child mentally, physically or sexually is to damage God's creation and to abuse the trust placed in you by God.

Substance abuse

Although there is no Jewish law saying that drug-taking is wrong, rabbis teach abstinence (restraint). The belief of Jews that God, rather than a person, owns their body, is a further deterrent. Jews should not deliberately harm the body that God has given them.

Capital punishment

Judaism teaches that human life is sacred and the Tenakh contains strict instructions for anyone committing sins, such as murder and adultery (Genesis 9:6). Although Jewish law does not agree with capital punishment in all cases, it says that the death penalty is allowed in extreme cases, provided it is not illegal in the land (although not every Jew agrees with this).

Poverty

Tzedakah (righteousness) is not only about helping people financially, it is also about making people feel valued. A Jew believes that if food is given to a hungry person resentfully then the act loses its value. However, the Talmud also recognises the importance of people helping themselves.

Unemployment

Judaism teaches that everyone should work hard in order to receive wealth, but this should be done in an ethical way. The Torah and Talmud encourage loans, but only interest-free loans as interest would take advantage of someone else (Ezekiel 18:8a). The Torah also gives instructions for fair trading. Jews are known for excelling in business – this is in part due to their strong work ethic.

Prejudice and discrimination

Judaism teaches that everyone is equal in the eyes of God and that everyone should be treated well. Jews therefore see prejudice and discrimination as wrong.

Violence, vandalism and war

Judaism teaches the value of life. Unnecessary violence, vandalism and war are always considered wrong. However, some feel that fighting evil is sometimes necessary, such as during the Second World War when Jews were being persecuted. A Jew must first try to make peace, but as stated in Deuteronomy 20:12, 'If they refuse to make peace and prepare to fight, you must attack the town.'

Treatment of the mentally and physically challenged

Jews believe that all human beings are descended from one man and woman (Adam and Eve) created in the image of God, and because of this, each person (regardless of whether they are mentally or physically challenged) has a God-given right to live and should be treated as equal to everybody else.

Individuals' roles, responsibilities and rights in family life

Marriage and divorce

In Judaism, marriage is viewed as a contractual bond commanded by God. A Jewish marriage is expected to fulfil the commandment to have children. **Halakha** (Jewish law) allows for divorce, but this should be a last resort. If it is required, Orthodox Jews often have a religious ceremony for divorce to be recognised.

> If he doesn't care about himself, then you're not required to care about him either.
>
> Baba Metzia 32b

> When an alien lives with you in your land, do not ill-treat him. The alien living with you must be treated as one of your native-born. Love him as yourself, for you were aliens in Egypt. I am the Lord your God.
>
> Leviticus 19:33–34

In the Second World War, many Jews were killed at concentration camps such as Dachau

In Judaism, as in other religions, marriage is regarded as a lifetime contractual bond, made before God

Family life

The family unit is at the heart of the Jewish community. A secure and loving home built on moral and ethical values is viewed as the building block of society. Each family has a responsibility to the community to act as good Jewish role models and each member of the family has a distinct role to fill.

Parenthood

The Tenakh describes children as a blessing from God. This blessing also carries responsibilities. The main role of the parent is to nurture children and teach them to love and fear God. Jewish mothers in particular are very influential in their children's lives – even into adulthood.

Children

Jewish children should obey the fifth commandment: 'Honour thy father and mother'. They must respect their parents and abide by their rules. When they reach adulthood, children should care for their parents as their parents have cared for them.

Gender roles and responsibilities

Status of women

The role of the Jewish woman is very important since she is the **Akeret Habayit.** The woman is the foundation of the home and largely determines the character and atmosphere of the household. The Tenakh teaches that women should be respected and cherished by their husbands.

Responsibilities of the husband

A married Jewish man is required to work to provide food, clothing and shelter for his family. Throughout the first year of marriage, the husband must stay close to his wife and not let any obstacles keep him from her. It is the husband's responsibility to protect and take care of his wife. He must also support his wife financially should they divorce.

Obligations of genders to the commandments

The law was designed to liberate women of obligations that they would find difficult. For instance, a woman is not required to pray in the morning because she may need to attend to children. Nevertheless women are required to recite the prayer over the wine on Shabbat as all Jews must 'remember the Sabbath Day' (Exodus 20:8). Jewish tradition requires that men study the Torah in order to become holier and closer to God.

Concept of the reign of God in the Tenakh

Israel as God's special care

The Tenakh tells of how God chose Abram and the Jews to be His chosen people. He promised to make Abram's descendants (the Jews) into a great nation. This nation is Israel and the Tenakh speaks of God's special care for this nation.

The family unit is very important in Jewish culture, with the mother forming the Akeret Habayit or backbone of the home, on which everything else is built

The whole world belongs to God

Although Israel is God's chosen nation and is under God's special care, Judaism teaches that the whole world belongs to God, including everyone in it. God cares for and loves all of His creation. This is reflected in Genesis 12, which speaks of how all people on earth will be blessed through the Jews.

Medical and health issues

Autopsies

Jewish law requires that the dead be buried as close to the time of death as possible. The practice of routine **autopsies** is against Jewish law, since autopsies are viewed as a desecration of the body and will delay burial. In cases where the law requires an autopsy, it should be carried out under the supervision of a rabbi who is familiar with the procedures.

Abortion

Judaism does not forbid abortion, but it is only allowed in serious circumstances, as all human life is considered precious. Every case should be considered separately and a decision should be made after consulting with a rabbi. Strict Jews only allow abortion to take place in cases where continuing the pregnancy would put the mother's life in serious danger.

Euthanasia (termination of life) and life support

Judaism teaches that all life comes from God and that there is a destined time for everything (Ecclesiastes 3). Putting control of life and death into human hands is something that most religions disagree with. For this reason, it is seen as wrong to terminate life. Although Judaism is opposed to **euthanasia**, some Jews and rabbis believe that a person should not be kept alive artificially if there is no chance of recovery.

> **The earth is God's and Israel is His treasured possession**
> Now if you obey me fully and keep my covenant, then out of all nations you will be my treasured possession. Although the whole earth is mine.
> Exodus 19:5

> If there is anything which causes a hindrance to the departure of the soul then it is permissible to remove it.
> Rabbi Moses Isserles (1520–72)

CASE STUDY | The greatest gift?

Benjamin and Jacob's father has just returned from donating blood. Saving the life of another person is considered to be the greatest act a Jew can perform. Benjamin wonders if this means that Jews should donate their organs to others when they die.

Benjamin's dad explains that although in theory a Jewish person could donate their organs, Jewish law makes this difficult. Desecrating a body is only allowed if it will save another human life – but there is no way to be sure that this will happen since some organs are used for research. Also, as most organs need to be removed while the heart is still beating, this presents a problem for Jews. Jews believe that a person is still alive as long as their heart beats and, therefore, removing an organ would constitute murder.

In medicine, a person is considered dead when their brain stops functioning, even if their heart is still beating. Choosing to donate your organs is not a straightforward decision. Jacob and Benjamin's dad explains that it is for each Jewish person to make this decision for themselves.

> **DID YOU KNOW?**
> The Talmud teaches that a body should be buried whole. However, since life is sacred and saving it is a sacred act, donating an organ to save a life after death takes precedence over this teaching.

The Tenakh

LEARNING OUTCOMES

In this section you will learn to:

- describe how the Tenakh (Torah, Nev'im, Ketuvim) was transmitted
- identify the different types of writings in the Tenakh
- explain how passages from the Tenakh are used as instruction for Jewish teaching and practices
- relate teachings of the Tenakh to personal and social experiences.

Transmission of the Tenakh

The Dead Sea Scrolls

The Dead Sea Scrolls are a collection of around 972 ancient texts from the Hebrew Bible and other biblical documents. They were discovered Qumran between 1947 and 1956 in caves along the north-west shore of the Dead Sea. These texts are of great religious and historical importance as they include the oldest-known surviving copies of biblical documents. They are written in Hebrew, Aramaic and Greek on parchment and papyrus. Most of the manuscripts date from between 150 BCE and 70 CE.

The oral tradition

The Jewish oral tradition is the teachings passed down by Jews through the ages. This includes laws that were transmitted orally from Mount Sinai by Moses but which were not written in the Torah. Instead, they were passed on orally from generation to generation. The oral tradition was eventually recorded in the Talmud and the Midrash. Another term for the oral tradition is the oral Torah or oral law.

Today, as in the past, Jews also use oral tradition to pass on stories, Jewish folklore and wisdom to their children and grandchildren.

One of the caves in Qumran where the Dead Sea Scrolls were found

CASE STUDY	Just for fun

Benjamin and Jacob enjoy evenings spent with their grandfather listening to the stories he tells of Jews throughout history and Jewish folklore. Some of these stories are from the Tenakh and Talmud and have great meaning and wisdom. Others are stories told just for fun, like the humorous stories of the Jews who lived in Chelm. Many popular stories are told about the foolish things these Jews did. Jacob's favourite story is of a Jewish resident in Chelm who bought a live fish to cook for Shabbat. He stored the fish underneath his coat, from where the fish slapped his face with his tail. The Jew took the fish to Chelm court and the court sentenced the fish to death by drowning!

DID YOU KNOW?

There is a type of folktale called 'noodleheads' about kindly but foolish people. In Yiddish tradition, many such stories are based in the city of Chelm. This is a real city in Eastern Poland, but in Jewish folklore it is a mythological village of fools. 'Tevye the Milkman' is a well-known folktale based in Chelm that was made into the famous film and musical called *Fiddler on the Roof*.

Names of the books in the Torah, Nev'im and the Ketuvim

Together, the Torah (T), Nev'im (N) and Ketuvim (K) make up the TeNaKh (the letters T, N and K are used to form the word 'Tenakh'). Christians refer to the Tenakh as the Old Testament. The Torah, Nev'im and Ketuvim are made up of different types of writing:

- Torah – the law books: made up of Genesis (Beresheet), Exodus (Shemot), Leviticus (Vayikra), Numbers (Bamidbar) and Deuteronomy (Devarim).
- Nev'im – the prophets: includes Isaiah, 1 and 2 Samuel, Hosea and Daniel.
- Ketuvim – the poetic writings: includes Psalms, Proverbs and Ecclesiastes.

The books of teaching

The Torah

The Five Books of Moses that make up the Torah were given to the Jewish people at Mount Sinai approximately 3,500 years ago. They include Genesis, Exodus, Leviticus, Numbers and Deuteronomy. These books record the beginning of God's relationship with the Jews, including His covenant with Abram, Isaac and Jacob. They also record the laws passed down by God to Moses at Mount Sinai, most significantly, the Ten Commandments. God gave these to Moses on Mount Sinai when the Jews were escaping the slavery of Egypt (the Exodus).

> **ACTIVITY**
>
> How many of the Ten Commandments can you remember? Look them up in Exodus 20 and make sure you know them all.

The Nev'im

Prophets (Nev'im) are direct prophecies or recordings of what God said to the prophets. The books of the prophets are 1 and 2 Samuel; 1 and 2 Kings; Joel, Isaiah and Jeremiah. The text tells of direct prophecies given by God to the prophets that Jews believe have been or will be fulfilled (come true). These books also record events in the lives of the prophets.

> **DID YOU KNOW?**
>
> Prophecies mean different things to different people. Most Jews are still waiting for prophecies in the Tenakh to come true. Christians believe that Old Testament (or Tenakh) prophecies were fulfilled through Jesus. Some Jews, called Messianic Jews, believe that the Messiah has come; most are still waiting.

The Ketuvim

Writings (Ketuvim) are books written by the prophets with the guidance of God. They are the books of Psalms, Esther, Proverbs, Nehemiah and Daniel. These writings, also known as the Hebrew literary books, are divided into three major parts – Literature, Megillot (scrolls) and Histories. The Psalms in particular form a great deal of Jewish prayers. Many people, not just Jews, find comfort in the words of the Jewish Writings.

Instruction on Jewish teachings and practices

Beliefs about human nature

Judaism teaches that humans were made from the earth and the breath of God. The Hebrew for man (adam) may be related to the Hebrew for ground (adamah), emphasising the point that we were formed from the dust of the ground. Since God made us in His likeness, parts of our human nature reflect God's nature – qualities such as love, kindness and morality. However, aspects of human nature, such as selfishness, greed and violence stem from our sinfulness, which is a result of **the Fall.**

The well-known story of Daniel in the lion's den is recorded in the Book of Daniel, which forms part of the Ketuvim in the Tenakh

> **DID YOU KNOW?**
>
> Because the books included in the Tenakh were mainly written in Hebrew and form the Old Testament books of the Bible, the Tenakh is sometimes referred to as the Hebrew Bible.

The breath of life
Then the Lord God formed a man from the dust of the ground and breathed into his nostrils the breath of life, and the man became a living being.
Genesis 2:7

LINK

There is more on the pilgrim festivals in Festivals and observances, starting on page 160.

Belief in Yahweh (God)

Deuteronomy 6:4 says: 'Hear, O Israel: The Lord our God, the Lord is one'. This verse, known as the Shema, states that there is one God and reminds Jews that they are God's chosen people (elected). This verse is said twice a day and emphasises that Judaism is a monotheistic faith.

The observance of the Sabbath

The eighth commandment tells the Jewish people to 'Remember the Sabbath day by keeping it holy.' Sabbath is kept from sundown on Fridays to sundown on Saturdays and during this time no work can be done. This command is based upon the fact that God made all of creation in six days and rested on the seventh day (Exodus 20:8).

Observances of the three pilgrim festivals

Leviticus 23:24–36 outlines the three pilgrim festivals that Jewish people celebrate. The three pilgrimage festivals are outlined below.

- Pesach celebrates the Jewish people being freed from slavery in Egypt (the Exodus). At home, on the eve of the seven- or eight-day festival, the service of Seder is held. Traditional symbolic foods are prepared and, after dinner, the youngest child asks four traditional questions to which the oldest man present replies with the story of Israel's escape from Egypt.
- Shavuot takes place exactly seven weeks after Pesach and it is a celebration of the giving of the Torah to Moses on Mount Sinai.
- Sukkoth is when the journey of the Jews through the desert to the Promised Land is remembered. A hut is erected in the synagogue and in private gardens to remember God's provision. The hut is decorated with fruit and flowers and the family gathers in it to eat meals. At the synagogue, palm, myrtle, willow and citron are waved to symbolise God's presence and in keeping with the requirements outlined in Leviticus 23:40.

DID YOU KNOW?

During the First World War in Poland, people made use of sweet tea (instead of the traditional four cups of wine) in the Seder meal. This was because during wartime it was very difficult to find kosher wine, so the rabbinical authorities in those areas gave this special decree.

Beliefs about the Jewish afterlife

An early common theme within Judaism is that death means being reunited with your ancestors. Abram, Isaac, Jacob, Moses and other patriarchs are 'gathered to their people' after death (Genesis 25:17, 35:29, 49:33). Other imagery emphasises how final death is: the dead are like dust returning to dust (Genesis; Ecclesiastes 3:19–20) or water poured out on the ground (2 Samuel 14:14). However, most Jews believe that these verses refer only to the body, while the soul lives on.

During Sukkoth (the Feast of Tabernacles) Jewish families remember God's provision by spending time in tabernacles (or tents) as their ancestors did in the wilderness

The Torah is surprisingly silent on what happens to people after they die. Many think this is to distinguish the Torah from Egyptian religious texts that were obsessed with the afterlife. Since there is no definitive teaching about the afterlife in the Torah, some Jews argue that it cannot be known whether there is life after death or not. Whether or not Jews believe in an afterlife, the Torah stresses that living a good life in Olam Ha Ze (this world) is what is important.

ACTIVITY

Using the examples above, create a drawing that evokes the Jewish afterlife.

Beliefs about the Messiah

Around the time that Jesus came to earth, the Jews were waiting for a Messiah that they believed would be a great political leader descended from King David (Jeremiah 23:5). They believed he would know Jewish law and observe its commandments (Isaiah 11:2–5). The Jews hoped that he would be a great military leader who would win battles for Israel and free them from Roman rule. They also believed he would be a great judge who would make righteous decisions (Jeremiah 33:15). Jews today still wait for their Messiah, although some believe that this will be an age (period) rather than a person. During this age, Jews believe the world will be at peace, Jewish law will rule (Jeremiah 33:15) and Jerusalem will be restored (Hosea 3:4–5).

Belief in worship and prayer

Jews worship in synagogues and attend services there every Sabbath. Men and women traditionally sit separately, although this is changing in some progressive synagogues. Men are required to cover their heads. In most cases worship takes place in Hebrew. Hymns, prayers and readings from the Tenakh take place. When praying, Jews turn to face Jerusalem, their ancient religious centre. Jews believe that God commands His people to worship Him and that prayer is a means of communicating with God.

Belief in the Resurrection of the Dead and the Judgement

Based on Rabbi Hiyya ben Joseph's teachings, many Jews believe that the righteous dead will be brought back to life one day during the reign of the Messiah or the Messianic age. These righteous dead will be given the opportunity to experience a perfect world that their righteousness helped to create. The wicked dead will not be resurrected.

The dead will come up through the ground and rise up in Jerusalem … and the righteous will rise up fully clothed.

Rabbi Hiyya ben Joseph in Babylonian Talmud, tractate Ketubot 111b

Beliefs about Jews

Jews believe that they are the 'elect', God's chosen people elected by Him for a special purpose. The Jewish people are faithful to God and in return God looks after them as a sign of the covenant (promise) made between God and the Jewish race.

Teachings of the Tenakh applied to personal and social experiences

Relationship with family and peers

Although the Tenakh was written thousands of years ago, its teachings are still relevant for life today. Genesis 4:7 (the story of Cain and Abel) teaches Jews to do what is right and not to be tempted to sin. Cain kills his brother Abel and, because of this, God punishes him harshly. This encourages Jewish people to have good relationships with their family and to resolve conflicts peacefully since the family is at the centre of the Jewish community.

Guidelines for living

Exodus 20:1–17 outlines the Ten Commandments that Jews must follow. These are essential guidelines for living. Many of these commands form the basis of laws put in place by governments throughout the world. For example, 'Do not murder' (the sixth commandment).

Comfort in times of sorrow and suffering

Many Jews find comfort in the teachings of the Tenakh. One verse that offers comfort and strength in times of sorrow and suffering is Proverbs 4:20–22:

> My child, pay attention to what I say. Listen carefully to my words. Don't lose sight of them. Let them penetrate deep into your heart, for they bring life to those who find them and healing to their whole body.
>
> Proverbs 4:20–22

Protection in times of danger

Verses like these from the book of Psalms demonstrate how God's people are protected in times of danger:

> But let all who take refuge in you be glad; let them ever sing for joy. Spread your protection over them, that those who love your name may rejoice in you.
>
> Psalm 5:11

> The Lord is my rock, my fortress and my deliverer; my God is my rock, in whom I take refuge. He is my shield and the horn of my salvation, my stronghold.
>
> Psalm 18:2

Business and professional behaviours

Psalm 15 encourages Jewish people to be 'blameless and to do what is righteous'. Jews believe that trusting in the Lord and obeying His commands will help them to do what is right, both at home and at work. Proverbs 3:1–12 commands Jews to 'Honour the Lord with your wealth, with the first fruits of all your crops; then your barns will be filled to overflowing, and your vats will brim over with new wine.' In other words, be generous with the money that you earn and God will reward you.

Dietary regulations and health issues

Jews may only eat meat from animals that have a cloven hoof and chew the cud (grass) – they may not eat meat that has come from a pig. All meat must be kosher (meet Jewish dietary requirements) and be removed of all blood, since Deuteronomy 12:23 states: 'be sure you do not eat the blood, because the blood is the life, and you must not eat the life with the meat.' Orthodox Jews will not mix meat and dairy products (such as milk or cheese) at the same meal, and will use separate plates and sinks to wash and serve the two types of food.

These days many well-known restaurants around the world offer kosher food

ACTIVITY

Research kosher meat and answer the questions that follow.

1 What animals are Jews permitted to eat?

2 How is the animal slaughtered and the meat prepared?

3 Are there Jewish laws concerning eating fish and seafood?

Morals and ethics

In Judaism, morality includes a person's inner thoughts, emotions, intentions, attitudes and motives as well as their actions. The Torah warns against being jealous of others (Exodus 20:14; Deuteronomy 5:18), against hating others (Leviticus 19:17), and against hardness of heart (Deuteronomy 15:9–10 commands Jews to show compassion to those who are poor). Mishpat (justice), tzedakah (righteousness), hesed (kindness) and rahamim (compassion) are all encouraged, as they are characteristics of a moral and ethical person.

Death and mourning

In Judaism death is not a tragedy, even when it occurs early in life or through unfortunate circumstances. Death is a natural process and has meaning because it is part of God's plan. Most Jews have a firm belief in an afterlife, a world to come, where those who have lived a worthy life will be rewarded. Jewish practices relating to death and mourning have two purposes: to show respect for the dead (kavod ha-met) and to comfort the living (nihum avelim).

God

In this section you will learn to:

- describe the nature of God
- discuss the understanding of the name and the significance of the titles for God
- explain the significance of the idea of God as a covenant maker
- explain the attributes of God.

The nature of God

God is limitless

> Can you probe the limits of the Almighty? They are higher than the heavens – what can you do? They are deeper than the depths of the grave – what can you know? Their measure is longer than the earth and wider than the sea.
>
> Job 11:7–9

These verses highlight how God's power is limitless and exceeds anything on the earth. Jews draw comfort and confidence from this fact.

God is one

Jews believe in one God. Unlike Christians, they do not believe that He is one part of a trinity. The Shema, which Jews recite every day, reminds Jews of this fact:

> Hear, O Israel: The Lord our God, the Lord is one.
>
> Deuteronomy 6:4

God is creator

Genesis 1:1 says: 'In the beginning, God created the heavens and the earth.' Genesis also tells of how, before God's creation, the earth was formless and empty. This shows how God is the creator of everyone and everything. Jews, like followers of most religions, believe that creativity comes from God.

God is moral

As a God of justice, His actions and decisions are true, right, kind and moral (Job 34:12). As Lord and Judge, God brings justice to nations (Psalm 67:4) and acts on behalf of the poor, the oppressed, and victims of injustice (Psalm 103:6, 146:6–9). Morality and justice is part of God's nature. Frequently in the Tenakh, God's people are commanded to show this same justice and morality.

God is personal

Jews believe that God is not a distant God but rather that He cares about and interacts with His creation. Psalm 139 demonstrates this point, since it explains that God knows each person intricately – He knew a person in their mother's womb and knows the number of hairs on their head. He also knows what the future holds for each person. Isaiah 46:4 encourages Jews by reminding them of God's personal care for them:

> Even to your old age and gray hairs I am He, I am He who will sustain you. I have made you and I will carry you; I will sustain you and I will rescue you.
>
> Isaiah 46:4

Many verses in the Tenakh talk about God's personal care for individuals. Some verses talk about God carrying His people, others state that their names are engraved on the palm of His hand. This imagery brings people comfort and strength.

The name of God and titles for God

Judaism does not prohibit writing the name of God, but it does not allow for erasing or defacing the name of God. Many Jews avoid writing any name of God because of the risk that the written name might later be defaced or destroyed accidentally by somebody who does not know better. Jews often write G-d instead. The commandment not to erase or deface the name of God comes from Deuteronomy 12:3. In that passage, the people are commanded that when they take over the **Promised Land,** they should destroy all things related to the idolatrous religions of that region and should destroy the names of the local gods. Immediately afterwards, the Jews were commanded not to do the same to their God. From this, the rabbis commanded Jews not to erase or deface the name of God.

God is known by many names. These include:

- Yahweh. Roughly translated as 'I am', this is the answer that God gave to Moses when Moses asked for his name.
- Ha 'Shem. In conversation, many Jewish people, even when not speaking Hebrew, will call God 'Ha 'Shem', which is Hebrew for 'the Name'.
- El. The word 'El' comes from a root word meaning 'might, strength, and power'.
- Adonai. Jews also call God Adonai, Hebrew for 'my lords', from 'adon', which means 'lord, owner'.
- Eliyah sh' Eliyah. This was the first of three responses given to Moses when he asked for God's name (Exodus 3:14). It is roughly translated as 'I am that I am' and means that God cannot be compared to anything else. He is above all things.
- Zebaot. This means 'the Lord of hosts, the God of the armies of Israel'.

Every name that the Jewish people use to refer to God says something about His character as the divine, perfect and holy God.

> **ACTIVITY**
>
> Find out whether there are any other names that Jews use for God and what they mean.

God and covenant

As examined in Section 2 of this guide, a covenant is an agreement between God and His people. It is a solemn promise with responsibilities on both sides. The Old Testament contains many covenants between God and people such as Noah, Abram, Isaac and Moses. Although these covenants are between God and individuals, they form essential promises for all Jews to come and they are one of the central themes of the Jewish faith.

God's covenant with Noah

God's promise to Noah was that He would never again destroy the world by flood (Genesis 9). God made an everlasting covenant with Noah and his descendants and sent the rainbow as the sign of His promise (Genesis 9:1–17).

A rainbow was a sign of God's covenant with Noah that He would never again destroy the earth with a flood

God's covenant with Abram

In making a covenant with Abram (Abraham), God promised that Abram would be the father of a great nation, although it seemed impossible for him and his wife Sarah to have children since Sarah was past childbearing age. God also promised to bless Abram's descendants and make them His own special people. In return, Abram was to remain faithful to God and keep his laws, including the law of circumcision. Abram also had to follow God to a 'promised land' that would be shown to him (Genesis. 12:1–4). This took a great deal of faith on the part of Abram.

> **God's promise to Abram**
> I will make you into a great nation
> And I will bless you;
> I will make your name great,
> And you will be a blessing.
> I will bless those who bless you,
> And whoever curses you I will curse;
> And all peoples on earth will be blessed through you.
> Genesis 12:2–3

DID YOU KNOW?

The Hebrew word for covenant is 'ber'it', meaning promise or pledge.

Jews as God's special people

Life within the covenant

The covenant that God gave to Moses at Mount Sinai reinforced the covenant that God had given to Abram, and told the Jews what they would have to do to keep their side of the covenant. God again promised to stay with the Jews and never to abandon them, because they were His chosen people. God told the Jewish people, that for their part, they must:

- dedicate themselves to serving God forever
- make it known to the world that they were God's people
- make the world a better and holier place by obeying God's laws.

The covenant is made with the Jewish people as a whole, not with each individual Jew.

Jewish identity as God's special people

One of the most important beliefs of Jews is the idea of there being one God and Jews being God's special people – something reflected in Jewish culture and Jewish identity. People find their identity in lots of ways, including through their history and nationality as well as their family, hobbies, religion and ancestry. A Jew's ancestry, as part of the Jewish race, goes all the way back to Abram. Jewish identity, as a race and a culture, is something that is common to all Jews, whether or not they follow the Jewish religion.

Attributes of God

- Eternal. Jews believe that God has always existed and will always exist. He is outside time and, in that sense, can be everywhere and in the past and future, as well as the present, simultaneously. God has no beginning and no end.
- Omniscient. God knows all things – past, present, and future. His 'omniscience' means that he is all-knowing.
- Omnipresent. God is all-present. In other words, He is present in every place.
- Loving. Jews believe that it is God's nature to love. Attributes of love include patience, kindness, protection, trust and perseverance. Jews believe that they are especially loved by God.
- Just. In Micah 6:8, the prophet Micah tells the Jewish people what God wants from them: 'to be fair and just and merciful and to walk humbly with your God.' This shows the importance of fairness and justice to God.
- Holy. In Exodus 3:5 when Moses comes into the presence of God, God tells him: 'Take off your shoes for you are standing on holy ground.' This illustrates the Jewish belief that God cannot come near to sin. God's presence is something that sinful humans cannot draw close to.
- **Righteous**. God is righteous (moral and justified) in everything He does. God's faithfulness to His covenant, despite the failure of the Jews to uphold their part of the agreement, shows His righteousness.
- Merciful. Jews believe that God shows His mercy by not giving humanity the punishment they deserve, which is abandonment. Mercy can be translated as loyal and undeserved love.

In this section you will learn to:

- identify the festivals and holy days of Judaism
- discuss the purpose and ceremonial observance of the festivals and holy days
- explain the modern significance of each festival
- identify the months of celebration for each festival.

The Sabbath (Shabbos)

Exodus 20:1–14 commands that the Jewish people keep the Sabbath holy by not doing any work on this day. Sabbath lasts from sunset on Friday to sunset on Saturday. On the Friday, the mother lights the Sabbath candles and the father blesses the loaves of plaited bread and the wine at the family meal. On the Saturday, the family attends a synagogue service in the morning and spends the rest of the day quietly at home or visiting friends and relatives.

Purpose and observance

The Sabbath runs from sundown on Friday to sundown on Saturday every week of the year. It is a weekly day of rest for the Jewish people. The purpose of observing this day is to keep the covenant between the Jewish people and God, as outlined in Exodus 20:1–14. Observance of the Sabbath also helps the Jews to keep a healthy balance of work and rest and ensures that time is spent together as a family.

Modern significance

The Sabbath is a day dedicated to serious prayer and reading of the Torah. It is a chance for Jews to rest, remember their faith and make time to focus on their spirituality. It is also an opportunity for Jews to spend time with family. The strength and building up of the family unit is very important in Judaism.

The Sabbath is a time for Jews to rest from work, to focus on God and to spend time with their families

Rosh Hashanah

Rosh Hashanah is the Jewish New Year festival and commemorates the creation of the world. It lasts for two days starting on 1 Tishri or 2 Tishri for Jews in **diaspora** (September/October, the seventh month of the Jewish calendar).

It is also a time of judgement when Jews believe that God balances a person's good deeds over the last year against their bad deeds, and decides what the next year will be like for them. A ram's horn, or shofar, is blown at the synagogue service to call Jews to prayer, and apples dripped in honey are eaten to symbolise the hope for a good year ahead.

Purpose and observance

Rosh Hashanah is the beginning of the 10 Pentecostal days, which end on Yom Kippur. The ceremonial observance of this festival is seen through the blowing of the shofar 100 times by the rabbi, reminding each Jew to attend the synagogue and repent of their sins. Rosh Hashanah is a time of reflection and personal sacrifice. The story of the sacrifice of Isaac is retold and each Jew is reminded of the importance of personal sacrifice within their 'modern' lives.

Modern significance

The modern significance of Rosh Hashanah is to start the year in a positive way. During Rosh Hashanah, Jews make a personal sacrifice in **repentance** for past sins.

Yom Kippur

Also known as the Day of Atonement, this is the holiest day in the Jewish year and it is a day of atonement and fasting. It takes place on 9 and 10 Tishri (September/October, the seventh month of the Jewish calendar), 10 days after Rosh Hashanah.

The family eats before the sun sets, and then a fast lasting 25 hours begins. Jews attend the synagogue and ask God to forgive them for any sins they may have committed during the past year, whether they meant to sin or not.

The rabbi blows the shofar to call Jews to prayer

ACTIVITY

1 What do you think is the significance of fasting during Yom Kippur?

2 What effect might it have on a person to go without food for a whole day?

3 How might this help a person's relationship with God?

Instructions for the Day of Atonement
On the tenth day of this seventh month hold a sacred assembly. You must deny yourselves and do no work. Present as an aroma pleasing to the Lord a burnt offering of one young bull, one ram and seven male lambs a year old, all without defect. With the bull offer a grain offering of three-tenths of an ephah of the finest flour mixed with oil; with the ram, two-tenths; and with each of the seven lambs, one-tenth. Include one male goat as a sin offering, in addition to the sin offering for atonement and the regular burnt offering with its grain offering, and their drink offerings.

Numbers 29:7–11

In Israel it is considered rude to drive a vehicle on Yom Kippur

DID YOU KNOW?

In Israel Yom Kippur is a state holiday. Airports and public transport are shut down, there are no television or radio broadcasts and all businesses are closed.

DID YOU KNOW?

The word 'canon' refers to writings that are viewed as genuine scripture and used in worship. Writings that were not selected to be included in Jewish scriptures but were still considered important, such as 1 and 2 Maccabees, are known as deuterocanonical writings (which means 'belonging to the second canon'). These books are sometimes included in Jewish scriptures in their own section called the Apocrypha.

Purpose and observance

Yom Kippur is a solemn day of complete fasting and prayer. This follows the teaching in Leviticus 16:1–34, which describes how the Jews are to atone for their sins. Verses 29 and 30 state:

> This is to be a lasting ordinance for you: On the tenth day of the seventh month you must deny yourselves and not do any work, because on this day atonement will be made for you, to cleanse you. Then, before the Lord, you will be clean from all your sins.

Leviticus 16:29–30

Verse 34 then says: 'This is to be a lasting ordinance for you: Atonement is to be made once a year for all the sins of the Israelites.' This teaching is still followed by the Jews through the observance of Yom Kippur each year.

Modern significance

The modern significance of Yom Kippur is to concentrate on the spirit. Numbers 29:1–11 tells Jews to hold a spiritual assembly and do no regular work during Yom Kippur, allowing them to focus fully on their spirituality.

Sukkoth (Tabernacle)

Sukkoth is the Jewish harvest festival, which takes place on 15 Tishri (September/October), five days after Yom Kippur. At this festival, Jews remember the time when the Israelites had to live in tabernacles (during their journey through the desert). Jews remember and thank God for His provision for them.

> **Instructions for Sukkoth**
> The Lord said to Moses, 'Say to the Israelites: "On the fifteenth day of the seventh month the Lord's Festival of Tabernacles begins, and it lasts for seven days."'
> Leviticus 16:29–30

Purpose and observance

Sukkoth reminds Jews of the temporary and fragile nature of their lives on earth and reminds them that life and provision is a gift from God. Jews are reminded that they should use each day for the glory of God. Jews also take part in blessings for the gift of food to eat. Thanking God for His love and care is an important part of the Jewish faith.

Modern significance

Sukkoth allows for a Jew to change their behaviour and act in a more positive way. In this world, there is always someone who is in need, as shown within Leviticus 19:9–10. Succoth provides Jewish people with an opportunity to help others.

Chanukah

Chanukah, the Feast of Dedication (also known as the Festival of Lights), occurs on 25 Kislev (November/December, the ninth month of the Jewish calendar) and lasts for eight days. At home, a menorah (eight-branched candle) is lit so that on the eighth night the whole menorah is alight. Presents are often exchanged at this time because it is a happy festival.

Chanukah recalls the rededication of the Temple by Judas Maccabeus after he had seized it from the Syrians in 164 CE. An account of Maccabeus' defeat of the Syrians is found in the book of 1 Maccabees, which is a deuterocanonical book (meaning it does not form part of the Tenakh, the first and most important scriptural source, but is an additional text).

Purpose and observance

At the festival of Chanukah, Jews give thanks for the preservation of the Jewish faith and of the temple. Lighting the menorah on each of the seven nights of the festival reminds Jews of the miracle of the lamp burning for eight days in the temple when the Jews reclaimed it from Antiochus Epiphanes. Jews thank God for his protection and remember the sacrifice of others in order to preserve and protect the Jewish faith.

Modern significance

Chanukah shows the victory of the 'few' over the 'many', as in the case of the Jews fighting the Syrians. If the Jewish faith was not preserved then the modern life of each Jew would not exist. Therefore, observing this festival is significant and relevant to the lives of Jews now.

It also gives encouragement to all minorities. In a modern situation, these minorities take comfort and strength from Chanukah because it shows that what is right will win eventually over what is evil.

Purim

Purim, also known as the Festival of Lots, takes place on 14 Adar (February/March, the twelfth month of the Jewish calendar).

At Purim, the story of Esther is read to remember and celebrate the fact that the Jews were saved by her from death at the hands of the Persians. Jews fast the day before Purim in honour of Esther, who fasted before approaching the king to ask him to save her people. On Purim, many Jews dress up to commemorate Esther concealing her Jewish identity. Presents are exchanged, people enjoy sweet treats, and everyone rejoices.

On Purim, Jews eat sweet treats. They also use noisemakers and boo and hiss when the villain Haman is mentioned during the retelling of the Purim story of Esther.

Purpose and observance

The festival of Purim reminds Jews of the persecution they have faced, but also, in the case of Purim, their deliverance. The festival also remembers the courage and dedication of Esther in saving her people and the importance of taking action to make the world a better place. During Purim it is traditional for Jews to carry out acts of tzedakah or charity.

Modern significance

Purim teaches that those who spread hatred destroy themselves, and that salvation is the reward for the Jew who clings to their faith. This is demonstrated in the story of Esther who declared: 'If I die, I die', when facing the King to ask for the release of the Jews. Esther had complete faith in God and, as a result, the Jewish race was delivered from evil and destruction.

Pesach (Passover)

This is the festival during which the Jews remember their deliverance by God from slavery in Egypt (see Exodus 12:14–51). It takes place from 5 to 22 Nissan (March/April, the first month of the Jewish calendar). For Jews in **diaspora** the festival takes place from 15 to 23 Nissan.

During Pesach, a family meal, called Seder, is shared. Four glasses of wine are poured. Each glass represents one of the promises God made to Moses to save the people of Israel and form them into a nation. A glass of wine is also poured for Elijah, to remember that this prophet will return to earth to announce the coming of the Messiah. During the meal, while the family listen to the story of the Exodus, they dip parsley in salt water and bitter herbs in haroset (a paste made of chopped apples, nuts, cinnamon and red wine) to signify the sorrow and bitterness that their ancestors experienced in Egypt. Jews also use the festival of Pesach to pray for people trapped in slavery today.

Seder plate

1 A roasted egg reminds Jews of the animal sacrifices made at the temple in Jerusalem during Pesach.

2 Haroset symbolises the mortar Jews used to construct Egyptian buildings while in slavery.

3 Bitter herbs are a reminder of how bitter life was for Jews during slavery in Egypt. There are two types: maror, which is often horseradish, and chazeret, usually the romaine lettuce.

4 Green vegetables (usually parsley) remind Jews that Pesach is a spring festival.

5 A roasted lamb bone represents the lamb's blood that was used to mark Jewish houses so that the plague in Egypt would pass over them.

6 Salt water represents the tears of the Jews during their time in slavery.

Purpose and observance

The observation of Pesach acts as a remembrance of the Exodus of the Jews from Egypt. The main observance is in the form of the Seder Supper with its special meal and the reading of the Hagadah (Hebrew for 'telling') which retells the story of the Exodus and contains blessings, rituals and songs to be performed during Pesach. This ensures that the Jewish people never forget their past.

Modern significance

Pesach celebrates the delivery of the Jews from Egypt, one of the most important acts in Jewish history. It allowed Jews to be free to practise their religion and culture. This thankfulness for the actions of Jews in the past gives Pesach relevance and significance today.

Shavuot

Shavuot, also know as the Feast of Weeks, occurs on 6 Sivan (May/June, the third month of the Jewish calendar), seven weeks after Pesach. It celebrates the Jewish people receiving the Torah/Ten Commandments from God at Mount Sinai (Exodus 19:1–20; 23; Deuteronomy 16:9–12).

Purpose and observance

Observing the festival of Shavuot reminds the Jewish people that idolatry (such as that displayed by the Israelites worshipping the golden calf in Exodus 32) is a sin. It also commemorates the receipt of the Ten Commandments on Mount Sinai by Moses – these laws underpin Jewish belief.

Modern significance

The modern significance of Shavuot comes through the acknowledgement that the Ten Commandments are still relevant for life today and will always stand as basic requirements for good and godly living. The Ten Commandments underpin lawful society in most nations of the world.

> **DID YOU KNOW?**
>
> The months in a Jewish calendar, like the Muslim calendar, are determined by the appearance of the moon. This is known as a lunar calendar. Since there are more months in a lunar year than there are on a Gregorian (or Western) calendar, the dates of Jewish observances on Western calendars change each year.

> **DID YOU KNOW?**
>
> It is traditional on the eve of Shavuot to stay awake all night reading the Torah. This stems from the account in the Midrash of the Israelites almost missing the Torah being given to Moses because they overslept.

> **ACTIVITY**
>
> For a personal perspective, why not try to speak to a Jewish person about how they celebrate Jewish festivals in the Caribbean. Do they do anything differently to Jews celebrating the festivals in other parts of the world? Maybe there is a Jewish person at your school, or enquire at your local synagogue.

Exam tips

Exam and revision tips

Very few people in the world like exams. But they are a fact of life, and by following some basic revision techniques and tips for how to get the best out of yourself during an exam, you can make them work in your favour.

Revision

- Trying to force yourself to concentrate on anything for hours on end will not work. The human brain can only concentrate fully for around 30 minutes at a time. Try revising in 30-minute chunks, giving yourself 5–10-minute breaks in-between. However, make sure that you concentrate fully during your 30 minutes of revision.

- To help your concentration, make sure you have everything nearby that you might need – drinks, snack, pen, paper, computer, books. This will stop you wandering around the house and getting distracted.

- Do not revise in front of the TV or while listening to the radio, and make sure your mobile phone is turned off so that you are not tempted to start texting or calling friends.

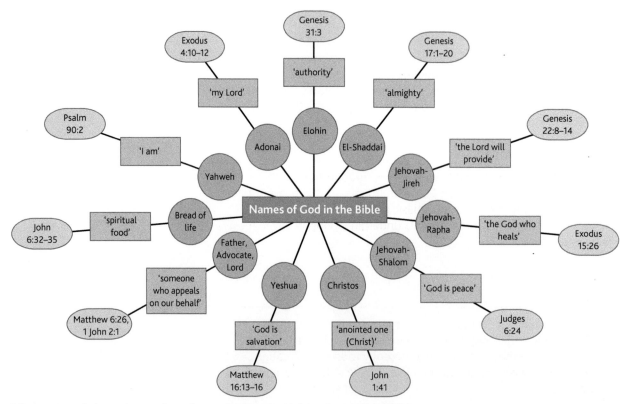

Mind maps can help you to organise and remember important information and how it links up

- Do not look at everything you have got to revise/remember in one go – you will end up feeling overwhelmed. Work through your notes, revision guide and/or textbook bit by bit. Break it down into manageable chunks.

- Try to summarise what you need to know into bullet points. Or make a mind map. To do this, write the topic in the middle of a sheet of paper and draw lines coming from this topic with any associated information. This information may, in turn, have a line coming from it with secondary information. This can be a useful way of organising facts that you need to know.

- Use old exam papers, or set yourself questions on topics and practise answering them without your notes and within a set amount of time.

Exams

- It is tempting to dive in and frantically start answering questions. Take a few minutes to read through the whole paper first and work out roughly how long you have to spend on each section. Make sure you leave enough time for questions that will take longer.

- Answer a question that you are comfortable with first. It will boost your self-confidence.

- Read through questions carefully before answering, and make sure you do what you are asked. If you are asked to discuss, make sure you present different points of view, and give your opinion only if it is required. If a question asks you just to state facts, do not waste time discussing.

- Always aim to have a go at every question – it is better to gather one or two marks from a question by having a go than to gain no marks by leaving the answer blank.

- For multiple-choice questions, if you do not know the answer, have a guess. You might get lucky!

- Roughly plan out essay questions (or questions requiring longer answers) before answering. Use a sentence or two to identify the points you want to make and list these points in order. Also outline what your introduction and conclusion will be. Finally, note down any scriptural references or quotes that you want to use. Once you have a plan for your essay, then start writing, making sure you follow your plan. This way, if you run out of time, the examiner will see, from your planning, that you knew the main points. Having a guide to work from when writing your essay will also help you to stay calm.

- Where possible use references from scripture to back up and illustrate your points.

- If there is time, read through your answers before submitting your paper – this gives you a chance to make any final tweaks and correct any errors.

And finally...

Prepare as well as you possibly can, and during the exam give everything you have got. Stay calm and have confidence in yourself. Make sure you can know, at the end of the exam, that you have done your best. And remember – there is life after exams!

Three final points to leave you with:

- Make sure you have eaten a nutritional meal before your exam. A rumbling tummy will be a big distraction. You are going to need all the brain energy you can get.
- Take more than one pen.
- It has been said before, but it is so important that we are saying it again – stay calm and do your best. Then, whatever the result, you can be proud of yourself.

Good luck!

SECTION 1: Multiple-choice questions

1 Which of the following is the most accurate definition of the term 'denomination'?

  a A term that describes the various beliefs and practices in different religions

  b A term that describes the various beliefs and practices in different branches of the same religion

  c A term that describes the different clothes and markings people use to identify themselves within a religion

  d A term that describes a recently created new religion, often with a charismatic and radical leader

2 Which of the following options matches the religion with its correct place of worship, written in English and Sanskrit/Arabic?

  a Hinduism – temple/masjid, Islam – mosque/mandir

  b Hinduism – temple/mandir, Islam – mosque/masjid

  c Hinduism – river/mandir, Islam – shrine/masjid

  d Hinduism – mosque/masjid, Islam – temple/mandir

3 Which of the following are examples of rituals?

  a Offering fruit or flowers to gods

  b Taking part in a christening service

  c Praying

  d Studying scripture

4 Which of the following statements about symbols are correct?

  a Christians, Muslims and Hindus use symbols to remind themselves of what they believe

  b Christians, Muslims and Hindus use symbols during worship

  c Christians and Jews use symbols to represent their religion and remind themselves of key beliefs

  d Islam does not use symbolism

5 What is the purpose of sacred writings?

  a To help people to understand God and His purposes for humankind

  b To give guidance about how we should live

  c To receive inspiration

  d All of the above

6 At what times of year do many religions hold festivals?

  a Birthdays

  b Harvest

  c The start of summer

  d At the start of a new year

7 How can religion help to contribute to a sense of personal identity?

  a It provides a reason for why we are on the earth and gives beliefs to live by

  b It explains why bad things happen

  c It can help us to forgive

  d It encourages moral living

8 Why is religion good for the environment?

  a God created the world

  b Religious people must give to environmental charities

  c Religion teaches that people should respect and protect the earth

  d Religious people limit their car use

9 Which of the following are examples of rites of passage?

  a Sacred Thread ceremonies

  b Bar and bat mitzvah

  c The Aqeeqah

  d All of the above

10 Which of the following are examples of religious moral codes?

  a The Ten Commandments, karma and the Sermon on the Mount

  b The Ten Commandments, mantra and the Sermon on the Mount

  c The Ten Commandments, karma and wudu

  d The Ten Commandments, wudu and the Parable of the Sower

Further practice questions and examples can be found on the accompanying CD.

SECTION 2: Multiple-choice questions

1 Which of the following religions believe in a single God?
  a Christianity, Islam and Hinduism
  b Christianity, Judaism and Hinduism
  c Christianity, Islam and Judaism
  d All of the above

2 Which of the following is the term used to describe belief in a single God?
  a Monogamy
  b Polytheism
  c Polygamy
  d Monotheism

3 What is the Trinity in Christianity?
  a Three different Christian gods
  b Three different aspects/forms of one God
  c A type of prayer
  d Another name for the Holy Spirit

4 Which three central Hindu gods make up the Brahman Trinity?
  a Brahma, Vishnu and Shiva
  b Brahma, Vishnu and Shakti
  c Brahma, Shiva and Shakti
  d Brahma, Lakshmi and Shiva

5 Why do many Hindu students worship the goddess Saraswati during examinations?
  a Saraswati is the goddess of good fortune
  b Worshipping Saraswati brings relief from stress
  c Worshipping Saraswati is thought to aid concentration
  d Saraswati is the goddess of knowledge

6 What term describes belief in the Oneness of God in Islam?
  a Tawhid
  b Shahadah
  c Salah
  d Assalamu alaikum

7 What does the word 'Islam' mean?
  a Respect for all
  b Submission to Muhammad
  c Submission to Allah
  d There is no God but Allah, and Muhammad is His messenger

8 Which word describes the belief that Jews are God's chosen people?
  a Shema
  b Covenant
  c Election
  d Incorporeal

9 What is a covenant?
  a An agreement between God and a person or people
  b A promise from God to provide protection
  c A percentage of money given to God
  d An offering made to God

10 What are orishas?
  a Smaller gods or spirits connected to one supreme God
  b Statues of gods
  c Qualities attributed to gods
  d Short prayers uttered to gods

1 Choose from the words below to fill the gaps in the following sentences:

chapels   church   tabernacle   cathedral

a A bishop is based at a _____

b A _____ is a building set aside for the worship of God

c Hospitals, airports and funeral homes often contain _____

d The ark of the covenant was carried in a _____ as it was thought to be too holy to touch

2 Why might the Pope name a building a basilica?

a It is a pilgrimage site

b It is in Italy

c It is a beautiful building

d It contains certain features such as a nave and a dome

3 Which Hindu tree is thought to have received a drop of heavenly nectar?

a The banyan tree

b The neem tree

c The tulsi tree

d The lotus tree

4 Why is the cow considered sacred in Hinduism?

a Because its dung is useful for a variety of purposes

b Because the Hindu god Vishnu came to earth as a cow

c Because of its sacrifice in providing milk to drink and to make ghee for worship

d Because of its provision of meat

5 In Islam, what is the name of the masjid that contains the Kaaba?

a Masjidul Aqsa

b Masjidun Nabi

c Masjid al-Haram

d Jama masjid

6 What is the purpose of the minbar in a masjid?

a It allows worshippers to see and hear the imam

b It shows the direction of Makkah

c It provides a dividing line between the imam and the worshippers

d It elevates the imam to show his authority and status

7 What is the significance of the Ner Tamid (the perpetual light) in a synagogue?

a It represents the light in the original Temple in Jerusalem, which burned continually

b It provides light to read the Torah by

c It represents Judaism as being the true light

d It symbolises light always shining in darkness

8 What is contained inside the Ark in a synagogue?

a The Tenakh

b Instructions for worship

c Jewish holy garments

d The scroll of the Torah

9 Which Caribbean indigenous religions use poles to attract the spirits?

a Vodun and Orisha

b Vodun and spiritual Baptists

c Vodun and Rastafari

d Rastafari and Spiritual Baptists

10 What is a Casa de Santo?

a A small Vodun temple

b The home of a senior Santeria priest in which followers meet

c A type of food eaten in Vodun worship ceremonies

d A castle used for Santeria ceremonies

Further practice questions and examples can be found on the accompanying CD.

SECTION 4: Multiple-choice questions

1 What was the cause of people converting from Roman Catholic Christianity to Protestant Christianity in the Caribbean during the 17th century?

   a They were disillusioned with Roman Catholicism

   b The British invasion banned Roman Catholicism

   c They were attracted to Protestant Christianity because it allowed them to also practise their traditional religions

   d Protestant Christianity allowed them to divorce

2 When did Christian missionaries arrive in the Caribbean?

   a Beginning of the 1700s

   b Middle of the 1700s

   c End of the 1700s

   d Beginning of the 1800s

3 Why did Indian Hindus travel to the Caribbean?

   a To work as indentured labourers

   b To spread their religion

   c To work as slaves

   d To see the world and enjoy new opportunities

4 In which Caribbean countries is Hinduism mainly concentrated?

   a Trinidad and Tobago and Anguilla

   b Trinidad and Tobago, Belize, and Jamaica

   c Trinidad and Tobago, Suriname, and Guyana

   d Trinidad and Tobago and Cuba

5 What happened to many Muslim slaves when they arrived in the Caribbean?

   a They converted to Christianity and other religions

   b They converted local people to Islam

   c They were imprisoned

   d They built masjids

6 In which of the following geographical regions is Islam mainly concentrated?

   a Middle East, North Africa and South-East Asia

   b Middle East, South Africa and South-East Asia

   c Middle East, Europe and South-East Asia

   d Middle East only

7 Which countries of the world have the largest Jewish population?

   a The UK and Israel

   b The UK and France

   c The UK and Jamaica

   d Israel and North America

8 What was the most common reason for Jews immigrating to the Caribbean during the 15th and 17th centuries?

   a To take advantage of business opportunities

   b For better education opportunities

   c To flee persecution

   d To enjoy a warmer climate

9 Where did Rastafari begin?

   a Trinidad

   b Jamaica

   c Barbados

   d Haiti

10 In which Caribbean country is Vodun concentrated?

   a Dominican Republic

   b Haiti

   c Trinidad and Tobago

   d Grenada

1 What are the names of the two parts of the Bible?

  a The Old and Modern Testaments

  b The Ancient and Modern Testaments

  c The Old and New Testaments

  d Revealed and Hidden Testaments

2 Along with the Bible, what are the other main sources of authority for Christians?

  a The Holy Spirit and Christian leaders/teachers

  b The Holy Spirit and the Holy Piby

  c The Holy Spirit and the self/conscience

  d Christian leaders and the self/conscience

3 Which category of Hindu scriptures is believed to have been communicated directly from Brahman?

  a Smriti

  b Shruti

  c Swati

  d Shastras

4 Which holy Hindu story illustrates that, although adharma threatens order and happiness, dharma prevails?

  a *Ramayana*

  b Puranas

  c *Mahabharata*

  d All of the above

5 What is Shariah in Islam?

  a The laws that govern how a Muslim should behave and worship

  b A Muslim holy text

  c Advice given by a Muslim leader

  d Food that Muslims are permitted to eat

6 What is the English translation of the Arabic word 'Sunnah'?

  a The teachings

  b The revelations

  c The practical example

  d The sayings

7 Together, what do the Torah, the Nev'im and the Ketuvim form?

  a The Talmud

  b The Apocrypha

  c The Tenakh

  d The Bible

8 What is the most important source of authority for Jews?

  a The Torah

  b The Nev'im

  c The Talmud

  d The rabbi

9 Which Caribbean indigenous religion does not use the Bible as a source of authority?

  a Santeria

  b Vodun

  c Orisha

  d Spiritual Baptists

10 Why is spirit possession important to some followers of Caribbean indigenous religions?

  a The spirits give guidance and revelation about the future

  b The spirits provide a connection with past lives

  c Spirit possession gives a deeper understanding of life and death

  d All of the above

Further practice questions and examples can be found on the accompanying CD.

1 Which of the following are gifts of the Holy Spirit?

  a Speaking in tongues and patience

  b Preaching and compassion

  c Speaking in tongues and prophesying

  d Self-control and faithfulness

2 What is the term used to describe the Christian belief that Jesus Christ will return to earth?

  a The Rapture

  b The Resurrection

  c The Second Coming

  d The Ascension

3 What is dharma in Hinduism?

  a Religion, duty and law

  b The collective deeds of a person throughout their life

  c The soul

  d A blockage to spiritual enlightenment

4 What are the four goals in life for a Hindu?

  a Kama, artha, dharma and samsara

  b Kama, artha, dharma and grihastha

  c Kama, Maayaa, dharma and moksha

  d Karma, artha, dharma and moksha

5 What is the role of angels in Islam?

  a To announce the end of the world

  b To attend to the needs of Allah

  c To provide protection and blessing to Muslims and to carry out specific tasks

  d They have no role

6 What are the Five Pillars of Islam?

  a Declaration of faith, reproduction (having children), prayer, pilgrimage and fasting

  b Declaration of faith, prayer, charitable giving, fasting and pilgrimage

  c Baptism, prayer, charitable giving, fasting and pilgrimage

  d Declaration of faith, prayer, charitable giving, study of the Qur'an and pilgrimage

7 According to Jewish belief, what are the three parts of a human soul?

  a The I, the other and the Holy Spirit

  b The animating spirit, the you and the Holy Spirit

  c The animating spirit, the still spirit and the Holy Spirit

  d The animating spirit, the reflective spirit and the restored spirit

8 Which Jewish sects follow halakhah (Jewish law) either strictly or liberally?

  a Orthodox, Reconstructionist, Conservative and Flexidox

  b Orthodox, Reform, Humanist and Flexidox

  c Orthodox, Reform, Reconstructionist and Humanist

  d Orthodox, Messianic and Reconstructionist

9 Which Caribbean indigenous religion teaches that the universe is occupied by three groups of spirits?

  a Vodun

  b Orisha

  c Revivalism

  d Rastafari

10 Which Caribbean indigenous religion carries out degradation ceremonies?

  a Rastafari

  b Spiritual Baptists

  c Vodun

  d Santeria

Further practice questions and examples can be found on the accompanying CD.

1 Why is the day that Christians remember Jesus dying called Good Friday?

  a Jesus was good

  b It is the duty of all Christians to be good

  c It is the start of the Sabbath

  d Christians believe that Jesus' death was good because it paid the price of sin and allows human beings to have their relationship with God restored

2 What does the Day of Pentecost commemorate?

  a Jesus teaching that the Christian life will be costly

  b The coming of the Holy Spirit

  c The start of Jesus' teachings being written down

  d Jesus' ascension into heaven

3 Why do many Hindus stay awake all night on the night of Maha Sivaraatri?

  a To carry out all-night prayer vigils

  b To benefit from the high level of divine energy on this night

  c To practise self-denial

  d To extend celebrations for as long as possible

4 Why do Hindus throw colourful dye at each other during the festival of Phagwa/Holi?

  a To celebrate colour and diversity

  b To cover up past wrongdoing

  c To disguise themselves

  d To celebrate the god Krishna's playful side

5 How are the poor provided for during the Muslim festivals of Eid ul Fitr and Eid ul Adha?

  a Through donating a room of your house to a homeless person

  b Through giving a percentage of your wealth to charity and sharing your food with the poor

  c Through praying for the poor

  d Through creating employment for the poor

6 Which of these Muslim festivals commemorates the birthday of the Prophet Muhammad?

  a Miladunnabi

  b Lailatul Miraj

  c Lailatul Qadr

  d Lailatul Bara'at

7 What happens on the tenth day of Rosh Hashanah?

  a Jews commit the coming year to God

  b God judges each Jewish person to decide whether they should remain in the Book of Life

  c Jews share in a feast to celebrate the onset of a new year

  d Jews make a sacrifice to God

8 What does the name Passover refer to?

  a The passing over of one year into the next

  b The Jews passing over the Red Sea during their Exodus from Egypt

  c God's presence passing over creation

  d The angel passing over Jewish homes when he brought death to Egyptian firstborn sons

9 What event do Rastafari commemorate on 2 November each year?

  a Ethiopian Orthodox Christmas

  b The coronation of Emperor Haile Selassie

  c Haile Selassie's visit to Jamaica

  d Haile Selassie's birthday

10 Which god is honoured during the Orisha rain festival?

  a Olokun, the god of the ocean

  b Shango, the god of thunder

  c Osun, the river goddess

  d Yemaya, goddess of the ocean

1 What do the bread and wine symbolise in Holy Communion?

  a Jesus' words and actions while on earth

  b Jesus' body and blood

  c God's provision

  d Jesus' holiness

2 What earlier ritual is confirmation linked to?

  a Baptism/christening

  b Naming ceremony

  c Holy Communion

  d Marriage

3 What happens three days after a Hindu cremation?

  a The ashes of the body are gathered and ceremonies are performed to help the soul to find its new resting place

  b A service of remembrance is held

  c Mourners perform grieving ceremonies

  d The ashes of the body are planted in the ground

4 What is sapta-padi in a Hindu marriage?

  a Special food to signify the sweetness of the marriage

  b The patterns a Hindu has drawn on their hands with henna

  c The seven steps that a couple take around a fire while declaring promises to each other

  d The headdress that the woman wears

5 What is the first thing to happen to a Muslim baby when they are born?

  a The Shahadah is whispered into their ear

  b The adhan is whispered into their ear

  c Their head is shaved

  d A small piece of date is inserted into their mouth

6 After death a Muslim is wrapped in three plain sheets. What do the three plain sheets symbolise?

  a That the person is purified through faith in Allah

  b The simplicity of death

  c That all Muslims are equal in death

  d That we take nothing out of this world

7 Where in a Jewish home is the mezuzah placed?

  a In hallways

  b In the kitchen

  c At the entrance

  d In doorways

8 What do the words 'bar mitzvah' mean?

  a Son of the Commandment

  b Son of the Covenant

  c Son of the Law

  d Son of the Lord

9 What is the purpose of a mourning ceremony?

  a To mourn a dead relative or friend

  b To repent sins and seek forgiveness for them

  c To focus on your spiritual rather than your physical state

  d To mark the end of a particular stage of life

10 Which of the following lists the four Santeria initiation ceremonies in the correct order?

  a Receive eleke, create an elegguá, receive warrior implements, the Asiento

  b Create an elegguá, receive eleke, receive warrior implements, the Asiento

  c The Asiento, receive eleke, create an elegguá, receive warrior implements

  d Receive warrior implements, the Asiento, create an elegguá, receive eleke

1 Which religions believe in monotheism?
  a Christianity, Hinduism, Islam, Rastafari, Revivalism
  b Christianity, Islam, Judaism, Rastafari, Revivalism, Spiritual Baptist
  c Christianity, Islam, Judaism, Rastafari, Revivalism, Orisha
  d Christianity, Judaism, Vodun, Hinduism, Orisha

2 Which religions are founded on the teaching of prophets?
  a Christianity, Islam, Judaism, Rastafari
  b Hinduism, Islam, Rastafari
  c Islam, Judaism, Hinduism
  d Christianity, Vodun, Hinduism, Islam

3 Which religions were introduced to the Caribbean through the slave trade or indentured workers?
  a Islam, Hinduism, Caribbean indigenous religions
  b Christianity, Islam, Caribbean indigenous religions
  c Judaism, Islam, Caribbean indigenous religions
  d Judaism, Hinduism, Caribbean indigenous religions

4 Which religion does not follow Old Testament teaching?
  a Hinduism
  b Islam
  c Revivalism
  d Judaism

5 Which religions use shrines (areas containing a holy statue, altar, offerings, etc.) in their worship?
  a All of them
  b None of them
  c Islam, Christianity, Judaism and Santeria
  d Christianity, Hinduism and Spiritual Baptist

6 In which major religions do worshippers sit on the floor?
  a Islam and Judaism
  b Islam and Hinduism
  c Hinduism and Judaism
  d Christianity and Judaism

7 Which of the following teachings do all religions accept?
  a Life after death
  b Communication with spirits
  c Sin and salvation
  d Reincarnation

8 What is the Hindu doctrine of sin and salvation?
  a The concept of sin does not exist in Hinduism
  b That paap (moving away from dharma) is sin, and moksha is salvation
  c That karma determines your spiritual progress on to moksha
  d There is no salvation in Hinduism

9 Which religions do not use symbols in worship?
  a Christianity and Rastafari
  b Christianity and Judaism
  c Islam and Judaism
  d Hinduism and Islam

10 Which religion does not have rules about which foods can and cannot be eaten?
  a Christianity
  b Rastafari
  c Judaism
  d Hinduism

Further practice questions and examples can be found on the accompanying CD.

Option A: Short-answer questions

1 Using examples, outline what the different names of God can tell us about what God is like.

2 Explain what stewardship means and how this influences Christians' views on child abuse and discrimination.

3 Explain what the Dead Sea Scrolls are and outline their relevance to the Bible today.

4 Describe what sin is and the effects it can have on quality of life. According to the Bible, what are the consequences of sin?

Option B: Short-answer questions

1 Outline the roles, responsibilities and rights that Hindus have in the following relationships, giving examples from Hindu scriptures where possible:

   a Children to parents

   b Parents to children

   c Husbands and wives

2 Explain how Shabari's story illustrates faith.

3 Describe Brahman as both Nirgun and Sagun Brahma, outlining the characteristics of these two views of God.

4 Outline the relationship between bondage and liberation in Hinduism.

Option C: Short-answer questions

1 Using examples and references from the Qur'an and Hadith, describe how a person can be a good vicegerent of God on the earth in the following circumstances:
   a Care for the environment
   b Attitude to fellow human beings
   c Role in the family

2 Outline some of the teachings of the main tenets (principles) in the Qur'an concerning Allah, man and Islamic law.

3 Discuss the role of one of the following in Islam:
   a Angels
   b Prophets
   c The hereafter (afterlife).

4 Define sin from an Islamic perspective and describe two possible consequences of sin as described in the Qur'an.

Option D: Short-answer questions

1 How does being made in the image of God bring meaning and purpose to life according to Jewish teaching?

2 Describe the three types of Hebrew writings that make up the Tenakh. State the name of at least one of the 'books' that appears in each type of writing.

3 Give translations for the following names for God:
   a Yahweh
   b Ha 'Shem
   c El

4 Choose one of the Jewish festivals discussed in this section and describe how and when it is celebrated, what its meaning is and what its modern significance is to Jews.

Further practice questions and examples can be found on the accompanying CD.

Glossary

A

Adhan the Islamic call to prayer.

Adharma the opposite of dharma, it means 'that which is not in accord with the law' – referring to both the human written law and the divinely given law of nature. It includes concepts such as wrongness, evil and immorality.

Admonition advice or correction. It is a term that comes up frequently in the Qur'an.

Advent the period that starts on the fourth Sunday before Christmas Day and ends on Christmas Day. During Advent, Christians remember Christ's promise that he will come to earth again to judge humanity.

Akeret Habayit Hebrew for 'mainstay', meaning the backbone or building block on which everything else is built. In the home, the mother is seen as the Akeret Habayit. She fills the central role and is responsible for the family and the home.

Al Qadr one of the six pillars of faith for Muslims. It is the belief in divine decree – that everything that happens is the will of Allah and that He sees every person's life before they live it.

Aranyakas Hindu sacred writings that focus on a category of rituals relevant to one who has renounced the world.

Atheism disbelief in the existence of a god or gods.

Atman the divine self.

Autopsy examination of a body to determine the cause of death. This procedure often involves examining internal organs.

Avatar the concept of God taking a human form.

B

Baptism by the Holy Spirit the moment that the Holy Spirit enters a person's body. This can cause a physical reaction – the person might shake, cry, laugh or speak in tongues. People also testify to a feeling of peace and joy.

Baptism by water also called baptism by immersion. This is the process of being submerged in water to symbolise the old, sinful self dying and then rising to a new spiritual life. This mirrors the actions of Christ dying and rising again.

Brahman the Ultimate Reality or Truth in Hinduism. It is considered to be the spirit that effects creation and creates and sustains all life. Hindus see Brahman as the 'Ultimate Reality' to have union with – the lifeblood and core of a person, creature or plant.

Brahmanas sacred writings added to the Samhitas or Vedas that detail the performance of rituals in domestic life.

C

Caste also caste system. This derives from the Portuguese word 'casta' meaning pure. It is a Western term used to describe the socio-economic grouping system in Hinduism. As a Hindu, the social group or class that you form part of is dependent on conduct, spiritual knowledge and profession. In the Caribbean the caste system only has ritual status; it is not generally acknowledged in day-to-day life.

Circumcision the removal of the foreskin (the tight skin covering the end of the penis).

Commentary a piece of writing that interprets and explains a usually well-known text. There are many different commentaries on most religious texts, including the Tenakh, the Bible, the Qur'an and the Vedas.

Cremation the act of burning a body after death. Christianity teaches that what happens to the body after death does not really matter as the soul (the core of a person) is no longer present.

Crucifix a cross with the figure of Jesus Christ on it.

D

Degradation a Vodun ceremony to remove abilities and pass them on to a successor.

Dharma a Sanskrit word meaning 'that which supports'. It refers to the duties, responsibilities, values and guiding principles that help Hindus to achieve moksha (the connection of one's soul with Brahman), while also maintaining order, peace and harmony on the earth. There are different types of dharma for different purposes.

Diaspora Jews living outside Israel.

Disciple the follower of a particular religion, movement or school of thought. Disciples live their lives according to the teachings and principles of their religion.

Divination the act of discerning or discovering future or unknown events through supernatural powers – usually spirit possession or communication.

E

Eid Mubarak this means 'blessed Eid'. Just like Christians at Christmas, as Eid Mubarak approaches Muslims send each other cards to wish each other a happy festival time.

Elected chosen by God for a special purpose.

Epiphany the holy day commemorating the manifestation of Christ to the Gentiles. It also marks the end of the 12 days of Christmas.

Euthanasia the painless killing of someone in an irreversible coma or suffering from an incurable disease.

Evangelise to tell others about your religion with the objective of converting them.

Fasting going without food (and sometimes drink) in order to focus on your spiritual state rather than your physical needs. Many people also fast to share in the suffering of a religious figure, or to show the earnestness of their prayers.

Fiqh methods of interpreting and applying Islamic law.

Free will the freedom and ability to make one's own decisions and choose between right and wrong.

Funeral pyre a structure made up of layers of wood. The body of the deceased is laid on this and the wood is set alight. Burning of funeral pyres still takes place in the open air in India and the Caribbean. In other parts of the world, funeral pyres are assembled inside buildings with an open roof.

Fusion the joining together of different beliefs, practices or traditions to create a new identity.

Gentiles people who are not Jewish.

Gifts of the Holy Spirit supernatural abilities that the Holy Spirit gives to people. These include speaking in tongues (a heavenly language), prophesy (predicting a future event) and words of knowledge (an understanding about a person or situation). Fruits of the Spirit are attributes such as patience, kindness and self-control, which can be strengthened in a person by the Holy Spirit.

Grand Maitre the Great Master/ Creator. It is the Vodun name for God.

Hadith the sayings, actions and silent approvals of Muhammad,

written down by his followers. They are part of a body of writings called the Sunnah.

Halakha Jewish law and jurisprudence, based on the writings in the Talmud.

Halal meat that has been slaughtered in line with the instructions outlined in Islam. Only meat that is halal can be eaten by Muslims.

Holy Communion participating in the Eucharist, the service at which bread and wine are consecrated (made sacred).

Home altar/shrine a specially demarcated space where one worships (individually or with the family) and keeps sacred objects.

I and the plural I-N-I the term Rastafari use instead of 'me' – this reflects the individuality and respect of each person. Using I and I (shortened to I-N-I) reflects that each Rastafari is an individual but that they are also all united under Jah.

Ihsan perfection. The highest state or level that a Muslim seeks to achieve.

Incarnations gods or spirits becoming flesh (living beings) on earth. This is often as a human, although in Hinduism many of the gods and goddesses have non-human features, such as Hanuman the monkey god and the many Hindu gods and goddesses that have multiple arms.

Indentureship a way for plantation landowners to obtain cheap labour once slavery was abolished. Workers (normally shipped in from other countries) were paid a small amount of money to work on the land. Workers had to sign a contract to say that they would work for the landowner for a set period of time – normally

five years. Although workers were promised good conditions, in reality, many workers were treated little better than slaves.

Inquisition (or Spanish Inquisition) an institution set up by the Roman Catholic Church in 1480. Its purpose was to protect Roman Catholicism in Catholic countries and remove other religions. The Inquisition spread from Spain to Spanish islands, Portugal and countries in South America. During the time of the Inquisition, anyone unwilling to convert to Roman Catholicism was expelled from the country or killed.

Jah the living God, believed by Rastafari to be Ras Tafari.

Jurisprudence the theory and philosophy of law. There are different branches of jurisprudence in society including medical jurisprudence and political jurisprudence. Islamic jurisprudence is called Fiqh, which literally means 'understanding', and relates to the laws and duties of Islam.

Kalaamullah the Perfect Words of Allah.

Karma the concept of a human being's actions causing that person to be bound to the cycle of birth and death.

Last Days the time leading up to the end of the world.

Lent the 40 days before Easter, when Christians traditionally show penitence and practise fasting and self-restraint to commemorate Christ's fasting in the wilderness.

Liturgy written prayers that congregations read together.

Glossary

Manifest that which is clear and seen. The Sanskrit word for manifest is vyakta.

Missionaries people sent on a religious assignment.

Mitzvah a commandment in Judaism.

Moksha the spiritual connection of one's soul (atman) with Brahman (the Ultimate Reality). Achieving moksha frees a person's soul from the continual cycle of death and rebirth on earth.

Monogamous being married to or having a relationship with only one person at a time.

Monotheism belief in a single god.

Moral a good human behaviour. If someone has good morals they have a good sense of what is right. Many people believe that human beings are born with a God-given conscience that helps them to discern between right and wrong.

New Testament one of the two parts of the Bible. The New Testament begins with the coming of Jesus to the earth. It records Jesus' teaching and actions while he was on the earth and records the history and teaching of the early church.

Night Journey when the Prophet Muhammad travelled from Makkah to Jerusalem in a single night. From Jerusalem, Muhammad was taken up to heaven by Allah.

Nisab the amount Muslims must have saved (after meeting basic requirements) for a year before paying zakah. Once a Muslim has saved this amount of money or more for a year, they pay zakah (2.5 per cent) on it.

Non-denominational churches churches that are open or acceptable to people of any Christian denomination.

Nyabhingi an orthodox celebration of Rastafari involving music and drumming.

Old Testament one of the two parts of the Bible. The Old Testament records the time before Jesus came to earth. It contains the story of creation and gives the history of the Jewish people and God's relationship with them. It also contains lots of prophecies about the future.

Oral transmission passing on information through speech.

Orishas gods or spirits smaller than the main god or gods in a religion. It is thought that it is often an orisha that possesses people during spirit possession. Orishas feature particularly in Caribbean indigenous religions.

Pacifist a person who believes that war and violence are wrong and refuses to fight.

Pan-Africanism the concept of a socially and politically united Africa. This single African community would include all native Africans and those of African descent. It is a goal of Rastafari to return to Africa, which is thought of as the motherland.

Parmatma the super soul in Hinduism that lives within the souls of all living beings.

Patriarchal a society ruled by men.

Penitence regret for sins committed.

Persecution sustained aggression and ill-treatment of a person or group.

Pilgrimage a journey to a sacred place.

Promised Land Canaan, the land promised to Abram and his descendants.

Prophecy the prediction of future events. Christians believe that the Old Testament prophesies about Jesus coming to earth. There are also prophecies in the New Testament that relate to the end of the world.

Purushartas four goals of human living in Hinduism designed to foster successful living on earth leading to moksha.

Qalb the Islamic word for the heart.

Qur'an the sacred book of Islam.

Ramayana the epic poem first penned by Valmiki and rewritten by others, including Tulsidas. It tells the story of the great Lord Rama and his epic war with Rawan to regain his wife who was kidnapped, and to restore moral and social order to society.

Reasoning the practice of Rastafari discussing an issue or a passage from the Bible. It is important that everyone has a chance to give their view during reasoning and the time must end with everyone reaching an agreed understanding.

Redemption to recover possession of something by paying a price. Christians believe that Jesus paid the ultimate price to recover God's 'possession' of us. The Bible teaches that Jesus died to pay for our sin. With sin removed, God could restore His relationship with humans forever.

Religion a system of beliefs and practices.

Repentance feeling or showing true regret or remorse for a sin committed.

Righteous to act according to high moral values. God cannot be anything but righteous since He is the source of all goodness, fairness and justice. God's righteousness means that He should judge humans according to His strict morals and cast them aside. However, Jews believe that God has chosen to show mercy and allow sinful people to have a relationship with Him.

Sacrament an outward religious act that shows an inward spiritual state or decision and which gives peace and grace to the soul. However, not all Christians believe in the sacrament.

Samhitas mantras of the Vedas – traditionally synonymous with the word Veda.

Samsara the concept of human beings being bound to repeated cycles of birth and death or reincarnation based on their karma.

Sanskrit an ancient ritual language of Hinduism.

Second Coming the prophesied return of Jesus Christ to earth.

Shahadah the Muslim declaration of faith, said several times a day. 'There is no god but Allah, and Muhammad is His messenger.'

Shariah the laws of Islam, based on the teachings of the Qur'an and the Prophet Muhammad.

Shema the statement of Jewish belief that begins: 'Hear, Israel, the Lord is our God, the Lord is One.'

Shruti this means 'what is heard or revealed'. It is knowledge revealed by God to spiritually evolved humans called rishis. These are the Vedas and they are the primary source of religious authority. They are traditionally passed on through the oral tradition.

Sin a wrong thought or action that rebels against God and His perfect standards. Christians believe that sin entered the world through Adam and Eve's disobedience. Ever since then, sin has been part of our world. All humans sin, but Christians believe that Jesus' death means humans can be forgiven and have a relationship with God despite their wrongdoing.

Smriti sacred texts written by enlightened human beings to analyse and communicate the teachings of Shruti to the masses.

Sovereign supreme ruler over all.

Stewardship 1. in the religious sense, the practice of being appointed by God to care for and nurture his world, including caring for the creatures, plants and people in it. Many people describe this responsibility as humans being God's 'hands and feet' in the world; 2. the role of taking personal responsibility for caring for one's own or another person's resources.

Sunnah writings made up of the Hadith and the biography of Muhammad.

Taqwah derived from the word 'waqaa', it means 'to shield'. One must shield against the punishment of Allah by carrying out his commandments and abstaining from any prohibited actions.

Tawhid the Islamic belief that there is just one God.

Teertha a sacred pilgrimage that many Hindus make (either internally or externally) for spiritual merit; for meeting holy persons; to perform specific rites; and for a general spiritual experience.

Tenakh the Jewish Holy Scriptures. They are grouped into three sections: the Torah, the Nev'im and the Ketuvim.

The Fall Adam and Eve's disobedience in the Garden of Eden, which resulted in humankind's descent into a state of sin.

Torah the law books of Jewish faith. It is made up of the first five books of the Old Testament (Genesis, Exodus, Leviticus, Numbers and Deuteronomy).

Trinity the three different persons of God: God the Father, who presides in heaven and rules over all; God the Son, who came to earth in human form as Jesus Christ; and God the Holy Spirit, who is God in spirit form, which enables Him to be with His people and to speak to, comfort and guide them.

Unmanifest that which is hidden – it cannot be clearly seen or understood. The Sanskrit word for unmanifest is avyakta.

Upanishads sacred writings that give deep philosophical explanations of Vedic teachings.

Usury a professional and formal term used to describe the action of lending money with interest attached (paying back more than you borrowed). This is the established practice of Western banks.

Vicegerents trustees or representatives. Vicegerent (vicegerency) is a word that is not used very often in everyday life, but it is used frequently in Islam to describe the responsibility that humankind has on the earth as the representatives of Allah.

Yoruba the language and belief system that originated in the West African countries of Nigeria, Benin and Togo.

Index

A

Abakua dance of the Ireme 73
abortion 108, 149
Abram (Abraham) 15, 158
Absolute, the 114
Adam and Eve 120–1
adhan 80
adharma 10, 116
admonition 125
Advent 58
agape love 97
Akeret Habayit 148
Al Akhirah 51
Al Qadr 51, 137–8
Allah 12–13, 134–9, 143
angels 51, 134
animals 21, 123
apocalyptic writing 100
Apocrypha 43
Aranyakas 38
Ark of the Covenant 18, 24, 84
Ascension Day 60
Ash Wednesday 59
Ashura 66
assembly halls 19
atheism 7
atman (atma) 48, 115
authority, sources of 89
   Caribbean indigenous
      religions 44–5
   Christianity 36–7
   Hinduism 38–9
   Islam 40–1
   Judaism 42–3
   see also sacred writings
autopsies 149
avatars 112, 114

B

baptism 77, 90
   by the Holy Spirit 57
   by water 45, 56, 87
bar mitzvah 84
basilicas 19
bat mitzvahan and bat chayil 85
belief systems 4
   see also teachings and beliefs
Bembe feasts 73
Bhagavad Gita 106, 108, 112
Bible 36–7, 44, 45, 97, 98–101
birth 75, 78, 80, 82
Blackman's Bible 44
Brahma 10, 114
Brahman 10, 114–15
Brahmanas 38

C

calendars 13, 165
camps, Rastafari 26
capital punishment 94, 108, 147
Casa de Santos 27
castes and caste system 48, 111
cathedrals 19
Chanukah 69, 163
chapelles 27
chapels 19
charity 50, 122, 127, 138
child abuse 93, 108, 126, 146
children 96, 110, 122, 124, 148
   see also birth
christenings 74
Christianity
   the Bible 36–7, 97, 98–101
   in the Caribbean 29, 30
   festivals 58–61
   and God 8–9, 46–7, 92, 97, 102–3
   human life issues 92–7
   locations in world 28
   places of worship 18–19
   practices and rites 74–7
   sin and salvation 47, 104–5
Christmas 58
churches 18, 26, 27
circumcision 80, 82
commentary 43
confirmation 77
Conservative Jews 54
Corpus Christi 61
covenants 15, 158, 159
creator 8, 12
cremation 75, 79
crucifix 77
cults 3

D

David, King 15
Day of Atonement 68, 161–2
Dead Sea Scrolls 98–9, 150
death
   Caribbean indigenous religions
      and 86, 87
   Christianity and 75
   Hinduism and 79
   Islam and 51, 80–1, 136
   Judaism and 83, 152, 155
degradation 57, 86
deities 5
   see also God
denominations 2
dharma 10, 48, 116
Dharma Shastras 38–9

diaspora 161, 164
disciples 106
discrimination 94, 109, 126, 147
dismissal, ceremony of 87
Divali (Deepavali) 62
divination 45, 57
Durga 11

E

Earth festival 73
Easter 59–60
Eid Mubarak 64
Eid ul Adha 65
Eid ul Fitr 64
Ekalavya 107
elected people 14, 153, 159
Epiphany 58–9
Eucharist 18, 59, 76
euthanasia 149
evangelise 19

F

Fall, the 151
family life 96, 110–11, 123–4,
   147–8, 153–4
fasting 50, 64, 139
Feast of Weeks 71, 152, 165
female roles 95, 109, 124, 126, 148
festivals 5, 90
   Caribbean indigenous
      religions 72–3
   Christian 58–61
   Hindu 62–3
   Islamic 64–7
   Jewish 68–71, 152, 160–5
fiqh 41
fish symbol 77
Five Pillars of Islam 50
Flexidox Jews 54
food 65, 85, 90, 154–5
forgiveness 47, 52
free will 92, 119, 144
funeral pyre 79
fusion of religions 34, 35

G

gambling 126
Ganesh 11
Ganges, River 20–1
Garvey, Marcus 34
Gemara 43
gender roles 95, 109, 124, 126, 148
Gentiles 58
Ghandi, Mahatma 106, 107
gifts of the Holy Spirit 47

God 5, 88
  Allah in Islam 12–13, 134–9, 143
  Caribbean indigenous religions
    and 16–17
  Christianity and 8–9, 46–7, 92, 97,
    102–3
  Hindu manifestations of 10–11,
    114–15
  Judaism and 14–15, 52, 148–9,
    156–9
Good Friday 59–60
Grand Maitre 17
Güiro 73
guruhood 106–8

H

Hadith 13, 40, 131–3
Haile Selassie, Emperor 16, 34
hajj 22, 50, 81
Halakha 147
halal meat 65
Hanafi 41
Hanbali 41
Hanuman 11
Hinduism
  in the Caribbean 31
  festivals 62–3
  holy scriptures 38–9, 107, 112–13,
    117
  human life issues 106–11
  locations in the world 28
  major beliefs 48–9
  manifestations of God 10–11,
    114–15
  practices and rites 78–9
  sacred places 20–1
  sin and liberation 116–19
HIV/AIDS 95
Holi 62
Holy Communion 18, 59, 76
Holy Piby 44
Holy Spirit 9, 46–7, 61, 103
Holy Week 59–60
home altar/shrine 20
hounfours 26
Howell, L.P. 34
human life
  meaning and purpose of 92, 106,
    120–1, 144
  sanctity of 111
  value and dignity of 93–5, 108–10,
    121–2, 126–7, 146–7
human relationships 13, 97, 111
Humanistic Jews 54
Hussein, Imam 66

I

I and I-N-I 44
ibaadah (worship) 125, 138
ihsan 143
incarnations 9, 48, 63
indentureship 30, 31, 32
initiation ceremonies 90
  Christian 77
  Hindu 79
  Jewish 84–5
  Santeria 87
inquisition 33
Islam
  and Allah 12–13, 134
  in the Caribbean 32
  festivals 64–7
  human life issues 120–7
  locations in the world 28
  places of worship 22–3
  practices and rites 80–1
  sacred writings 40, 128–31,
    135
  sin, punishment and reward 140–3
  sources of authority 40–1
  teachings and beliefs 50–1, 132–3,
    134–9

J

Jah 16
Jesus Christ 9, 46, 47, 103
Jonah 69
Judaism
  in the Caribbean 33
  festivals 68–71, 152, 160–5
  and God 14–15, 52, 144, 148–9,
    156–9
  human life issues 144–9
  locations in the world 28
  places of worship 24–5
  practices and rites 82–5
  sacred writings 42–3, 150–1
  sources of authority 42–3
  teachings and beliefs 52–5,
    151–5
judgement 47, 52, 153
jurisprudence, Islamic 41

K

Kaaba 22
kalaamullah 129
karma 48, 106
Ketuvim 42, 150, 151
kosher food 85, 154–5
Krishna Janam Ashtmi 63

L

Lailatul Bara'at 67
Lailatul Miraj 66–7
Lailatul Qadr 67
Lakshmi 11
Last Days 47, 53, 136–7
law, Islamic 40, 41, 121, 131
Lent 59
liberation (moksha) 48, 106, 116,
  118–19
life see human life
liturgy 3, 76
loas (lwas) 17
love, for others 97, 111

M

Maayaa (Maya) 49
Maha Sivaraatri 63
Mahabharata 39, 107
Mahesh (Shiva) 10, 114
male roles 95, 109, 124, 126,
  148
Maliki 41
mandirs 20
manifest, God 115
marriage
  Christianity and 75, 96
  Hinduism and 78–9
  Islam and 80
  Judaism and 82, 147, 148
masjids (mosques) 22–3
Maundy Thursday 59
menorah 83
mentally and physically challenged,
  the 95, 110, 147
Messiah 53, 153
Messianic Jews 54
mezuzah 83
Midrash 42
Mihrab arch 23
Miladunnabi 66
minarets 23
minbar 23
miracles 100
Mishnah 43
Mishneh Torah 43
mission houses 26
missionaries 30
mitzvah 145
moksha 48, 106, 116, 118–19
monogamous marriage 96
monotheism 8, 46
morals 145–6, 155
Moses 15
mosques (masjids) 22–3

Index

mourning ceremony 86
Muhammad 22, 40, 66–7, 128, 131, 136
Myalism 34

N
nation dance 86
Nava Raatri 63
Nev'im 42, 150, 151
New Testament 36–7, 97, 99
Night Journey 22
Nirgun Brahma 115
nisab 50
Noah 158
non-denominational churches 61
Nyabhingi 72

O
Odu Ifa 44–5
Old Testament 36, 97, 99
Olodumare 17
oral transmission 128, 150
Orisha
  beliefs 57
  concept of God 17
  development of 35
  festivals 72–3
  places of worship 26–7
  sources of authority 44–5
  spread of 29
orishas 17
Orthodox Jews 53
Oshun (Osun) festival 72

P
pacifists 95
palais 26
Palm Sunday 59
pan-Africanism 56
parables 36, 100
Parmatma 115
Paschaltide 60
patriarchal societies 95
peace, Islam and 122
penitence 68
Pentecost 61
persecution 33, 163
Pesach (Passover) 70, 152, 164–5
Phagwa/Holi 62
pilgrimage 19, 22, 50
places of worship 4, 90
  Caribbean indigenous
    religions 26–7
  Christian 18–19
  Hindu sacred places 20–1

Islamic 22–3
Jewish 24–5
plants and trees, sacred 21
poverty 94, 109, 126, 147
prayer 3–4
  Christianity 76
  Islam 23, 50, 125, 132, 138
  Judaism 24, 153
prejudice 94, 109, 126, 147
Promised Land 157
prophecy and **prophets** 42, 51, 100, 135, 151
Pukumina Revivalism 16, 44
punishment 47, 52, 133, 137
puranas 39
Purim 70, 163–4
purushartas (goals of life) 49, 109

Q
qalb 142
Qibla wall 23
Qur'an 40, 128–31, 132–3, 135

R
race relations 13, 146
Rain festival 73
Rama Naumi (Rama Navami) 63
Ramadan 50, 64, 139
Ramayana 39, 112–13, 117
Rastafari
  beliefs 56
  concept of God 16
  development of 34
  festivals 72
  places of worship 26
  sources of authority 44
  spread of 29
reasoning, worship through 26
Reconstructionist Jews 54
redemption 47
Reform Jews 53, 54
reincarnation 48
religion 2
  comparing religions 88–9
  reasons for following a 6
  throughout the world 28–9
renunciation, ceremony of 86
repentance 105, 161
resurrection 60, 153
Revealed Books 51
revelation 134–5
Revivalism
  beliefs 56
  concept of God 16
  development of 34

festivals 72
places of worship 26
practices and rites 87
sources of authority 44
spread of 29
reward 47, 52, 137
righteous, God is 159
rites of passage 5
  Caribbean indigenous
    religions 86–7
  Christian 74–5
  Hindu 77–8
  Islamic 80–1
  Jewish 82–3
rituals 4
  Christian 76
  Hindu 79
  Islamic 81
  Jewish 85
rivers, holy 20–1
Rosh Hashanah 68, 161

S
Sabbath 54–5, 152, 160
sacrament 76
sacred writings 5
  Caribbean indigenous
    religions 44–5
  Christian 36–7, 98–101
  Hindu 38–9, 107, 112–13, 117
  Islamic 40, 128–33, 135
  Jewish 42–3, 150–1
Sagun Brahma 115
salah (prayers) 50, 125, 138
salvation 52, 104–5
Samhitas 38
samsara 48
samskaras 78–9
Sanskrit 38
Santeria
  beliefs 57
  concept of God 17
  development of 35
  festivals 73
  places of worship 27
  practices and rites 87
  sources of authority 45
  spread of 29
Saraswati 11
sawm (saum) 50, 139
scriptures *see* sacred writings
Second Coming 47, 53
sects 2–3
Sephardic Jews 33
sexual issues 96, 146

Shafei 41
Shahadah 50
Shakti 10, 63
Shariah 40, 122
Shavuot 71, 152, 165
Shema 14
Shiva (Mahesh) 10, 114
shrines 20
Shruti 38
Simchath Torah 69
sin
   Christianity and 47, 104
   Hinduism and 112, 116–18
   Islam and 140–2
   Judaism and 52
slavery 30, 32
Smriti 38–9
social responsibility, Islam and 125,
   127, 133
social status 111, 146
souls 48, 52, 115, 136
sovereign ruler 102
spirit possession 44, 45
Spiritual Baptists
   beliefs 57
   concept of God 17
   development of 35
   festivals 73
   places of worship 27
   practices and rites 86
   sources of authority 45
   spread of 29
Star of David 84
stewardship 92–3, 144–5
substance abuse 94, 108, 126, 146
Sukkoth 69, 152, 162
Sunnah 40
Surya 11

symbols 4–5, 90
   Christian 77
   Hindu 79
   Islamic 81
   Jewish 83–4
synagogues 24–5

T
tabernacles 18, 26
Table, the 26, 72
Talmud 43
tapasya (tapas) 116
taqwah 142–3
Tawhid 12, 50, 134
teachings and beliefs 91
   Caribbean indigenous
   religions 56–7
   Christianity 46–7
   Hinduism 48–9
   Islam 50–1, 134–9
   Judaism 52–5, 151–5
teerthas 20
temples 18, 20, 24, 26
Ten Commandments 15, 42, 154,
   165
Tenakh 42, 53, 148–9, 150, 153–5
tents 19
thanksgiving offerings 145
Torah 15, 25, 42, 69, 150, 151
transmission, ceremony of 86
Trinity 9, 46–7, 103
Trinity Sunday 61

U
unmanifest, God 115
Upanishads 38
usury 127

V
Vedas 38
vicegerents 120–1, 141, 142
violence and vandalism 95, 110, 127,
   147
Vishnu 10, 114
Vodun
   beliefs 57
   concept of God 17
   development of 34–5
   festivals 72
   places of worship 26
   practices and rites 86–7
   sources of authority 44
   spread of 29

W
war 95, 110, 127, 147
Whitsuntide 61
women 95, 109, 124, 126, 148
work 94, 96–7, 109, 124, 147
worship 4
   Christianity 36
   Islam 13, 125, 132, 138
   Judaism 153
   see also places of worship

Y
Yahweh 14–15, 52, 148–9, 156–9
Yom Kippur 68, 161–2
Yoruba 35, 57
yugas, the four 49

Z
zakah (charity) 50, 127, 138
zikr 125
Zion Revivalism 16, 44

Acknowledgements

The author and the publisher would also like to thank the following for permission to reproduce material:

Text

Throughout: *The Holy Bible*, New International Version®, NIV® Copyright © 1973, 1978, 1984, 2011 by Biblica, Inc.™ Used by permission. All rights reserved worldwide; *The Holy Qu'ran* translated by Abdullah Yusuf Ali. First US Edition 2008, Reprinted with permission of Tahrike Tarsile Qur'an, Inc.

p6 C.S. Lewis, *Mere Christianity* Copyright © C.S. Lewis Pte Ltd 1942, 1943, 1944, 1952; pp28 and 29 from Warren Matthews, *World Religions* (with InfoTrac), 4E © 2004 Cengage Learning; p32 from Dr Abdullah Hakim Quick, *Deeper Roots: Muslims in the Caribbean Before Columbus to the Present* published by Ta-Ha Publishers (1996). Reproduced with permission of the author; p69, Sukkoth prayer from Ray Colledge, *Mastering World Religions*, 1999, Macmillan Press Ltd. Reproduced with permission of Palgrave Macmillan.

Photos

p3 top Getty/ImagesBazaar; p3 bottom Alamy/Caro; p7 Getty/Yuri Cortez; p10 Alamy/Art Directors; p11 top Fotolia; p11 bottom left Alamy/Vinod Kurien; p11 bottom centre Art Archive/Victoria and Albert Museum London; p11 bottom right iStockphoto; p15 Getty/Bill Keefrey; p16 Rex Features/Everett Collection; p18 Corbis/Peter Turnley; p19 Alamy/imagebroker; p20 Alamy/Danita Delimont; p21 left Fotolia; p21 right iStockphoto; p22 top Corbis/Kazuyoshi Nomachi; p22 middle iStockphoto; p22 bottom Getty/Muhannad Fala'ah; p24 Sha'are Shalom synagogue; p25 Alamy/Danita Delimont; p26 Getty/Dario Mitidieri; p27 Getty/CON/Sean Drakes; p31 Getty/CON/Sean Drakes; p33 Getty/Mambo/Sven Creutzmann; p34 Getty/Hulton Archive; p35 Rex Features/Keystone; p37 Getty/Natalie Behring; p39 Art Directors/Helene Rogers; p41 Getty/Noah Seelam; p42 Catherine House; p43 Alamy/Design Pics Inc.; p46 iStockphoto; p48 Getty/Design Pics/Keith Levit; p50 Nelson Thornes International Collection/Colin Babb; p53 Alamy/dbimages; p55 Corbis/Sygma/Serge Attal; p56 Corbis/Kevin Fleming; p60 iStockphoto; p65 Getty/Adek Berry; p67 Corbis/Kazuyoshi Nomachi; p69 Fotolia; p71 Superstock; p75 Nelson Thornes International Collection/Shawn Banton; p76 Corbis/Karen Kasmauski; p84 Alamy/PhotoStock-Israel; p89 Alamy/PhotoStock-Israel; p94 Getty/Ted Russell; p96 Getty/Gen Nishino; p98 Corbis/John Trever; p103 Getty/Paul Hudson; p105 iStockphoto; p107 Getty/Hulton Archive; p109 Getty/Adrian Pope; p110 Dinodia; p112 Art Directors; p114 left iStockphoto; p114 middle Shutterstock; p114 right Fotolia; p118 Getty/Yuri Cortez; p122 Corbis/Reuters/Rafiqur Rahman; p124 Superstock; p126 Alamy/Jim West; p127 Alamy/Richard Levine; p129 Getty/Image Bank; p131 Getty/Elise Hardy; p135 Public domain (Wikipedia Commons); p137 Getty/Design Pics/Reynold Mainse; p139 Getty/Reza; p141 Getty/AFP; p147 top Getty/Maurice Zalewski; p147 bottom; Getty/Mario Tama; p148 Alamy/Noam Armonn; p150 Getty/Blend Images; p155 Getty/David Silverman; p158 Getty/Image Bank; p160 Corbis/NSI Agency/Demotix; p161 iStockphoto; p162 Corbis/Adam Reynolds; p163 Fotolia; p164.

Every effort has been made to trace the copyright holders but if any have been inadvertently overlooked the publisher will be pleased to make the necessary arrangements at the first opportunity.